A Bibliography of the City Coinage of Palestine

From the 2nd century B.C. to the 3rd century A.D.

Arie Kindler
and
Alla Stein

BAR International Series 374
1987

B.A.R.

5, Centremead, Osney Mead, Oxford OX2 0DQ, England.

BAR S374,1987 :'A Bibliography of the City Coinage of Palestine'

ISBN 9780860544821 paperback
ISBN 9781407346502 e-book
DOI https://doi.org/10.30861/9780860544821
A catalogue record for this book is available from the British Library
This book is available at www.barpublishing.com

C O N T E N T S

Preface

The idea to prepare a bibliography for the Palestinian city-coinage arose due to my constant involvement in the research of this field of numismatics during the last three decades.

It should be commune opinion that upon conducting research in any field of numismatics, besides the research on the coins proper, all the relevant literature ever published on the subject should be read carefully. First, one needs a comparison with previously published material which will enable to accept or reject former opinions and also one has to avoid the re-publication of 'hitherto unpublished coin-types'.

I am happy to have been ably assisted by Mrs. Alla Stein, whose endeavours towards perfection in accuracy made this volume an indispensible tool for the scholar of Palestinian Greek Imperials.

As the funds at our disposal did not enable us to check libraries outside Israel, this volume cannot claim to be complete. But leaning on rather well assorted numismatic libraries in Israel which have been carefully screened, it presents the reader with the close to exhaustive number of about 2700 entries. The respective literature from Patin (1671) onwards has been screened and the volume was brought up to date to the end of 1984. We kept strictly to the field of Palestinian city coins, 37 cities altogether on both sides of the river Jordan, and did not deal with affiliated material, such as the Greco-Persian issues of Gaza, the Hellenistic mints of Acco-Ptolemais, Joppe, Ascalon and Gaza and the Herodian mints of Caesarea Maritima, Tiberias and Paneas. We did on the other hand not restrict ourselves to pure numismatic entries, but dealt also with subjects relating to the history, mythology, archaeological comparison and the economic situation of a city, inasmuch as linked to the coins.

The present bibliography is published under the auspices of the Israel Numismatic Society.

Technical introduction

The bibliography of each of the 37 cities has been dealt with separately. Cities beyond the historical-geographical borders of the Provincia Judaea, later on the Provincia Syria-Palestina, such as Acco-Ptolemais and Dora (Phoenicia) and the cities of the Decapolis and the Provincia Arabia were incorporated.

In order to facilitate the perusal of this bibliography, the cities appear in strict alphabetical order and not in the frame of geographical entities, such as Judaea, Galilaea, Phoenicia, Arabia, etc.

The same idea was followed in the frame of each city proper, when the authors were arranged in alphabetical and not in chronological order. In cases of prefixes to names of authors, such as Le Rider, deSaulcy, de Veaux and Van der Vliet, it was decided to put the main name at the beginning, as for instance: Rider, G. Le.

Figures, such as plate numbers, etc. originally given in Roman numerals have been changed into Arabic numerals.

Periodicals have been listed in the commonly accepted abbreviations and the key to these is given on page 249.

Titles of Hebrew articles have been translated into English with the remark: (Hebrew).

As an appendix to the numismatic literature-bibliography of each city, a list of auction catalogues, price-lists, etc. in which relevant coins appear has been added. Also these appendices follow the alphabetical order. The order in these entries is as follows: name of the dealer, place and date. The number of the auction catalogue or running number of the price list is given in parentheses.

ABILA

ANONYMOUS, CH 1, 1975, p.34/123.

BARAG, D. "Tyrian currency in Galilee", INJ 6-7, 1982/3, p.10.

BELLINGER, A.R. "The Syrian tetradrachms of Caracalla and Macrinus", ANS NS 3, 1940, p.14.

DUSSAUD, R. "Le temple de Jupiter Damascénien", SYRIA 3, 1922, p.230, fig. 4.

ECKHEL, J. "Doctrina numorum veterum", vol. III, Vienna 1794, pp.345-346.

HEAD, B.V. "Historia numorum", Oxford 1911, p.786.

HERZFELDER, H. "Contribution a là numismatique de la Décapole", RN, 4th ser., 39, 1936, pp.291-295.

KADMAN, L. "Numismatic evidence of the architectonic revolution in the Second Century C.E.", INB 3-4, 1962, pp.72, 76, 77. Heb. ed. pp.65, 67, 68.

KELLNER, W. "Commodus-Münzen aus der Dekapolis", SM 77, 1970, pp.1-2, 3.

KINDLER, A. "Akko, a city of many names", BASOR 231, 1978, p.51.

KINDLER, A. "The status of cities in the Syro-Palestinian area as reflected by their coins", INJ 6-7, 1982/3, pp.80, 82.

KINDLER, A. "The coinage of Bostra", Warminster, England 1983, p.147.

KLAWANS, Z.H. "An outline of ancient Greek coins", Wisconsin, USA 1959, p.50.

ABILA

KLIMOWSKY, E.W. "The monetary function of city coins", International numismatic convention in Jerusalem (1963), proceedings (A. Kindler, ed.), Tel-Aviv 1967, pp.164, 172.

MESHORER, Y. "A hoard of coins from Migdal", ATIQOT, Es 11, 1976, pp.55, 56, 71, pl.15/152.

MESHORER, Y. "The city coins of Eretz-Israel and the Decapolis in the Roman period", Jerusalem 1984, pp.78, 119 (Hebrew).

MESHORER, Y. and SPAER, A. "Some additional apparently unpublished city coins", INJ 3, 1965/6, p.75.

MIONNET, T.E. "Description de médailles antiques, grecques et romaines", Paris 1806-1837, vol. V, p.318; vol. VII (Notes et obs.), p.109; vol. VIII, suppl., pp.223-224.

PRICE, M.J. and TRELL, B.L. "Coins and their cities", London 1977, pp.34, 164, 282, fig. 288.

RIDER, G. le "Les ateliers monétaires de la côte Syrienne, Phénicienne, Palestinienne, Égyptienne et Cyrénéenne", Congresso Internazionale di numismatica (Roma 1961), vol. I, Relazioni, Roma 1961, p.87.

ROSENBERGER, M. "The coinage of Eastern Palestine", Jerusalem 1978, pp.1-4.

SAULCY, F. de "Numismatique de la Terre Sainte", Paris 1874, pp.308-312, pl.16/1-7.

SEAR, D.R. "Greek imperial coins and their values", London 1982, nos. 1673, 1797, 1872, 2047, 2266, 2453, 2665, 3104.

SESTINI, D. "Classes generales geographiae numismaticae sev monetae urbium, populorum et regum", Lipsiae 1797, part I, p.67.

SESTINI, D. "Classes generales sev moneta vetus urbium, populorum et regum", Florentiae 1821, p.143.

SESTINI, D. "Descrizione delle medaglie antiche Greche del Museo Hedervariano", part 3, Firenze 1829, p.73, pl.31/2.

SEYRIG, H. "Antiquités Syriennes 73. Temples, cultes et souvenirs historique de la Décapole", SYRIA 36, 1959, pp.60-62, 67, 68, 75-76, pl.12/1-5.

SNG ANS part 6, "Palestine-South Arabia", 1981, pl.38/1119-1128.

SNG FM vol. IV, part 8, "Syria-Nabathaea", 1971, pl.132/5977.

SPIJKERMAN, A. "An unknown coin-type of Pella Decapoleos", LA 20, 1970, p.356.

SPIJKERMAN, A. "The coins of the Decapolis and provincia Arabia", Jerusalem 1978, pp.48-57, 280, pls.7-9.

VLIET, N. van der "Monnaies inédites ou très rares du médaillier de Sainte-Anne de Jérusalem", RB 57, 1950, pp.243-244, pl.4/1.

WICZAY, C.M. "Musei Hedervarii numi antiqui ..", Vindobonae 1814, part I, p.278/6028.

WROTH, W. BMC, Galatia, Cappadocia and Syria, 1899, pp.lxxix, lxxxiii.

ABILA

<u>Auction Catalogues and Price Lists</u>

AGORA, Tel-Aviv 1974(1), p.26, nos.161-162, pl.9
1975(2), no. 219, pl. 9.

BETTER, Jaffo 1974(7), no.293.

CAHN, A.E., Frankfurt 1931(71), p.64, no.1056, pl.32.

HESS-LEU, Luzern 1965(28), p.41, no.297, pl.13.

HOLZER, H. "The Thomas Ollive Mabbott collection", part I, New York 1969, p.102, nos.2626-2627.

MALTER, J.L. "Journal of Numismatic Fine Arts", Encino, CA, USA 1973(2/2), p.35/B 55.

MONNAIES ET MÉDAILLES, Basel 1954(13) p.71, no.929, pl.33.
1966(32), p.47, no.450, p.27.
1970(41), p.77, nos.605-607, pl.38.

MÜNZEN UND MEDAILLEN, Basel 1978(398), p.1, no.2

STERNBERG, F. Zürich, 25-26 Nov. 1976, pp.65-66, nos.495-499, pl.20.

SUPERIOR STAMP AND COIN CO., Los-Angeles, June 1976, p.22, no.225.

TAMAR, Tel-Aviv 1975(9), p.8, no.183.
Tel-Aviv 1975(10), p.10, no.167.
Ramat-Gan, Israel 1976(11), p.12, no.151.
Ramat-Gan, Israel 1976(12), p.52, no.877.

ACCO-PTOLEMAIS

AKERMAN, J.Y. "Numismatic illustrations of the New Testament", Chicago, 1966 (rp) p.35.

ANONYMOUS *CH* 1, 1975, p.34/123,124.

ANONYMOUS "A new coin-type of the Acco series" (A. Kindler), *INJ* 2(3-4), 1964, p.65, pl.4/16.

ANONYMOUS "City coins of ancient Israel", *JIN* 1(4), 1966, pp.115-116.

ARIEL, D.T. "A survey of coin finds in Jerusalem", *LA* 32, 1982, pp.281, 283, 292, 317, 321.

ARRIGONI, O. "Numismata quaedam cujuscunque formae..", Tarvisii, part I (1741), Numismata in coloniis percussa a J. Vaillant non relata, pls.2/22,26; 6/90; 10/153.

AVIGAD, N. "Beth-She'arim, III: The archaeological excavations during 1953-8. The catacombs 12-23", Jerusalem, 1971, p.55 (Hebrew).

AVI-YONAH, M. "Syrian gods at Ptolemais-Accho", *IEJ* 9 (1), 1959, pp.1-12.

BABELON, E. "Les Rois de Syrie, d'Arménie et de Commagène", Paris, 1890, pp.ciii-civ, cxxii, cliii-cliv.

BABELON, E. "Les Perses Achéménides ... Cypre & Phénicie", Paris, 1893, pp.218-228, pl.29/1-18.

BALDUS, H.R. "Eine Münzprägung auf das Ehepaar Mark Anton - Kleopatra VII", *SM* 129, 1983, pp.5-10.

ACCO-PTOLEMAIS

BARAG, D. "Hanita, Tomb XV - A tomb of the 3rd and early 4th century C.E.", ATIQOT, Es 13, 1978, pp.47, 53, pl. 10/176.

BARAG, D. "Tyrian currency in Galilee", INJ 6-7, 1982/3, pp.9, 10, 11, 12, 13.

BARAMKI, D.C. "The coin collection of the American University of Beirut Museum. Palestine and Phoenicia", Beirut, 1974, pp.168-173, pl.21.

BELLINGER, A.R. "Coins from Jerash, 1928-1934", NNM 81, 1938, pp.9, 24-25, nos.20-21.

BELLINGER, A.R. "The Syrian tetradrachms of Caracalla and Macrinus", ANS NS 3, 1940, pp.13, 14.

BENTINCK, de "Catalogue d'une collection de médailles antiques", Amsterdam, 1787, part I, p.499, part II, p.1070; suppl. (1788), p.207.

BERMAN, A. "A numismatic survey in Yotapatha", INB 2, 1962, pp.48-49, pl.1/20. Heb. ed. p.43, pl.1/20.

BRETT, A.B. "Seleucid coins of Ake-Ptolemais in Phoenicia", ANS MN 1, 1945, pp.17-35, pls.6-11.

CARSON, R.A.G. "The inflation of the third century and its monetary influence in Near East", International numismatic convention in Jerusalem (1963), proceedings (A. Kindler, ed.), Tel-Aviv, 1967, pp.240, 242.

CHAIX, E. "Recherche des monnaies coloniales Romaines non décrites dans l'ouvrage de H. Cohen", ASFN 16, 1892, p.200/7; 232/15; 233/3; vol. 17, 1893, p.24/15; p.27.

COHEN, H. "Médailles Imperiales", Leipzig, 1930 (rp), vol. I, pp.263/140; 309/431-433; vol. II, pp.93/709; 241-242/1580-1584; vol. III, pp.374-375/1182-1183; vol. IV, pp.95/928-933; 102/8; 134-135/332-334; 236/900-906; 286/309; 309/185; 317/47-48; 369-370/456-464; 383/18; 386/13; 474-475/708-712; pp.130/352-355; 156-157/115-116; 177/137-138; 260/197; 334-335/368-374; 488/1502-1503; 514/174-177.

DOWLING, T.E. "Coinage of Ptolemais and Sycaminum", PEFQSt 39, 1907, pp.158-159.

ECKHEL, J. "Doctrina numorum veterum", vol. III, Vienna, 1794, pp.408-409, 423-425.

ECKHEL, J. "Catalogus Musei Caesarei Vindobonensis numorum veterum..", Vindobonae, 1779, pars I, p.240.

ELGAVISH, J. "Pottery from the Hellenistic stratum at Shiqmona", IEJ 26 (2-3), 1976, pp.65-67, pl.16.

FLESCH, M. "Group of city coins", in 'Collector's choice', Bezalel National Museum, Jerusalem, 1964, p.16/79.

FLUSSER, D. "Gods, personifications and sea monsters", SEFUNIM 3, 1969/71, p.41, pl.7/11.

FORRER, L. "Weber collection", Vol. III, part 2: "Greek Coins", London, 1929, p.779-780, nos.8048-8049, pl.296.

FRANCESCO DE DOMINICIS "Repertorio numismatico", Napoli, t.I (1826), pp.237, 401, t.II (1827), pp.98, 176, 178, 229, 253, 363.

FROELICH, E. "Quatuor tentamina in re numaria vetere", 2nd ed., Viennae 1737, pp.91-92.

ACCO-PTOLEMAIS

FULCO, W.J. "Monnaies de Tell Keisan, 1971-1974", RB 82, 1975, pp.234, 236, pl.19/20-21.

GESSNER, J.J. "Numismata antiqua imperatorum Romanorum latina et graeca..", Tiguri (Zürich), 18th cent., pls.42/24, 79/70, 135/55-58, 145/26, 148/16-18, 152/54, 157/24, 158/40-42, 160/26, 41; 165/36; 180/36.

GILMORE, P.M. "Caracalla's silver mints in Syria", NCirc. 88 (3), 1980, p.90.

GOLDMAN, Z and SHAHAF, N. "The coinage of Akko" (guide), Municipal Museum of Akko, 1959/60.

HAMBURGER, H. "The coin issues of the Roman administraiton from the mint of Caesarea", IEJ 20 (1-2), 1970, pp.82, 85.

HAMBURGER, H. "A hoard of Syrian tetradrachms and Tyrian bronze coins from Gush Halav", IEJ 4 (3-4), 1954, pp.220/111, 222/127, 226/144, pl.21/144. Same in 'Recent studies and discoveries on ancient Jewish and Syrian coins', PINS 7, Jerusalem, 1954, pp.84, 86, 90, pl.21/144.

HANSON, R.S. "Meiron coins: 1974-75", AASOR 43, 1976, p.99.

HANSON, R.S. "Report on the coins from Gush Halav", in 'Preliminary report on the 1977 and 1978 seasons at Gush Halav', BASOR 233, 1979, p.52, fig. 17/R 77170.

HANSON, R.S. "Tyrian influence in the Upper Galilee", Cambridge, 1980, p.52.

HEAD, B.V. "Historia numorum", Oxford, 1911, p.793-794.

HENDIN, D. "Guide to ancient Jewish coins", New York, 1976, pp.96-97, pl.8/227.

HEYMANN, H. "Roman legionary coins from Phoenicia", *INJ* 1(3), 1963, p.49.

HILL, G.F. BMC, "Phoenicia", 1910, pp.lxxvii-lxxxvii, 128-138, pls.16/4-15, 17/1-11.

IMHOOF-BLUMER, F. "Zur syrischen Münzkunde", *NZ* 33, 1901, pp.10-12.

IMHOOF-BLUMER, F. "Zur griechischen und römischen Münzkunde. II Abteilung", *SNR* 14, 1908, p.129.

IMHOOF-BLUMER, F. "Apollon Karneios auf kyrenäischen und anderen griechischen Münzen und numismatische Miszellen", *SNR* 21, 1917, pp.52-54.

IMHOOF-BLUMER, F. "Fluss- und Meergötter auf grieschischen und römischen Münzen", *SNR* 23, 1923, pp.370-371, pl. 15/18-19.

JONAS, R. "Mythology on Palestinian coins", internal circular no. 2, Israel Num. Society, Haifa branch, 1959, pp.5, 6.

KADMAN, L. "The coins of Akko Ptolemais", Corpus Nummorum Palaestinensium, vol. IV, Jerusalem, 1961.

KADMAN, L. "Numismatic evidence of the architectonic revolution in the Second Century C.E.", *INB* 3-4, 1962, pp.72, 74, pl.1/15-16. Heb. ed. p.65.

KADMAN, L. "Coins of Akko as illustrations to passages in Mishnah and Talmud", *INJ* 3, 1963, pp.52-54, pl.3/6-7.

KADMAN, L. and KINDLER, A. "Coins in Palestine throughout the ages", Tel-Aviv, 1963, pp.29-30, pl.14/1-11 (Hebrew).

ACCO-PTOLEMAIS

KINDLER, A. "Thesaurus of Judaean coins from the fourth century B.C. to the third century A.D.", Jerusalem, 1958, no.38 (Hebrew).

KINDLER, A. "A new type of the coin series of Acco-Ptolemais", <u>ALON</u> 1 (3), 1967, p.59 (Hebrew).

KINDLER, A. "The coin issues of the Roman administration in the provincia Judaea during the reign of Domitian", <u>ALON</u> 3 (4), 1969, p.92, pl.6/22, 24 (Hebrew).

KINDLER, A. "New types of Palestinian city-coins", <u>ALON</u> 4 (2), 1969, pp.22-23, pl.3/2-3 (Hebrew).

KINDLER, A. "A coin hoard of the second half of the 2nd Century B.C.E.", <u>ALON</u> 4 (3), 1970, pp.41-46, pl.4 (Hebrew).

KINDLER, A. "An extraordinary coin of Acco-Ptolemais", <u>ALON</u> 5 (3), 1974, p.41, pl.6/1 (Hebrew).

KINDLER, A. "Akko, a city of many names", <u>BASOR</u> 231, 1978, pp.51-55.

KINDLER, A. "The coinage of Bostra", Warminster, England, 1983, pp.30, 33, 49, 61, 64, 66, 92.

KINDLER, A. "The status of cities in the Syro-Palestinian area as reflected by their coins", <u>INJ</u> 6-7, 1982/3, pp.82, 84.

KLAWANS, Z.H. "An outline of ancient Greek coins", Wisconsin, USA 1959, p.51.

KLIMOWSKY, E.W. "The monetary function of city coins", International numismatic convention in Jerusalem (1963), proceedings (A. Kindler, ed.), Tel-Aviv, 1967, pp.131, 146, 152, 155, 158, 160, 164, 166, 168, 170, 172, 174.

KLIMOWSKY, E.W. "Roman imperial 'Virtutes' on contemporaneous city coins", INJ 3, 1965/6, pp.22, 24, 25, pls.5/16, 24; 6/31, 34. Same in 'On ancient Palestinian and other coins, their symbolism and metrology", PINS 7, Tel-Aviv, 1974, pp.95, 96, 98, pls. 5/16; 6/24, 31, 34.

KLIMOWSKY, E.W. "The origin and meaning of Marsyas in the Greek Imperial coinage", INJ 6-7, 1982/3, p.98.

KONTORINI, V. "L'autonomie de Ptolémais-Akko de Phénicie", RN, 6th s., 21, 1979, pp.30-41, pl.11.

KRAFT, K. "Das System der kaiserzeitlichen Münzprägung in Kleinasien", Berlin, 1972, pp.98, 101.

KUBITSCHEK, W. "Zur Geschichte von Stadten des römischen Kaiserreiches. Epigraphisch-numismatische Studien", heft I, Wien, 1916, pp.80-94.

KUBITSCHEK, W. "Ptolemais", NZ 50 (10 Neue f.), 1917, pp.46-48.

LAMBERT, C. "Coins in the Palestine Museum, II", QDAP 1, 1931/2, p.134, pl.55/17-18.

LAPP, N.L. "The excavations at Araq El-Emir", AASOR 47, 1983, p.16, fig. 8/1.

LEDERER, P. "Two unpublished Greek coins", NC, 5th s., 18, 1938, pp.65-75.

LIEBE, C.S. "Gotha numaria, sistens Thesauri Fridericiani..", Amsterdam, 1730, pp.159-162.

MACDONALD, G. "Catalogue of Greek coins in the Hunterian collection", Glasgow, 1905, vol. III, p.248.

ACCO-PTOLEMAIS

MATSSON, G.O. "The gods, goddesses and heroes on the ancient coins of Bible Lands", Stockholm, 1969, pp.9, 28, 66, 71, 116, 119, 128, 129, 139, 142, 156, 159, 163, 167, 168, 173, 181, 184, 192, 193, 197, 214, 216, 220, 221, 224, 227, 231, 232, 235, 236, 240, 241, pls.1/7b; 3/54; 4/57b; 5/67a, 69, 77, 84, 85b; 6/95a, b; 7/100, 112, 114c.

MESHORER, Y. "A hoard of coins from Migdal", ATIQOT, Es 11, 1976, pp.54-55, 56, 64-65, pls. 12/92-95; 13/96-106.

MESHORER, Y. "The city-coins of Eretz-Israel and the Decapolis in the Roman period", Jerusalem, 1984, pp.11-15, 110 (Hebrew).

MESHORER, Y. and SPAER, A. "An apparently unpublished coin of Acco-Ptolemais", INJ 3, 1965/6, p.74, pl.14/1.

MESHORER, Y. "Coins of the Ancient World", Minneapolis 1975, pp.74-76. Heb. version (Jerusalem 1979), pp.51-52; same in "Münzen, Zeugen der Vergangenheit", Zürich - Köln, 1979, pp.74-76.

MIONNET, T.E. "Description de médailles antiques grecques et romaines", Paris, 1806-1837, vol. V, pp.473-481, vol. VIII, suppl., pp.324-331.

NEWELL, E.T. "Late Seleucid mints in Ake-Ptolemais and Damascus", NNM 84, 1939, pp.3-4.

PATIN, C. "Imperatorum Romanorum numismata ex aere mediae et minimae formae descripta et enarrata..", Amsterdam(?). 1671, pp.299, 317.

PELLERIN, J. "Mélange de diverses médailles..", t.I, part 3, Paris 1764, p.324, pl.21/5, p.332, pl.22/8-9, p.340, pl.23/9.

PLANT, R. "Greek coin types and their identification", London, 1979, nos. 608, 1934, 2374.

PRICE, M.J. and TRELL, B.L. "Coins and their cities", London 1977, p.44, 280, figs. 73, 463, 480, 515.

REICHARDT, H.C. "Unpublished Greek Imperial coins", NC, Ns 2, 1862, pp.108-109.

REICHARDT, H.C. "Remarks on some Jewish coins, and on some inedited coins of Phoenicia, Judaea, etc.", NC, Ns 4, 1864, pp.187-188.

RIDER, G. le "Monnaies grecques récemment acquises par le cabinet des médailles", RN, 6th ser., 3, 1961, p.23, pl.2/D.

ROSENBERGER, M. "The Rosenberger Israel collection", vol. I, Jerusalem 1972, pp.17-32.

ROSENBERGER, M. "City-coins of Palestine", vol. III, Jerusalem 1977, pp.69-72.

ROUVIER, J. "Ptolémais-Acé, ses noms et ses ères sous les Séleucides et la domination romaine..", RB 8, 1899, pp.393-408.

ROUVIER, J. "Numismatique des villes de la Phénicie", JIAN 4, 1901, pp.193-232.

SAULCY, F. de "Numismatique de la Terre Sainte", Paris 1874, pp.153-169, 405-406, pl.8/2-11.

SAULCY, F. de "Sur les monnaies des Antiochéens frappées hors d'Antioche", NC, Ns 11, 1871, pp.69-92.

ACCO-PTOLEMAIS

SCHNITZLER, O. "The Syrian Triad on coins of Akko", INJ 1 (4), 1963, pp.70-74.

SEAR, D.R. "Greek imperial coins and their values", London 1982, nos. 479, 626, 1086, 1244, 1678, 2269, 2456, 2675, 2899, 3114, 3187, 3197, 3254, 3371, 3963, 4061, 4151, 4507, 4625, 4693, 5203.

SELLERS, O.R. "Coins of the 1960 excavation at Shechem", BA 25 (3), 1962, p.96, fig. 12/83-86.

SESTINI, D. "Classes generales geographiae numismaticae sev monetae urbium, populorum et regum..", Lipsiae 1797, pars I, pp.69-70, pars II, pp.101-102.

SESTINI, D. "Descrizione delle medaglie Greche e Romane del Fu Benkowitz", Berlino 1809, p.35.

SESTINI, D. "Lettere e dissertazioni numismatiche", vol. IX, Firenze 1820, pp.97-101, pl.2/9-11.

SESTINI, D. "Classes generales sev moneta vetus urbium, populorum et regum", Florentiae 1821, pp.148-149.

SESTINI, D. "Descrizione delle medaglie antiche Greche del Museo Hedervariano", part 3, Firenze 1829, pp.102-103, pl.31/11-14.

SEYRIG, H. "Antiquités Syriennes, 10. Note sur le culte de Déméter en Palestine", SYRIA 13, 1932, p.357.

SEYRIG, H. "Antiquités Syriennes, 80. Divinités de Ptolémais", SYRIA 39, 1962, pp.193-207, pls.13-14.

SEYRIG, H. "Notes on Syrian coins", NNM 119, 1950, pp.32, 34.

SEYRIG, H. "Le monnayage de Ptolémais en Phénicie", RN, 6th ser., 4, 1962, pp.25-50.

SNG DNM "Phoenicia", 1961, pl.5, figs.177-187.

SNG FM vol. IV, part 8, "Syria-Nabathaea", 1971, pl.134/6042.

SPERBER, D. "Roman Palestine 200-400. Money and prices", Jerusalem 1974, pp.133, 144.

SPIJKERMAN, A. "Cafarnao, III: Catalogo delle monete della città", Jerusalem 1975, p.51/430.

STEVENSON, S.W. "A dictionary of Roman coins", London 1964 (rp.), pp.666-668.

SUTHERLAND, G.H.V. "The pattern of monetary development in Phoenicia and Palestine during the Early Empire", International numismatic convention in Jerusalem (1963), proceedings (A. Kindler, ed.), Tel-Aviv 1967, pp.90, 91, 94, 95, 96, 99.

TIEPOLO, L. and F. "Musei Theupoli antiqua numismata..", Venetiis 1736, series 4, pp.679, 681, 690, 764.

TRELL, B. "Phoenician Greek Imperial coins", INJ 6-7, 1982/3, pp.133-134, pl.28/62-63.

VAILLANT, J. "Numismata aera imperatorum, augustarum et caesarum in coloniis, municipiis et urbibus", Paris 1688, pars I, pp.161, 181, 215, 230-232, pars II, pp.18-20, 29, 59-60, 73, 83, 123-125, 145, 150, 175, 250, 333-334.

VAILLANT, J. "Numismata imperatorum, augustarum et caesarum a populis Romanae ditionis graece loquentibus..", Paris 1698, pp.12-13, 247.

ACCO-PTOLEMAIS

VLIET, N. van der "Monnaies inédites ou très rares du médaillier de Sainte-Anne de Jérusalem", RB 57, 1950, pp.432-433, pl.6/3-4.

WICZAY, C.M. "Musei Hedervarii numi antiqui", Vindobonae 1814, pars I, 286-287, nos. 6181-6185.

Auction Catalogues and Price Lists

AGORA, Tel-Aviv 1974 (1), pp.23-24, nos. 141-145, pl.8.
1975 (2), nos. 159-162, pl.7.

BETTER, Haifa 1972 (1), nos. 147-150.
Haifa 1972 (2), nos. 245-248.
Haifa 1973 (3), nos. 288-293.
Haifa 1973 (4), nos. 183-183A.
Jaffo 1974 (5), nos. 128-130A.
Jaffo 1974 (7), nos. 177-178.
Haifa 1974 (8), nos. 104-105.

CAHN, A. Frankfurt 1931 (71), p.65, nos. 1064-1068, pl.32.

EGGER BRÜDER, (price list), Wien 1930 (56), p.7, no. 219.

EIDELSTEIN AND HOLLAND Haifa, 10 Nov. 1975, no. 147.

EIDELSTEIN AND HOLLAND (Price list), Haifa, summer 1976, nos. 157-158.

GANS, E. "Numismatic Fine Arts" (mail bid sale), Berkeley CA, USA 1955 (15), p.23, nos. 366-368, pl.8.

GANS, E. "Numismatic Fine Arts", Berkeley CA, USA 1956 (20), p.16, no. 4981.

GLENDINING, London, 10 March 1965, p.22, no. 169.

HESS, A. Frankfurt 1936 (224), p.57, no. 1718.

HOLZER, H. "The Thomas Ollive Mabbott collection", part 1,
New York 1969, p.105, nos. 2699-2708.

MALTER, J.L. "Journal of Numismatic Fine Arts", Encino Ca, USA
1973 (2/2), p.35/B 56.
1977 (6/1), p.13/S 65-66.

MONNAIES ET MÉDAILLES, Basel
1962 (25), pp.19-20, nos. 508-515, pl.8.
1966 (32), pp.37-38, nos. 291-297, pl.22.

MÜNZEN UND MEDAILLEN, Basel 1963 (236), p.10, no. 378.
1965 (252), p.13, no. 231.
1969 (305), p.3, nos. 35-37.
1973 (342), p.14, nos. 248-249.
1981 (436), p.14, nos. 150-151.
1982 (448), p.1, nos. 4-6.
1984 (468), p.14, no. 173.

MÜNZZENTRUM KÖLN, 1979 (36), p.28, no. 181.

RAUCH, H.D., Wien, 1985 (34), no. 260.

SCHLESSINGER, F. (price list), Amsterdam 1938 (9), p.2, no. 641.

SCHULMAN, H.M.F. New York, 6-7 Apr. 1971, p.45, no.451.

SEABY, London 1949 (373), p.288, no. A 1637.
1949 (378), p.536, nos. AM 349-350.

SPINK AND SON, London 1905 (13/153), nos. 18152-18154.
1927 (35/3), nos. 65437-65438.
1931 (39/8), nos. 9299-9300.
1934 (42/8-9), no. 35044.
1935 (43/12), nos. 47191-47194.

ACCO-PTOLEMAIS

SPINK AND SON (con't) 1939 (47/3), nos. 78545-78546.
1981 (89/6), p.205, no. 4525.

STERNBERG, F. Zürich, 25-26 Nov. 1976, pp.88-90, nos. 683-697, pl.29.

SUPERIOR STAMP AND COIN CO., Los-Angeles, June 1976, p.29, nos. 322-327.

TAMAR, Tel-Aviv 1975 (9), p.6, nos. 114-115.
Tel-Aviv 1975 (10), p.8, no. 122.
Ramat-Gan, Israel 1976 (11), pp.9-10, nos. 109-113.
Ramat-Gan, Israel 1976 (12), p.50, nos. 820-831.

VINCHON, J. "Monnaies Juives", 13 Fév. 1970, no. 85.

ADRAA

BEN-DAVID, A. "Dinarei 'Arba' and silver coins called 'Harubim'", ALON 5 (2), 1974, pp.27-28 (Hebrew).

BREZINA, A. "Darstellung von Meteoriten auf antiken Münzen", Monatsblatt der numismatischen Gesellschaft in Wien, 70, 1889, p.314.

DUSSAUD, R. "Le culte de Dusarès d'après les monnaies d'Adraa et de Bostra", RN 4th ser., 8, 1904, pp.160-173.

ECKHEL, J. "Doctrina numorum veterum", vol. III, Vienna 1794, pp.499-500.

HEAD, B.V. "Historia Numorum", Oxford, 1911, pp.811-812.

HILL, G.F. BMG, Arabia, Mesopotamia and Persia, 1922, pp.xxiii-xxiv, 15, pl.3/4-5.

HILL, G.F. "Some Palestinian cults in the Graeco-Roman age", Proceedings of the British Academy, vol. 5, London, 1912, p.413.

KINDLER, A. "The coinage of Bostra", Warminster, England, 1983, pp.16, 33, 37, 38, 43, 44, 46, 48-49, 53, 56, 58, 71, 73, 78, 81, 82, 83, 85-86, 115, 142, 143.

MESHORER, Y. "The city-coins of Eretz-Israel and the Decapolis in the Roman period", Jerusalem, 1984, pp.84, 120 (Hebrew).

MIONNET, T.E. "Description de médailles antiques, grecques et romaines", Paris, 1806-1837, vol. V, pp.577-579, vol. VIII, suppl., p.382.

ADRAA

PATRICH, Y. "Prohibition of a graven-image among the Nabateans - the testimony of the Massebot-cult", CATHEDRA 26, 1982, pp.62, 63, fig. 11 (Hebrew).

PRICE, M.J. and TRELL, B.L. "Coins and their cities", London 1977, p.284, fig. 442.

ROSENBERGER, M. "The coinage of Eastern Palestine", Jerusalem, 1978, pp.5-6.

SAULCY, F. de "Numismatique de la Terre Sainte", Paris 1874, pp.373-377, pl.23/1-4.

SEAR, D.R. "Greek Imperial coins and their values", London, 1982, nos. 1685, 1913, 2062, 3130, 4509, 4627.

SESTINI, D. "Descriptio numorum veterum..", Lipsiae, 1796, p.548, pl.12/5.

SESTINI, D. "Classes generales geographiae numismaticae sev monetae urbium, populorum et regum..", Lipsiae, 1797, pars I, p.73, pars II, pp.103-104.

SESTINI, D. "Lettere e dissertazioni numismatiche..", vol. IX, Firenze, 1820, p.109.

SESTINI, D. "Classes generales sev moneta vetus urbium, populorum et regum..", Florentiae, 1821, p.155.

SPIJKERMAN, A. "Yarmouk-coins of Adraa Arabiae", LA 21, 1971, pp.327-330.

SPIJKERMAN, A. "The coins of the Decapolis and provincia Arabia", Jerusalem, 1978, pp.58-65, 281, pls. 10-11.

SNG ANS part 6, "Palestine-South Arabia", 1981, pl.38/1129-1135.

SNG DNM "Palestine-Characene", 1961, pl.5, figs 136-138.

<u>Auction Catalogues and Price Lists</u>

AGORA, Tel-Aviv 1974 (1), p.27, no. 172, pl.10.
1975 (2), no. 225, pl.10.

MALTER, J.L. "Journal of Numismatic Fine Arts", Encino, CA, USA 1973 (2/2), p.35/B 57.

MUNZZENTRUM KOLN, 1981 (43), p.33, no. 197.

SCHLESSINGER, F. (price list), Amsterdam 1938 (9), p.5, no. 693.

STERNBERG, F. Zürich, 22-26 Nov. 1976, p.66, nos. 500-501, pl.20.

VECCHI, V.C. "Bonhams", London, 1982 (8), p.19, no. 218, pl.10.

AELIA CAPITOLINA

ANGLO-JEWISH HISTORICAL EXHIBITION, Catalogue, London 1888, p.161, plate/2379.

ANONYMOUS, *CH* 1, 1975, p.34/124.

ARIEL, D.T. "A survey of coin finds in Jerusalem", *LA* 32, 1982, pp.294-296, 309, 311, 317, 318, 319-320.

BARAG, D. "The countermarks of Legio Decima Fretensis", International numismatic convention in Jerusalem (1963), proceedings (A. Kindler, ed.), Tel-Aviv, 1967, pp.117, 118.

BARAG, D. "Tyrian currency in Galilee", *INJ* 6-7, 1982/3, p.11.

BARAMKI, D. "The coins exhibited in the Archaeological Museum of the American University of Beirut", Beirut, 1968, pp.94-95, nos. 312-315, pl.8.

BARAMKI, D. "The coin collection of the American University of Beirut Museum. Palestine and Phoenicia", Beirut, 1974, pp.34-43, pls.6/11-15; 7; 8/1-5.

BARAMKI, J. "Coins in the Palestine Archaeological Museum, III", *QDAP* 8, 1939, p.78, pl.41/4-6.

BELLINGER, A.R. "The Syrian tetradrachms of Caracalla and Macrinus", *ANS NS* 3, 1940, pp.11, 13, 15, 17, 18, 20, 95-97, pl.24/1-16.

BELLINGER, A.R. "The excavations at Dura-Europos. Final report VI. The coins", New Haven, USA 1949, p.16, nos. 283-285, pl.9; p.18 no. 347, pl.10; p.183.

BENTINCK, de "Catalogue d'une collection de médailles antiques", Amsterdam, 1787, part I, pp.272-273, 438, part II, p.1074.

BERNHART, M. "Dionysos und seine Familie auf Griechischen Münzen", JNG 1, 1949, p.64, nos. 209, 210.

BREZINA, A. "Darstellung von Meteoriten auf antiken Münzen", Monatsblatt der numismatischen Gesellschaft in Wien 70, 1889, p.314.

CARSON, R.A.G. "The inflation of the third century and its monetary influence in the Near East", International Numismatic convention in Jerusalem (1963), proceedings (A. Kindler, ed.), Tel-Aviv, 1967, p.242.

CAVEDONI, C. "Biblische Numismatik", vol. II, Hannover, 1856 (Italienisches Original: Appendice alla Numismatica, Modena, 1855), pp.68-73, pl.1/18.

CHAIX, E. "Recherche des monnaies coloniales Romaines non décrites dans l'ouvrage de H. Cohen", ASFN 16, 1892, pp.192/6, 10; 194/7; 195/5; 200/8.

COHEN, H. "De la numismatique de Pescennius Niger", RN, Ns 13, 1868, pp.437-438, pl.15/8.

COHEN, H. "Médailles Imperiales", Leipzig, 1930 (rp), vol. II, pp.242-243/1590-1595; 403-405/1249-1263; 412/42-44; vol. III, pp.124/1216-1220; 128/3; 131-132/2-8; 134/6-7; 213/421-422; 375/1192; 413/82, vol. IV, pp.95/934; 135/339; 138/3; 238/919-921; 286/311; 318/50-52; 370-371/468-477; 383/20; 475/715, vol. V, pp.85/565; 203-205/167-178; 223/1-2; 234-235/81-82; 335/376.

AELIA CAPITOLINA

DECLOEDT, A. "Monnaies inédites ou peu connues du médaillier de Sainte-Anne-de-Jérusalem", RN, 4th s., 16, 1912, pp.472-479, pl.13/10-13.

DURAND, G. "Aelia Capitolina", RB 1, 1892, pp.379-380, 384-385.

ECKHEL, J. "Doctrina numorum veterum", vol. III, Vienna 1794, pp.441-443.

ECKHEL, J. "Catalogus Musei Caesarei Vindobonensis numorum veterum", Vindobonae, 1779, pars I, p.249, pl.4/14.

FLESCH, M. "Group of city coins", in 'Collector's choice', Bezalel National Museum, Jerusalem, 1964, p.15, no. 72.

FORRER, L. "Weber collection, vol. III, part 2: Greek coins", London, 1929, pp.796-797, no. 8109, pl.299.

FRIEDLANDER, J. "Die Erwerbungen d. Kgl. Münzkabinets vom April 1878 bis April 1879", ZN 7, 1880, p.219.

FRIEDLANDER, J. "Erwerbungen des Königl. Münzkabinets im Jahre 1883", ZN 12, 1885, pp.4-5.

FROELICH, E. "Quatuor tentamina in re numaria vetere", 2nd ed., Viennae 1737, p.93.

GESSNER, J.J. "Numismata antiqua Imperatorum Romanorum latina et graeca..", Tiguri (Zürich), 18th cent., pls.101/67-70, 102/70, 11/45-49, 118/41, 155/66-67.

GILMORE, P.M. "The formulae of Antioch and Tyre", NCirc. 86 (2), 1978, p.76.

GILMORE, P.M. "Syrian officinae under Caracalla and Macrinus", NCirc. 87 (6), 1979, p.288.

GILMORE, P.M. "Caracalla's silver mints in Syria", NCirc. 88 (3), 1980, pp.89, 90.

HAMBURGER, A. "Gems from Caesarea", ATIQOT, Es 8, 1968, pp.9/54, 12/85-88.

HAMBURGER, H. "A hoard of Syrian tetradrachms and Tyrian bronze coins from Gush Halav", IEJ 4 (3-4), 1954, pp.203, 205. Same in 'Recent studies and discoveries on ancient Jewish and Syrian coins', PINS 1, Jerusalem 1954, pp.67, 69.

HEAD, B.V. "Historia Numorum", Oxford, 1911, p.803.

HENDIN, D. "Guide to ancient Jewish coins", New York 1976, pp.114-115, pl.9/264-267.

HEYMANN, H. "Roman legionary coins from Phoenicia", INJ 1 (3), 1963, pp.47-49.

HILL, G.F. "Some Palestinian cults in the Graeco-Roman age", Proceedings of the British Academy", vol. V, London, 1912, pp.413, 414, 418-419, pl./11.

HILL, G.F. BMC, Palestine, 1914, pp.xli-xlv, pp.82-102, pls.8/16-18; 9; 10; 11/1-5.

JOHNSON, S.E. "Catalogue of Roman coins - The excavation at Herodian Jericho, 1951", AASOR, 32-33, 1952-4, p.28, no. 8.

JONAS, R. "Mythology on Palestinian coins", internal circular no. 2, Israel Num. Society, Haifa branch, 1959, pp.3, 6, 7.

AELIA CAPITOLINA

KADMAN, L. "An unpublished commemorative medallion of Aelia Capitolina and the riddle of the re-naming of the city", NCirc. 62 (1), 1954, pp.9-11.

KADMAN, L. "The coins of Aelia Capitolina", Corpus Nummorum Palaestinensium, vol. I, Jerusalem, 1956.

KADMAN, L. "The coins of Aelia Capitolina", Congrès International de numismatique, (Paris, 6-11 juillet 1953), Paris, 1957, vol. II, pp.249-258.

KADMAN, L. "When was Aelia Capitolina named 'Commodiana' and by whom?", IEJ 9 (2), 1959, pp.137-140.

KADMAN, L. "Numismatic evidence of the architectonic revolution in the Second Century C.E.", INB 3-4, 1962, pp.71, 72, pl.1/14. Heb. edition p.65.

KADMAN, L. and KINDLER, A. "Coins in Palestine throughout the ages", Tel-Aviv, 1963, p.39, pl.17/7-17 (Hebrew).

KANAEL, B. "Book review on L. Kadman 'The coins of Aelia Capitolina'", IEJ 7 (4), 1957, pp.268-272.

KENNETH, A.J. "Coins and Christianity", London, 1959, p.10, fig. 6.

KINDLER, A. "Thesaurus of Judaean coins from the fourth century B.C. to the third century A.D.", Jerusalem, 1958, no.23 (Hebrew).

KINDLER, A. "The coin issues of the Roman administration in the provincia Judaea during the reign of Domitian", ALON 3 (4), 1969, p.92, pl.6/18 (Hebrew).

KINDLER, A. "A new city coin type of Aelia Capitolina", ALON 4 (1), 1969, p.12, pl.2/6 (Hebrew).

KINDLER, A. "Coins of the land of Israel. Bank of Israel collection", Jerusalem, 1971, p.129, no. 198 (Hebrew).

KINDLER, A. "Was there a detachment of the Third Legion Cyrenaica at Neapolis in A.D. 251-253?", INJ 4, 1980, p.58.

KINDLER, A. "The status of cities in the Syro-Palestinian area as reflected by their coins", INJ 6-7, 1982/3, pp.81, 84.

KINDLER, A. "The coinage of Bostra", Warminster, England, 1983, pp.30, 32, 33, 34, 43, 51, 61, 64, 66, 67, 79, 92, 145.

KIRKBRIDE, A.S. "Currencies in Transjordan", PEQ 1939, p.155.

KLAWANS, Z.H. "An outline of ancient Greek coins", Wisconsin, USA 1959, p.54.

KLIMOWSKY, E.W. "The monetary function of city coins", International Numismatic convention in Jerusalem (1963), proceedings (A. Kindler, ed.), Tel-Aviv, 1967, pp.131, 146, 154, 155, 162, 164, 166, 168, 170, 172, 177.

KLIMOWSKY, E.W. "Roman imperial 'Virtutes' on contemporaneous city coins", INJ 3, 1965/6, pp.22, 23, 24, 25, pl.6/33, 37. Same in 'On ancient Palestinian and other coins, their symbolism and metrology", PINS 7, Tel-Aviv 1974, pp.95, 96, 97, 98, pl.6/33, 37.

KRAFT, K. "Das System der kaiserzeitlichen Münzprägung in Kleinasien", Berlin, 1972, p.101.

LAMBERT, C. "Coins in the Palestine Museum", QDAP 1, 1931/2, pp.71-73, pl.37/9-16.

AELIA CAPITOLINA

LEDERER, P. "Neue Beiträge zur antiken Münzkunde aus schweizerischen öffentlichen und privaten Sammlungen", SNR 30, 1943, p.83, pl.6/98.

LEVY, M.A. "Geshichte der jüdischen Münzen", Leipzig, 1862, pp.108-109.

LIEBE, C.S. "Gotha numaria, sistens Thesauri Fridericiani..", Amsterdam, 1730, pp.313-315.

MADDEN, F.W. "History of Jewish coinage", London, 1864, pp.211-230.

MADDEN, F.W. "Jewish numismatics § VII", NC, Ns 16, 1876, pp.55-68.

MADDEN, F.W. "Coins of the Jews", London, 1881, pp.247-275.

MANNS, F. "Gemmes de l'époque Gréco-Romaine provenant de Palestine", LA 28, 1978, pp.154, 155, 156, 159, 160, pls.25/1, 2, 7, 8; 27/25-28.

MATSSON, G.O. "The gods, goddesses and heroes on the ancient coins of Bible Lands", Stockholm, 1969, pp.3, 47-48, 65, 66, 72, 121, 124, 134, 142, 168, 169, 175, 180, 183, 207, 222, 225, 227, 237, 238, 240, pls.2/38c, d; 5/71-72, 85a; 7/104b, 107, 111.

MENDELSSOHN, E. "Dating of the 'Judaea' coins of Hadrian", SHEKEL 7 (2), 1974, pp.20 (fig. 4), 26.

MESHORER, Y. "An unpublished coin of Aelia Capitolina", IEJ 13 (1), 1963, pp.59-60, pl.8.

MESHORER, Y. "Jewish coins of the Second Temple period", Tel-Aviv 1967, pp.92-93. Hebrew version, Tel-Aviv 1966, pp.60-61.

MESHORER, Y. "The hoard of coins in the Hebron Mountains district", in 'The Hebron Mountains. Collected sources and articles' (S. Dar, ed.), Dept. of local studies of the Kibbutz movement, Tel-Aviv 1970, p.68 (Hebrew).

MESHORER, Y. "Catalogue of coins", in 'Ships and parts of ships on ancient coins', (Ben-Eli, A.L., ed.), part I, National Maritime Museum of Haifa, 1975, p.54, no.44.

MESHORER, Y. "Coins of the Ancient World", Minneapolis 1975, pp.63-65. Hebrew version (Jerusalem 1979) pp.48-50. Same in "Münzen, Zeugen der Vergangenheit", Zürich - Köln 1979, pp.63-65.

MESHORER, Y. "The city coins of Eretz-Israel and the Decapolis in the Roman period", Jerusalem, 1984, pp.59-63, 117 (Hebrew).

MIONNET, T.E. "Description de médailles antiques, grecques et romaines", Paris, 1806-1837, vol. V, pp.516-522, vol. VIII, suppl., pp.360-363.

MEYSHAN, J. "Unpublished and unusual Jewish coins", NUMISMATIST 72 (7), 1959, p.787. Same in 'Essays in Jewish numismatics', Jerusalem 1968, pp.157-158, pl.5/10.

MEYSHAN, J. "The legion which reconquered Jerusalem in the war of Bar-Kochba (A.D.132-135)", PEQ 1958, pp.22-24, pl.1. Same in 'Essays in Jewish numismatics', Jerusalem, 1968, pp.146-148, pl.5/10.

MILDENBERG, L. "Bar Kokhba coins and documents", Harvard Studies in Classical Philology 84, 1980, p.333.

MILDENBERG, L. "The coinage of the Bar Kokhba War", Aarau-Frankfurt am Main-Salzburg 1984, pp.99-101.

AELIA CAPITOLINA

MÜNSTERBERG, R. "Neuerwerbungen der Sammlung antiker Münzen 1920 bis 1924", NZ, Nf 18 (58), 1925, p.32.

NARKISS, M. "From the numismatic collection", OMANUTH, Quarterly of the Bezalel Museum, Jerusalem, vol. I (3), 1940, pp.56-57.

PATIN, C. "Imperatorum Romanorum numismata ex aere mediae et minimae formae descripta et enarrata..", Amsterdam(?), 1671, pp.195-196, 200, 235, 396.

PELLERIN, J. "Mélange de diverses médailles..", t.I, part 3, Paris 1764, pp.273, 286, pl.17/5.

PELLERIN, J. "Second supplément aux six volumes de recueils des médailles", Paris 1766, p.54, pl.2/7, 12-13.

PLANT, R. "Greek coin types and their identification", London, 1979, nos. 942, 2039, 2059.

PRICE, M.J. and TRELL, B.L. "Coins and their cities", London 1977, p.284, figs. 311, 312.

RAFFAELI, S. "Jewish coinage and the date of the Bar-Kokhbah revolt", JPOS 3, 1923, p.195.

RAFFAELI, S. "Coins of the Jews", Jerusalem 1913, pp.183-199, pls.30-35 (Hebrew).

RAHMANI, L.Y. "The coins from Nahal Scelim and Nahal Hardof", IEJ 11 (1-2), 1961, p.64, pl.10/F.

RAHMANI, L.Y. "Roman tombs in Nahal Raqafot", ATIQOT, Es 11, 1976, p.81.

REICHARDT, H.C. "Unpublished Greek Imperial coins", NC, Ns 2, 1862, pp.114-116.

REICHARDT, H.C. "Remarks on some Jewish coins and on some inedited coins of Phoenicia, Judaea, etc.", NC, Ns 4, 1864, pp.182-183.

REICHARDT, H.C. "Dreizehn Münzen von Aelia Capitolina (Jerusalem) die bei de Saulcy nicht vorkommen", NZ 1, 1869, pp.79-88.

REIFENBERG, A. "Denkmäler der jüdischen Antike", Berlin 1937, taf.31/1.

REIFENBERG, A. "Israel's history in coins", London 1953, p.42, no.49.

REINACH, T. "Jewish coins", London 1903, pp.59-60, pl.9/1-2.

RIDER, G. le "Les ateliers monétaires de la côte Syrienne, Phénicienne, Palestinienne, Égyptienne et Cyrénéenne", Congresso Internazionale di numismatica (Roma 1961), vol. I, Relazioni, Roma 1961, pp.95, 96.

ROGERS, E. "A handy guide to Jewish coins", London 1914, pp.59-60, pl.7/5.

ROSENBERGER, M. "The Rosenberger Israel collection", vol. I, Jerusalem 1972, pp.1-17, 67.

ROSENBERGER, M. "City-coins of Palestine", vol. III, Jerusalem 1977, pp.68-69.

ROSENTHAL-HEGINBOTTOM, R. "The Mampsis hoard - A preliminary report", INJ 4, 1980, pp.42, 48.

SAULCY, F. de "Recherches sur la numismatique Judaique", Paris 1854, pp.171-187, pls.15/5-9; 16-18; 19/1-5; 20/11.

AELIA CAPITOLINA

SAULCY, F. de "Numismatique de la Terre Sainte", Paris 1874, pp.83-109, 404-405, pl.5/5-11.

SEAR, D.R. "Greek Imperial coins and their values", London 1982, nos. 1249, 1272, 1274, 1275, 1507, 1518, 1526, 1683, 1697, 1712, 1717, 1877, 1885, 1886, 2059, 2070, 2273, 2297, 2462, 2688-2689, 2903, 2970-2971, 3028, 3124, 3145, 3189, 3376, 4212, 4254, 4285, 4288, 4304.

SESTINI, D. "Descriptio numorum veterum", Lipsiae 1796, pp.544-545.

SESTINI, D. "Classes generales geographiae numismaticae sev monetae urbium, populorum et regum..", Lipsiae 1797, part I, p.71, part II, p.103.

SESTINI, D. "Classes generales sev moneta vetus urbium, populorum et regum..", Florentiae 1821, p.151.

SESTINI, D. "Descrizione d'alcune medaglie Greche del museo del signore Carlo D'Ottavio Fontana", Firenze 1822, p.13.

SESTINI, D. "Descrizione delle medaglie antiche Greche del Museo Hedervariano", part 3, Firenze 1829, p.111.

SNG ANS part 6, "Palestine - South Arabia", 1981, pls. 18-19, figs. 593-634.

SNG DNM "Palestine-Charracene", 1961, pl.1/23-26.

SNG FM vol. IV, part 8, "Syria-Nabathaea", 1971, pl.136/6106.

SOLOVEICHIK, M. "The world of the Bible", London 1895, p.75, nos. 296-298 (Hebrew).

SPERBER, D. "Roman Palestine 200-400. Money and Prices", Jerusalem 1974, pp.133, 143.

SPIJKERMAN, A. "Cafarnao, III: Catalogo delle monete della città", Jerusalem 1975, pp.15, 48, 50, nos. 23, 400, 423.

SPIJKERMAN, A. "A supplemental study of the coinage of Aelia Capitolina", *LA* 7, 1956/7, pp.145-164.

SPIJKERMAN, A. "Chronique du musée de la Flagellation", *LA* 12, 1961/2, p.328.

SPIJKERMAN, A. "Observations on the coinage of Aelia Capitolina", *LA* 14, 1963/4, pp.245-260.

SPIJKERMAN, A. and STARCKY, J. "Un nouveau lot de monnaies palestiniennes", *RB* 65, 1958, pp.580-581, pl.20/79, 80.

STEVENSON, S.W. "A dictionary of Roman coins", London 1964 (rp), p.15.

STIEGLITZ, R.R. "Maritime history on Jewish coins", *SHEKEL* 10 (2), 1977, p.32.

SUKENIK, E.L. "Some unpublished coins of Aelia Capitolina", *Jewish Quarterly Review,* 1947.

SUTHERLAND, C.H.V. "The pattern of monetary development in Phoenicia and Palestine during the Early Empire", International numismatic convention in Jerusalem (1963), proceedings (A. Kindler, ed.), Tel-Aviv 1967, pp.89, 95, 96, 99.

TIEPOLO, L. and F. "Musei Theupoli antiqua numismata..", Venetiis 1736, series 4, pp.684, 689, 696, 706, 720.

VAILLANT, J. "Numismata aera imperatorum, augustarum et caesarum in coloniis, municipiis et urbibus", Paris 1688, part I, pp.220-222, 237-239, 251-253, 282-283, part II, pp.1-2, 100-102, 106-107, 275-276, 295-296, 299-300.

AELIA CAPITOLINA

VAILLANT, J. "Numismata imperatorum, augustarum et caesarum a populis Romanae ditionis Craece loquentibus", Paris 1698, p.89.

VLIET, N., van der, "Monnaies inédites ou très rares du médaillier de Sainte-Anne de Jérusalem", RB 57, 1950, pp.110-116, pl.1/1-10.

WAAGE, D.B. "Antioch on-the Orontes, IV. Part 2: Greek, Roman, Byzantine and Crusaders' coins", Princeton 1952, p.87, no.929.

WACKS, M. "Aelia Capitolina", SHEKEL 1 (3), 1968, pp.16-17.

WACKS, M. "Jerusalem: Mirrored in coins", World coins 9 (103), 1972, Sydney, Ohio, pp.882-885.

WICZAY, C.M. "Musei Hedervarii numi antiqui", part I, Vidobonae 1814, p.289, nos. 6213, 6214, pl.27/575.

<u>Auction Catalogues and Price Lists</u>

AGORA Tel-Aviv 1974 (1), p.24, nos. 149-150, pl.9.
1975 (2), nos. 191-194, pl.8.

BETTER
Haifa 1972 (1), nos. 190-213.
Haifa 1972 (2), nos. 282-290A.
Haifa 1973 (3), nos. 314-329.
Haifa 1973 (4), nos. 163-181.
Jaffo 1974 (5), nos. 131-135.
Jaffo 1974 (7), nos. 158-175.
Haifa 1974 (8), nos. 98-102.

CAHN, A.E. Frankfurt 1930 (68), pp.95-96, nos. 1588-1589.
1931 (71), pp.66-67, nos. 1093-1097, pls.32-33.

COIN GALLERIES (mail bid sale), New York, 13 July 1954, no. 1193.

COIN GALLERIES (price list), New York 1959 (17), p.16, nos. A 238.

EIDELSTEIN and HOLLAND, Haifa, 10 Nov. 1975, no. 148.

GALERIE DES MONNAIES, Genève, 15-16 Fév. 1977, no. 347.

GANS, E. "Numismatic Fine Arts" (Stock cat.), New York
1943 (2), pp.17 (nos. 6645, 7352, 7354), 19 (no.7340), 25 (no. 1370), 27 (no. 7341).
1943 (3), p.10, nos. 6645, 7352, 7354, 7340, 7341b.

GANS, E. "Numismatic Fine Arts", (Mail bid sale), Berkeley CA, USA, 1955 (15), p.23, nos. 374-378.

GANS, E. "Numismatic Fine Arts", Berkeley CA, USA,
1956 (18), p.1, no.4209.
1956 (20), p.15, nos. 4959-4960.
1960 (26), p.9, no. 6219.

GLENDINING, London, 25 March 1957, p.34, no. 441.
10 March 1965, p.21, no. 161.

HAMBURGER, L. Frankfurt, 1932 (96), p.9, no. 176, pl. 6.

HOLZER, H. "The Thomas Ollive Mabbott collection", part I, New York 1969, pp.105-106, nos. 2709-2718.

KRESS, K. München 1955 (98), p.67, no. 1989.
1958 (108), p.2, no. 65.

MALTER, J.L. "Journal of Numismatic Fine Arts", Encino CA, USA
1972 (1/5), p.100 (Asc. hoard), nos. A 17-18.
1973 (2/2), p.37, no. B 58, pl.10.

AELIA CAPITOLINA

MONNAIES ET MÉDAILLES, Basel
1954 (13), p.72, nos. 934-935, pl.33.
1962 (25), p.21, nos. 534-536, pl.9.
1966 (32), pp.43-44, nos. 381-407, pls.24-25.
1970 (41), p.77, no. 610, pl. 38.

MÜNZEN UND MEDAILLEN, Basel 1950 (96), p.2, no. 24
1955 (151), p.13, nos. 243-248.
1958 (176), p.3, nos. 51-54.
1968 (293), p.4, no. 47.
1972 (336), p.3, no. 47.
1978 (398), p.2, no. 8.
1980 (424), p.17, nos. 220-221.
1981 (436), p.14, no. 157.
1984 (468), p.14, no. 179.

MÜNZZENTRUM KÖLN 1980 (42), p.33, nos. 196-197.
1984 (53), p.79, nos. 2023-2024.

MYERS, R.J. New York 1972 (2), p.14, no. 168.

NUMISMATIC FINE ARTS, Beverly Hills, CA, USA 1979 (6), no. 407.

RAUCH, H.D. Wien 1971 (7), p.10, no. 101.
1985 (34), nos 182-184.

SCHLESSINGER, F., Berlin-Charlottenburg, 26 Feb. 1934, p.20, no. 363.

SCHLESSINGER, F., (price list), Amsterdam 1938 (9), p.4, nos. 668-672.

SCHULMAN, H.M.F., New York, 7-9 July 1970, p.19, no. 397.
14-15 Dec. 1970, p.18, no. 956.

SEABY, London 1956 (453), p.65, no. AG 198.
1956 (456), p.199, no. AG. 499.
1956 (462), p.448, no. AG 978.
1967 (584), p.162, no. A 476.

SEABY, London (con't)

1968 (593), p.29, no. A 69.
1973 (658), p.218, no. A 652.

SPINK and SON, London 1905 (13/153), nos. 18199-18214.
1925 (33/3-4), nos. 37924-37925.
1930 (38/11), no. 1785.
1931 (39/1), no. 3452.
1931 (39/9), nos. 10045-10051.
1934 (42/11), no. 36995.
1936 (44/1), nos. 48040-48043.
1939 (47/4), nos. 79413-79421.
1952 (60/4), p.214, no. 3379.
1960 (68/1), p.12, nos. 1-2.
1979 (87/12), p.560, no. 11234.

STERNBERG, F. Zürich, 25-26 Nov. 1976, pp.66-67, nos. 502-507, pl.20.

SUPERIOR STAMP AND COIN CO., Los-Angeles, June 1976, pp.22-23, nos. 226-246.

TAMAR Tel-Aviv 1975 (9), p.6, nos. 110-112.
Tel-Aviv 1975 (10), p.8, nos. 123-124.
Ramat-Gan, Israel 1976 (11), p.9, nos. 106-107.
Ramat-Gan, Israel 1976 (12), p.52, nos. 863-868.

ANTHEDON

ANONYMOUS CH 1, 1975, p.34/124.

BELLINGER, A.R. "The Syrian tetradrachms of Caracalla and Macrinus", ANS NS 3, 1940, p.13.

BENTINCK, de "Catalogue d'une collection de médailles antiques", Amsterdam, 1787, part II p.1070.

ECKHEL, J. "Doctrina numorum veterum", vol. III, Vienna 1794, pp.443-444.

FRANCESCO DE DOMINICIS, "Repertorio numismatico", Napoli 1826, vol. I, p.492.

HEAD, B.V. "Historia numorum", Oxford 1911, p.804.

HENDIN, D. "Guide to ancient Jewish coins", New York 1976, p.118.

HILL, G.F. "Some Palestinian cults in the Graeco-Roman age", Proceedings of the British Academy, vol. V, London 1912, p.413.

HILL, G.F. BMC, Palestine, 1914, pp.xlv-xlvii, p.103, pl.11/6-8.

JANIS, E. "The other coin cities of Israel", SHEKEL 3 (3), 1970, p.14.

KADMAN, L. "Numismatic evidence of the architectonic revolution in the Second Century C.E.", INB 3-4, 1962, p.72, Heb. ed. p.65.

KADMAN, L. and KINDLER, A. "Coins in Palestine throughout the ages", Tel-Aviv 1963, p.34, pl.15/12-13 (Hebrew).

KINDLER, A. "New types of Palestinian city-coins", ALON 4 (3), 1970, p.47, pl.4/1 (Hebrew).

KLIMOWSKY, E.W. "The monetary function of city coins", International numismatic convention in Jerusalem (1963), proceedings (A. Kindler, ed.), Tel-Aviv, 1967, pp.166, 172.

MATSSON, G.O. "Two unpublished Roman city coins of Palestine", NCirc. 64 (1), 1956, pp.9-10, fig. 1.

MESHORER, Y. "The city coins of Eretz-Israel and the Decapolis in the Roman period", Jerusalem 1984, pp.31, 112 (Hebrew).

MIONNET, T.E. "Description de médailles antiques, grecques and romaines", Paris, 1806-1837, vol. V, pp.522-523, vol. VIII, suppl., p.364.

RIDER, G., le "Les ateliers monêtaires de la côte Syrienne, Phénicienne, Palestinienne, Égyptienne et Cyrénéenne", Congresso Internazionale di numismatica (Roma 1961), vol. I, Relazioni, Roma 1961, p.96.

ROSENBERGER, M. "The Rosenberger Israel collection", vol. I, Jerusalem 1972, pp.32-33, 68.

SAULCY, F., de "Numismatique de la Terre Sainte", Paris 1874, pp.234-236, pl.12/1-4.

SEAR, D.R. "Greek imperial coins and their values", London 1982, no. 3377.

SESTINI, D. "Classes generales geographiae numismaticae sev monetae urbium, populorum et regum..", Lipsiae 1797, part I, p.71.

ANTHEDON

SESTINI, D. "Lettere e dissertazioni numismatiche..", vol. VI, Firenze 1819, pp.103-104.

SESTINI, D. "Classes generales sev moneta vetus urbium, populorum et regum..", Florentiae 1821, p.151.

SUTHERLAND, C.H.V. "The pattern of monetary development in Phoenicia and Palestine during the Early Empire", International numismatic convention in Jerusalem (1963), proceedings (A. Kindler, ed.), Tel-Aviv 1967, p.96.

<u>Auction Catalogues and Price Lists</u>

AGORA Tel-Aviv 1975 (2), no. 212, pl.9.

MALTER, J.L. "Journal of Numismatic Fine Arts", Encino, CA, USA 1973 (2/2), p.37/B 59.

SCHLESSINGER, F. (price list), Amsterdam 1938 (9), p.4, no. 673.

SPINK AND SON London, 1931 (39/9), no. 10052.
1939 (47/4), no. 79422.

SUPERIOR STAMP AND COIN CO., Los-Angeles, June 1976, p.23, no. 247.

ANTIPATRIS

ARIEL, D.T. "A survey of coin finds in Jerusalem", LA 32, 1982, p.318.

BELLINGER, A.R. "The Syrian tetradrachms of Caracalla and Macrinus", ANS NS 3, 1940, p.13.

HEAD, B.V. "Historia numorum", Oxford, 1911, p.802.

HENDIN, D. "Guide to ancient Jewish coins", New York, 1976, p.110, pl.9/258.

HILL, G.F. BMC, Palestine, 1914, pp.xv-xvi, p.11, pl.2/7.

JANIS, E. "The other coin cities of Israel", SHEKEL 3 (3), 1970, p.14.

KADMAN, L. "Numismatic evidence of the architectonic revolution in the Second Century C.E.", INB 3-4, 1962, p.72. Heb. ed. p.65.

KADMAN L. and KINDLER, A. "Coins in Palestine throughout the ages", Tel-Aviv 1963, p.38, pl.17/1-2 (Hebrew).

KINDLER, A. "The status of cities in Syro-Palestinian area as reflected by their coins", INJ 6-7, 1982/3, pp.84 (note 35), 85 (note 46).

KINDLER, A. "The coinage of Bostra", Warminster, England, 1983, p.61.

KLIMOWSKY, E.W. "The monetary function of city coins", International numismatic convention in Jerusalem (1963), proceedings (A. Kindler, ed.), Tel-Aviv, 1967, pp.166, 172.

ANTIPATRIS

MESHORER, Y. "The city coins of Eretz-Israel and the Decapolis in the Roman period", Jerusalem 1984, pp.53-54, 116 (Hebrew).

PRICE, M.J. and TRELL, B.L. "Coins and their cities", London 1977, p.283.

ROSENBERGER, M. "The Rosenberger Israel collection", vol.I, Jerusalem 1972, p.34.

SEAR, D.R. "Greek imperial coins and their values", London 1982, no. 3118.

SNG ANS part 6, "Palestine-South Arabia", 1981, pl.20/635.

SUTHERLAND, C.H.V. "The pattern of monetary development in Phoenicia and Palestine during the Early Empire", International numismatic convention in Jerusalem (1963), proceedings (A. Kindler, ed.), Tel-Aviv 1967, p.96.

VLIET, N., van der, "Monnaies inédites ou très rares du médaillier de Sainte-Anne de Jérusalem", RB 57, 1950, pp.116-117, pl.1/11-12.

Auction Catalogues and Price Lists

SCHLESSINGER, F. (price list), Amsterdam 1938 (9), p.3, no. 645.

STERNBERG, F. Zürich, 25-26 Nov. 1976, p.68, no. 519, pl.21.

ASCALON

ANONYMOUS — CH 1, 1975, p.34/124.

ANONYMOUS — "Numismatic finds: Coin finds from Masada", (L. Kadman), INB 6-7, 1964, p.28 (Hebrew).

ANONYMOUS — "Numismatic finds: Coin finds from the excavations at Ein-Gedi", (L. Kadman), INB 6-7, 1964, p.28 (Hebrew).

ANONYMOUS — "New coin finds at Masada", (L. Kadman), INJ 1 (3), 1963, p.61.

ANONYMOUS — "Roman legionary coins", (L. Kadman), INJ 1 (4), 1963, p.88.

ANONYMOUS — "City-coins of ancient Israel", JIN 1 (2), 1966, pp.49, 50.

ARIEL, D.T. — "A survey of coin finds in Jerusalem", LA 32, 1982, pp.280, 283, 288, 292, 312, 318, 321.

ARRIGONI, O. — "Numismata quaedam cujuscunque formae..", Tarvisii, part I (1741), Numismata Imperatoria in graecis urbibus percussa a J. Vaillant non edita, pl.3/31; part II (1744), Numism. Imper. in graecis urbibus percusa a J. Vaillant non relata, pl. 2/12.

BABELON, J. — "Catalogue de la collection de Luynes", vol. IV, Paris 1936, p.48, no. 3477, pl.129.

BARAG, D. — "The countermarks of the Legio Decima Fretensis", International numismatic convention in Jerusalem (1963), proceedings (A. Kindler, ed.), Tel-Aviv, 1967, pp.119, 120, pl.10/15-17.

BARAG, D. — "Tyrian currency in Galilee", INJ 6-7, 1982/3, p.11.

ASCALON

BARAMKI, D.C. "The coins exhibited in the Archaeological Museum of the American University of Beirut", Beirut 1968, pp.95-96, nos. 316-319, pl.8.

BARAMKI, D.C. "The coin collection of the American University of Beirut Museum. Palestine and Phoenicia", Beirut 1974, pp.44-57, pls.8/6-19; 9/1-10.

BARAMKI, D.C. "Note on a cemetery at Karm al-Shaikh, Jerusalem. Summary of coins found", QDAP 1, 1931/2, p.6.

BARAMKI, J. "Coins in the Palestine Archaeological Museum, III", QDAP 8, 1939, p.78, pl.41/7-8.

BELLINGER, A.R. "The Syrian tetradrachms of Caracalla and Macrinus", ANS NS 3, 1940, pp.11, 13, 15, 18, 19, 20, 100-101, pl.25/15-17.

BELLINGER, A.R. "The excavations at Dura-Europos. Final report VI. The coins", New Haven, USA 1949, pp.16/291; 89/1895-1896; 175; 183, pl.9.

BEN-DOR, S. "A Roman gem from Palestine", BIES 13 (3-4), 1947, p.171, pl.4/4 (Hebrew).

BENTINCK, de "Catalogue d'une collection de médailles antiques", Amsterdam, 1788, suppl., p.207.

BRETT, A.B. "A new Cleopatra tetradrachm of Ascalon", AJA 41, 1937, pp.452-463, pl.9.

BRETT, A.B. "The mint of Ascalon under the Seleucids", ANS MN 4, 1950, p.54.

CARRADICE, I. "Coinage in Judaea in the Flavian period, AD 70-96", INJ 6-7, 1982/3, p.17, pl.2/9.

CARSON, R.A.G. "The inflation of the third century and its monetary influence in the Near East", International numismatic convention in Jerusalem (1963), proceedings (A. Kindler, ed.), Tel-Aviv 1967, p.242.

CHABACHOFF, B. "Un rare bronze de Julia Domna d'Ascalon avec une date inédite(?)", CN 59-61, 1979, p.261.

ECKHEL, J. "Catalogus Musei Caesarei Vindobonensis numorum veterum..", Vindobonae, 1779, part I, p.250.

ECKHEL, J. "Doctrina numorum veterum..", vol. III, Vienna, 1794, pp.444-447.

FLESCH, M. "Group of city coins", in 'Collector's choice', Bezalel National Museum, Jerusalem 1964, p.16/82.

FLUSSER, D. "Gods, personifications and sea monsters", SEFUNIM 3, 1969/71, pp.37, 45, pls.6/20; 8/8. Heb. ed. pp.34, 42.

FORRER, L. "Weber collection, vol. III, part 2: Greek coins", London 1929, pp.797-798/8110-8116, pl.299.

FRANCESCO DE DOMINICIS, "Repertorio numismatico..", Napoli, t.I (1826), pp.43, 260-261, 492.

GESSNER, J.J. "Numismata antiqua imperatorum Romanorum latina et graeca..", Tiguri (Zürich), 18th cent., pls.27/11; 36/28; 48/18; 62/19; 68/49-51; 102/6; 136/1; 158/68.

GILMORE, P.M. "The formulae of Antioch and Tyre", NCirc. 86 (2), 1978, p.76.

GILMORE, P.M. "Syrian officinae under Caracalla and Macrinus", NCirc. 87 (6), 1979, p.288.

ASCALON

GILMORE, P.M. "Caracalla's silver mints in Syria", NCirc. 88 (3), 1980, pp.88, 89, 90.

GROSE, S.W. "Catalogue of the McClean collection of Greek coins in the Fitzwilliam Museum", vol. III, Cambridge 1929, pp.380-381/9543-9545, pl.354/6-8.

HAMBURGER, H. "A hoard of Syrian tetadrachms and Tyrian bronze coins from Gush Halav", in 'Recent studies and discoveries on ancient Jewish and Syrian coins', PINS 1, 1954, pp.67, 69. Same in IEJ 4 (3-4), 1954, pp.203, 205.

HAMBURGER, H. "The coin issues of the Roman administration from the mint of Caesarea", IEJ 20 (1-2), 1970, pp.82, 85.

HEAD, B.V. "Historia numorum", Oxford, 1911, p.804.

HEAD, B.V. and SVORONOS, J. "The illustrations of the 'Historia numorum'", Chicago, 1968 (rp), p.55, pl.28/9.

HENDIN, D. "Guide to ancient Jewish coins", New York 1976, pp.121-123, pl.9/278-281.

HEYMANN, H. "Roman legionary coins from Phoenicia", INJ 1 (3), 1963, pp.49, 50, 51, pl.3/2-3.

HILL, G.F. "Some Palestinian cults in the Graeco-Roman age", Proceedings of the British Academy, vol. V, London 1912, pp.419-423, pl./12-18.

HILL, G.F. BMC, Palestine, 1914, pp.xlviii-lxiv, pp.104-140, pls.11/9-19; 12; 13; 14/1-16.

IMHOOF-BLUMER, F. "Griechische Münzen aus dem Museum in Klagenfurt und anderen Sammlungen", NZ 16, 1884, pp.293-294.

IMHOOF-BLUMER, F. "Zur griechischen und römischen Münzkunde, II", SNR 14, 1908, pp.129-131.

JONAS, R. "Mythology on Palestinian coins", internal circular no. 2, Israel Num. Society, Haifa branch, 1959, pp.1, 2, 4, 6, 7.

KADMAN, L. and KINDLER, A. "Coins in Palestine throughout the ages", Tel-Aviv 1963, p.33, pl.15/3-11 (Hebrew).

KINDLER, A. "Thesaurus of Judaean coins from the fourth century B.C. to the third century A.D.", Jerusalem 1958, no. 28 (Hebrew).

KINDLER, A. "Imperial portraits on the coins of Ascalon", MHB 5, 1963, pp.45-47. Heb. ed. pp.43-44.

KINDLER, A. "A hoard of coins of Ascalon", ALON 2 (3), 1968, p.59 (Hebrew).

KINDLER, A. "A hoard of coins of Ascalon from the area of Hebron", ALON 2 (4), 1968, pp.66-75, pl.5 (Hebrew).

KINDLER, A. "A hoard of coins of Ascalon and Gaza", ALON 3 (2), 1968, p.55 (Hebrew).

KINDLER, A. "Numismatic documentation of Hadrian's visit to Gaza", MHB 17-18, 1975, pp.61-67, pl.12 (Hebrew).

KINDLER, A. "Two remarks", CATHEDRA 8, 1978, p.67 (Hebrew).

KINDLER, A. "Coins of the land of Israel. Bank of Israel collection", Jerusalem 1971, pp.128, 130, no. 199 (Hebrew).

KINDLER, A. "The status of cities in the Syro-Palestinian area as reflected by their coins", INJ 6-7, 1982/3, p.81.

ASCALON

KINDLER, A. "The coinage of Bostra", Warminster, England 1983, pp.28, 42.

KIRKBRIDE, A.S. "Currencies in Transjordan", PEQ 1939, p.155.

KLAWANS, Z.H. "An outline of ancient Greek coins", Wisconsin, USA 1959, p.65.

KLIMOWSKY, E.W. "The monetary function of city coins", International numismatic convention in Jerusalem (1963), proceedings (A. Kindler, ed.), Tel-Aviv, 1967, pp.130, 140, 141, 144, 147, 150, 153, 154, 155, 158, 160, 164, 166, 168, 170, 172, 175, 177.

KLIMOWSKY, E.W. "Roman imperial 'Virtutes' on contemporaneous city coins", INJ 3, 1965/6, p.24, pl.6/40. Same in 'On ancient Palestinian and other coins, their symbolism and metrology', PINS 7, Tel-Aviv, 1974, p.97, pl.7/40.

KUBITSCHEK, W. "Zur Geschichte von Städten des römischen Kaiserreiches. Epigraphisch-numismatische Studien", heft 1, Wien 1916, pp.29-31, 59-64, 65-66, 100.

LAMBERT, C. "Coins in the Palestine Museum, II", QDAP 1, 1931/2, pp.130-131, pl.54/1-7.

LEDERER, P. "Neue Beiträge zur antiken Münzkunde aus schweizerischen öffentlichen und privaten Sammlungen", SNR 30, 1943, pp.83-84, pl.6/99.

LIEBE, C.S. "Gotha numaria, sistens Thesauri Fridericiani..", Amsterdam 1730, pp.310-311.

MACDONALD, G. "Catalogue of Greek coins in the Hunterian collection", Glasgow 1905, vol. III, pp.280-281, pl.77/28-29.

MANNS, F. "Gemmes de l'époque Gréco-Romaine provenant de Palestine", LA 28, 1978, pp.158, 160, 162, 163, 165, 166, 167, 169, pls.27/18; 28/29; 29/41-42; 30/51; 31/56, 59; 32/66; 33/76.

MATSSON, G.O. "The gods, goddesses and heroes on the ancient coins of Bible Lands", Stockholm 1969, pp.9, 12, 30, 54, 57, 65, 73, 159, 160, 166, 182, 186, 192, 193, 197, 203, 209, 210, 232-233, 240, 243, pls.1/7a, 8b; 2/25d; 3/41c 43; 6/98a; 7/113a, b; 8/116.

MESHORER, Y. "Catalogue of coins", in 'Ships and parts of ships on ancient coins', (Ben-Eli, A.L., ed.), part I, National Maritime Museum of Haifa, 1975, p.74/66-67.

MESHORER, Y. "Coins of the Ancient World", Jerusalem 1979, p.58 (Hebrew).

MESHORER, Y. "The city coins of Eretz-Israel and the Decapolis in the Roman period", Jerusalem 1984, pp.26-28, 111-112 (Hebrew).

MEYSHAN, J. "The symbols on the coinage of Herod the Great and their meanings", PEQ 1959, p.117. Same in 'Essays in Jewish numismatics' Jerusalem 1968, p.93.

MILDENBERG, L. "Numismatische Evidenz zur Chronologie der Bar Kochba-Erhebung", SNR 34, 1948/9, p.22.

MIONNET, T.E. "Description de médailles antiques, grecques et romaines", Paris 1806-1837, vol. V, pp.523-533, vol. VIII, suppl., pp.365-370.

PATIN, C. "Imperatorum Romanorum numismata ex aere mediae et minimae formae descripta et enarrata..", Amsterdam(?), 1671, pp.45, 151, 227.

ASCALON

PICCIRILLO, M. "Le monete della Fortezza di Macheronte", LA 30, 1980, pp.403, 406-407, pl.103/12.

PLANT, R. "Greek coin types and their identification", London 1979, nos. 183x, 446, 1592, 2244.

PRICE, M.J. and TRELL, B.L. "Coins and their cities", London 1977, pp.166, 284, fig. 466.

RAPPAPORT, U. "Ascalon and the coinage of Judaea", Studies in the history of the Jewish people and the Land of Israel, IV, Haifa Univ., 1978, pp.77-88 (Hebrew).

REICHARDT, H.C. "Unpublished Greek Imperial coins", NC, Ns 2, 1862, pp.117-119.

REICHARDT, H.C. "Remarks on some Jewish coins and on some inedited coins of Phoenicia, Judaea, etc.", NC, Ns 4, 1864, p.188.

ROSENBERGER, M. "The Rosenberger Israel collection", vol. I, Jerusalem 1972, pp.34-67.

ROSENBERGER, M. "City-coins of Palestine", vol. III, Jerusalem 1977, pp.73-78.

ROSENBERGER, M. "The coinage of Eastern Palestine", Jerusalem 1978, pp.81, 82, 84.

ROSENTHAL-HEGINBOTTOM, R. "The Mampsis hoard - A preliminary report", INJ 4, 1980, p.48.

SAULCY, F., de "Numismatique de la Terre Sainte", Paris 1874, pp.178-208, 406, pls.9/5-19; 10/1-11.

SAULCY, F., de "Note sur quelques monnaies inédites d'Ascalon", RN, Ns 15, 1875/77, pp.124-135.

SCHONWALTER, R. "Numismatic evidence from the Dead Sea", NUMISMATIST 71 (7), 1958, p.796.

SEAR, D.R. "Greek imperial coins and their values", London 1982, nos. 119, 296, 404, 482, 631, 740, 783, 884, 1093, 1250, 1508, 1803, 2274, 2690, 2972, 3125, 3378, 5216.

SESTINI, D. "Descriptio numorum veterum..", Lipsiae 1796, pp.545-546.

SESTINI, D. "Classes generales geographiae numismaticae sev monetae urbium, populorum et regum", Lipsiae 1797, part I, p.71, part II, p.103.

SESTINI, D. "Classes generales sev moneta vetus urbium, populorum et regum..", Florentiae 1821, pp.151-152.

SESTINI, D. "Descrizione d'alcune medaglie Greche del museo del Signore Carlo D'Ottavio Fontana", Firenze 1822, p.13.

SESTINI, D. "Descrizione delle medaglie antiche Greche del Museo Hedervariano", part 3, Firenze 1829, pp.112-114.

SEYRIG, H. "Antiquités Syriennes 3. Numismatique supposée de Chalcis au Liban", SYRIA 12, 1931, p.324.

SEYRIG, H. "Antiquités Syriennes 11. Sur certain tétradrachmes provinciaux de Syrie", SYRIA 13, 1932, p.367.

SEYRIG, H. "Antiquités Syriennes 25. Sur quelques monnaies provinciales de Syrie et de Cilicie", SYRIA 20, 1939, p.42, fig. 3.

ASCALON

SEYRIG, H. "Antiquités Syriennes 89. Les dieux armés et les Arabes en Syrie (4. Les dieux armés hors de Palmyre)", SYRIA 47, 1970, pp.96-97, Fig. 18.

SEYRIG, H. "Notes on Syrian coins", NNM 119, 1950, p.32.

SNG ANS part 6, "Palestine - South Arabia", 1981, pls.20-23, figs. 636-743.

SNG DNM "Palestine-Characene", Copenhagen 1961, pl.2/27-42.

SPAER, A. "Ascalon: from royal mint to autonomy", in 'Festschrift für Leo Mildenberg', (A. Hougton, S. Hurter, P.E. Mottahedeh and J.A. Scott, eds.), Wetteren, Belgium 1984, pp.229-239, pls.35-37.

SPANHEMIUS, E. "Dissertationes de praestantia et usu numismatum antiquorum", new ed., t.I, London 1706, p.723 (addenda).

SPERBER, D. "Roman Palestine 200-400. Money and prices", Jerusalem 1974, p.143.

SPIJKERMAN, A. "Herodion III. Catalogo delle monete", Jerusalem 1972, p.98.

STAHL, Z. "The Flavian Emperors and their coins in Eretz-Israel", special brochure of Israel Num. Society, Tel-Aviv branch, 1976, p.7 (Hebrew).

STAHL, Z. "Roman coins of Palestine cities issued during the Jewish War, 66-70 C.E.", special brochure of Israel Num. Society, Tel-Aviv branch, 1979, pp.12, 22-23, 25 (Hebrew).

STIEGLITZ, R.R. "Maritime history on Jewish coins", SHEKEL 10 (2), 1977, p.33.

SUTHERLAND, C.H.V. "The pattern of monetary development of Phoenicia and Palestine during the Early Empire", International numismatic convention in Jerusalem (1963), proceedings (A. Kindler, ed.), Tel-Aviv 1967, pp.89, 90, 91, 94, 95, 96, 97.

THIERCH, H. "Archäologischer Jahresbericht", ZDPV 37, 1914, p.73, pl.33/4-10.

TIEPOLO, L. and F. "Musei Theupoli antiqua numismata..", Venetiis 1736, series 6, pp.842, 851, 887.

TRELL, B. "Phoenician Greek Imperial coins", INJ 6-7, 1982/3, p.132, pl.28/52.

VAILLANT, J. "Numismata imperatorum, augustarum et caesarum a populis Romanae ditionis, Greace loquentibus..", Paris 1698, pp.2, 8, 11, 14-15, 20, 21, 42, 92, 152, 163, 232, 330-335.

VAUX, R., de "Fouilles au Khirbet Qumrân, IV. Les monnaies", RB 61, 1954, p.230.

VLIET, N., van der "Monnaies inédites ou très rares du médaillier de Sainte-Anne de Jérusalem", RB 57, 1950, p.117, pl.2/13.

WAAGE, D.B. "Antioch on-the-Orontes, IV. Part two: Greek, Roman, Byzantine and Crusaders' coins", Princeton 1952, p.87, no.930.

WALCHER de MOLTHEIN, L. "Catalogue de la collection des médailles grecques de M. Le Chevalier", Paris - Vienne 1895, pp.269-271, nos.3171-3199, pl.30/3174, 3180, 3184-3185, 3199.

ASCALON

WICZAY, C.M. "Musei Hedervarii numi antiqui..", Vindobonae 1814, part I, p.289, nos. 6215-6227, pl.27/576-577.

YADIN, Y. "The excavation of Masada, 1963/4. Preliminary report", IEJ 15 (1-2), 1965, p.81.

ZURI, N. "A hoard of bronze and silver coins from Ain Hanaziv", INB 1962 (3-4), p.105. Heb. ed. p.88.

<u>Auction Catalogues and Price Lists</u>

AGORA Tel-Aviv 1974 (1), pp.24-25, nos. 151-153, pl.9.
1975 (2), nos. 195-211, pls.8-9.

ANTIQUITY IMPORTS, (price cat.), Minneapolis MN, USA 1976 (1), p.8, no.135.

BETTER Haifa 1972 (1), nos. 151-154.
Haifa 1972 (2), nos. 249-251A.
Haifa 1973 (3), nos. 267, 294-301.
Haifa 1973 (4), nos. 224, 234.
Jaffo 1974 (5), nos. 137-139.
Jaffo 1974 (7), nos. 179-203.
Haifa 1974 (8), nos. 106-114.

BUTTON, E. (price list), Frankfurt 1938 (35), p.5, nos.3050-3057.

CAHN, A.E. Frankfurt 1930 (68), p.96, nos. 1590-1592.
1931 (71), p.67, nos. 1098-1107, pls.21, 33.

COIN GALLERIES (mail bid sale), New York, 13 July 1954, nos.1194-1196.

COIN GALLERIES (auc), New York, 24-25 May 1963, p.36, no. 755.

COIN GALLERIES (price list), New York 1959 (17), p.16, nos. A 230-234.

EIDELSTEIN and HOLLAND, Haifa, 10 Nov. 1975, nos. 153-162.

EIDELSTEIN and HOLLAND, (price list), Haifa, summer 1976, no. 164.

GANS, E. "Numismatic Fine Arts" (Stock cat.), New York
1943 (2), p.17, no. 7349.
1943 (3), p.10, nos. 6305, 8765, 8766, 7349.

GANS, E. "Numismatic Fine Arts" (mail bid sale), Berkeley CA, USA 1955 (15), p.24, nos. 381-383.

GANS, E. "Numismatic Fine Arts", Berkeley CA, USA
1956 (18), p.1, no.4210.
1956 (20), p.15, nos. 4961-4966.
1958 (24), p.12, no. 5832.

GLENDINING London, 19 July 1950, p.46, nos. 334, 336.
21-23 Feb. 1961, p.99, no. 3005.
10 March 1965, pp.21 (nos. 162-164, pl.6),
26 (nos. 217-218, pl.8).

HAMBURGER, L. Frankfurt 1932 (96), p.10, nos. 177-178, pl.6.

HESS, A. Frankfurt 1936 (224), p.58, no. 1748.

HIRSCH, G. München 1963 (37), p.28, no. 555, pl.12.
1965 (45), p.67, no. 1802, pl.15.
1971 (75), p.17, no. 295, pl.4.
1973 (84), p.11, no. 159.

HOLZER, H. "The Thomas Ollive Mabbott collection", part I, New York 1969, p.106, nos. 2719-2721.

KRAUS, F.F. (price list), Braunschweig, Germany,
1928 (2), p.47, nos. 1085-1086.
1929 (1-2), p.54 nos. 1244-1246.

ASCALON

KRESS, K. München 1955 (98), p.67, no. 1990.
1958 (108), p.2, no. 66.
1961 (119), p.6, no. 388, pl.4.
1962 (124), p.6, nos. 369-375.
1967 (139), p.8 no. 420.

MALLOY, A. (price list), New York 1970/71 (20), p.20, no. 428.

MALTER, J.L. "Journal of Numismatic Fine Arts", Encino CA, USA.
1972 (1/5), p.100 (Asc. hoard), nos. A 1-14.
1973 (2/2), p.37, no. B 60.

MALTER, J.L. "Constantinopole Fine Arts", Encino CA, USA 1970 (1), p.10, no. 183.

MONNAIES ET MÉDAILLES, Basel 1954 (13), p.72, no. 936, pl.33.
1962 (25), p.20, nos. 516-517, pl.8.
1966 (32), pp.38-39, nos. 298-327, pl.22.

MÜNZEN UND MEDAILLEN, Basel 1952 (112), p.6, no. 135.
1955 (152), p.12, nos. 225-234.
1958 (176), p.3, nos. 55-56.
1968 (293), p.4, nos. 40-41.
1969 (305), p.3, no. 39.
1979 (412), p.14, no. 271.
1979 (417), p.2, no. 22.
1980 (424), p.17, nos. 222-225.
1981 (435), p.21, no. 234.
1984 (468), p.14, nos. 180-183.

MÜNZZENTRUM KÖLN, (price list), 1970 (2), p.9, no. 184d.

MÜNZZENTRUM KÖLN, (auc.), 1981 (43), pp.35-36, nos. 210-213.
1983 (48), p.31, nos. 200-205.

MYERS, R.J. New York 1971 (1), no. 305.
1973 (5), no. 270.

NUMISMATICA WIEN, 1975 (9), p.23, no. 129.

NUMISMATIC FINE ARTS, Beverly Hills, CA, USA
1976 (3), nos. 165/3, 167/1.
1979 (6), no. 408.
1983 (12), nos. 104-105.

PEUS, B. (price list), Frankfurt 1970 (14), p.3, nos. 39-40.

RAUCH, H.D. Wien 1971 (7), p.10, no. 100.
1985 (34), nos. 185-200.

SCHLESSINGER, F. (price list), Amsterdam 1938 (9), p.4, nos. 674-678.

SCHULMAN, H.M.F., New York, 18-19 Nov. 1955, p.71, no. 1922.
7-9 July 1970, p.19, nos. 395-396.
6-8 Oct. 1970, p.19, no. 229.
14-15 Dec. 1970, p.18, nos. 957-959.
6-7 Apr. 1971, p.24, nos. 436-437.

SEABY, London 1958 (478), p.118, no. AG. 264.
1962 (528), p.206, no. A 368.
1962 (534), p.436, no. A 971.
1965 (567), p.317, nos. A 766-767.
1966 (575), p.216, no. A 473.
1967 (591), p.435, no. A 1131.
1968 (595), p.146, no. A 331.
1968 (599), p.261, no. A 575.
1971 (635), p.261, no. A 640.
1971 (637), p.336, nos. A 857-860.
1979 (736), p.402, no. C 1351.

SPINK AND SON, London 1905 (13/154), nos. 19019-19051.
1925 (33/3-4), nos. 37837-37848.
1925 (33/9-10), no. 43258.
1925 (33/11-12), nos. 45382, 45424.

SPINK AND SON, London (con't)

1930 (38/11), no. 1786.
1931 (39/9), nos. 10053-10063.
1934 (42/7), no. 34225.
1934 (42/8-9), nos. 34997, 35017-35019.
1934 (42/10), nos. 36181-36183.
1934 (42/11), nos. 37006-37008.
1936 (44/1), nos. 48044-48081.
1939 (47/4), nos. 79423-79443.
1952 (60/4), p.214, no. 3382.
1960 (68/1), p.12, nos. 4-6, p.13, no. 27.
1963 (71/7-8), p.151, no. 5748.
1977 (85/7-8), p.318, nos. 6650-6652.
1977 (85/12), p.553, nos. 13059-13060.
1980 (88/11), p.408, no. 9122.
1981 (89/6), nos. 4528-4529.
1981 (89/7-8), no. 5231.

STACK'S New York, 23 Sept. 1961, p.41, no. 864.
10-11 June 1970, p.37, no. 457.

STERNBERG, F. Zürich, 25-26 Nov. 1976, pp.70-72, nos. 534-557, pls.22-23.

STERNBERG, F. Zürich 1977 (7), p.27, no. 173, pl.8.

SUPERIOR STAMP AND COIN CO., Los-Angeles, June 1976, pp.23-24, nos. 248-257.

TAMAR Tel-Aviv 1975 (9), p.6, nos. 116-125.
Tel-Aviv 1975 (10), p.9, nos. 126-129.
Ramat-Gan, Israel 1976 (12), p.52, no. 871.

VINCHON, J. "Monnaies Juives", Paris, 13 Fév. 1970, no. 86.

BOSTRA

ARIEL, D.T. "A survey of coin finds in Jerusalem", LA 32, 1982, p.318.

BABELON, J. "Catalogue de la collection de Luynes", vol. IV, Paris 1936, p.55, no. 3506, pl.130.

BARAG, D. "Tyrian currency in Galilee", INJ 6-7, 1982/3, pp.9, 11.

BELLINGER, A.R. "Coins from Jerash 1928-1934", NNM 81, 1938, pp.9, 27-29, nos. 32-39, pl.2.

BELLINGER, A.R. "The excavations at Dura-Europos. Final report IV. The coins", New Haven, USA 1949, p.87, nos. 1853-1854.

BEN-DAVID, A. "'Dinarei Arba' and silver coins called 'Harubim'", ALON 5 (2), 1974, pp.27-28 (Hebrew).

BENTINCK, de "Catalogue d'une collection de médailles antiques", Amsterdam, 1787, part I, pp.294, 476; part II, p.1076.

BERNHART, M. "Dionysos und seine Familie auf griechischen Münzen", JNG 1, 1949, p.167, nos. 1455-1456.

CHAIX, E. "Recherche des monnaies coloniales Romaines non décrites dans l'ouvrage de H. Cohen", ASFN 17, 1893, p.24, no. 16.

COHEN, H. "Médailles Imperiales", Leipzig 1930 (rp), vol. IV, pp.238/922-925, 371/478, 475-476/716-722; 501/115-120; vol. V, pp.132/372-374; 205/179-180; 214/47; 223-224/3-7.

DREXLER, W. "Bemerkungen zu einigen Münzen", ZN 13, 1885, pp.280-281.

BOSTRA

DUSSAUD, R. "Le culte de Dusarès d'après les monnaies d'Adraa et de Bostra", RN, 4th s., 8, 1904, pp.160-173.

ECKHEL, J. "Numi veteres anecdoti ex museis Caesareo Vindobonensi, Florentino Magni Ducis Etruriae..", Viennae 1775, p.289.

ECKHEL, J. "Catalogus Musei Caesarei Vindobonensis numorum veterum..", Vindobonae 1779, part I, p.252.

ECKHEL, J. "Doctrina numorum veterum..", vol. III, Vienna 1794, pp.500-503, vol. V, p.289.

FLUSSER, D. "Gods, personifications and sea monsters", SEFUNIM 3, 1969/71, p.28, pl.4/3. Heb. ed. p.26.

FORRER, L. "Weber collection. Vol. III, part 2: Greek coins", London 1929, p.809, no. 8150, pl.300.

FROELICH, E. "Quatuor tentamina in re numaria vetere", 2nd ed., Viennae 1737, p.127.

GESSNER, J.J. "Numismata antiqua Imperatorum Romanorum latina et graeca..", Tiguri (Zürich), 18th cent., pls. 136/62; 164/38; 165/25-27; 167/6-8; 180/32.

HAMBURGER, H. "A hoard of Syrian tetradrachms and Tyrian bronze coins from Gush Halav", in 'Recent studies and discoveries on ancient Jewish and Syrian coins', PINS 1, 1954, p.71. Same in IEJ 4 (3-4), 1954, p.207.

HANSON, R.S. and BATES, M.L. "Numismatic report" in 'Ancient synagogue excavations at Khirbet Shema, Upper Galilee, Israel, 1970-1972', AASOR 42, 1976, p.154, pl.6.2/R1404.

HANSON, R.S. "Tyrian influence in the Upper Galilee", Cambridge 1980, p.52.

HARDING, L. "Recent work on the Jerash Forum. The coins", PEQ 1949, p.18.

HEAD, B.V. "Historia numorum", Oxford 1911, p.812.

HILL, G.F. BMC, Arabia, Mesopotamia and Persia, 1922, pp.xxiv-xxx, 16-26, pls. 3/6-17; 4/1-13; 49/13-16.

HILL, G.F. "Greek coins acquired by the British Museum in 1922", NC, 5th s., 3, 1923, p.238.

JESSELSOHN, D. "The two-humped camel drachms of Trajan, the reason for its issue, a new variant", ALON 5 (4), 1976, p.72 (Hebrew).

KADMAN, L. "Numismatic evidence of the architectonic revolution in the Second Century C.E.", INB 1962 (3-4), p.73. Heb. ed. p.65.

KINDLER, A. "Two coins of the Third Legion Cyrenaica struck under Antoninus Pius", IEJ 25(2-3), 1975, pp.145-147, pl.14.

KINDLER, A. "The status of cities in the Syro-Palestinian area as reflected by their coins", INJ 6-7, 1982/3, pp.82, 84 (note 34).

KINDLER, A. "The coinage of Bostra", Warminster, England 1983.

KIRKBRIDE, A.S. "Some rare coins from Transjordan", BASOR 106, 1947, p.8, figs.3-4/6.

KIRKBRIDE, A.S. "Currencies in Transjordan", PEQ 1939, p.155.

BOSTRA

KLAWANS, Z.H. "An outline of ancient Greek coins", Wisconsin, USA 1959, p.69.

KLIMOWSKY, E.W. "The monetary function of city coins", International numismatic convention in Jerusalem (1963), proceedings (A. Kindler, ed.), Tel-Aviv 1967, pp.164, 168, 172, 177.

KLIMOWSKY, E.W. "The origin and meaning of Marsyas in the Greek Imperial coinage", INJ 6-7, 1982/3, pp.95, 98.

KUBITSCHEK, W. "Bostra", NZ, Nf 9 (49), 1916, pp.182-194.

LAMBERT, C. "Coins in the Palestine Museum, II", QDAP 1, 1931/2, pp.135-136, pls.55/22-23, 56/24.

MACDONALD, G. "Catalogue of Greek coins in the Hunterian collection", Glasgow 1905, vol. III, p.299, pl.78/21.

MESHORER, Y. "The city-coins of Eretz-Israel and the Decapolis in the Roman period", Jerusalem 1984, pp.87-88, 120-121 (Hebrew).

MIONNET, T.E. "Description de médailles antiques, grecques et romaines", Paris 1806-1837, vol. V, pp.579-585, vol. VII (notes et observations), p.110, vol. VIII, suppl., pp.383-386.

MOREY, C.R. "Une nouvelle représentation de Dusarès et autres types monétaires de Bostra (Arabie)", RN, 4th s., 15, 1911, pp.69-85, pl.3.

PRICE, M.J. and TRELL, B.L. "Coins and their cities", London 1977, pp.38, 145, 284, fig. 257.

PATIN, C. "Imperatorum Romanorum numismata ex aere mediae et minimae formae descripta et enarrata", Amsterdam(?), 1671, pp.264, 343.

PATRICH, J. "Prohibition of a graven-image among the Nabateans - the testimony of the Massebot-cult", CATHEDRA 26, 1982, pp.62, 64-65, fig. 12 (Hebrew).

PELLERIN, J. "Mélange de diverses médailles..", t.I, part 3, Paris 1764, p.308, pl.19/6; p.324, pl.21/7.

PELLERIN, J. "Recueil de médailles de peuples et de villes", part 6, suppl., Paris 1763, p.246, pl.134/10-11.

PLANT, R. "Greek coin types and their identification", London 1979, nos. 285, 794, 2043.

RAHMANI, L. and SHARABANI, M. "List of coins", in 'Hammath Tiberias' by M. Dothan, Jerusalem 1983, p.72, pl.22/23.

ROSENBERGER, M. "The coinage of Eastern Palestine", Jerusalem 1978, pp.7-17.

SAULCY, F., de "Numismatique de la Terre Sainte", Paris 1874, pp.361-372, pl.21.

SEAR, D.R. "Greek imperial coins and their values", London 1982, nos. 1510, 1539, 1686, 2063, 2278, 2296, 2464, 2694, 3131, 3380, 3482, 3968, 4063, 4155, 4213, 4255, 4289, 5218.

SESTINI, D. "Descriptio numorum veterum..", Lipsiae 1796, pp.548-549.

SESTINI, D. "Classes generales geographiae numismaticae sev monetae urbium, populorum et regum..", Lipsiae 1797, part I, p.73, part II, p.104.

BOSTRA

SESTINI, D. "Lettere e dissertazioni numismatiche", t.VI, Firenze 1819, pp.104, 95, pl.2/12.

SESTINI, D. "Classes generales sev moneta vetus urbium, populorum et regum..", Florentiae 1821, pp.155-156.

SESTINI, D. "Descrizione d'alcune medaglie greche del museo del Signore Carlo D'Ottavio Fontana", Firenze 1822, p.14.

SESTINI, D. "Descrizione delle medaglie antiche Greche del Museo Hedervariano", part 3, Firenze 1829, p.122, pl.32/1.

SEYRIG, H. "Antiquités Syriennes 89. Les dieux armés et les Arabes en Syrie (4. Les dieux armés hors de Palmyre)", SYRIA 47, 1970, pp.95-96, fig. 16.

SNG ANS part 6, "Palestine - South Arabia", 1981, pls.39-42, nos. 1153-1256.

SNG DNM "Palestine-Characene", Copenhagen 1961, pl. 5, figs. 139-149.

SPANHEMIUS, E. "Dissertationes de praestantia et usu numismatum antiquorum", new ed., t.I, London 1706, p.186.

SPIJKERMAN, A. "Cafarnao, vol. III: Catalogo delle monete della città", Jerusalem 1975, pp.16/30; 51/435.

SPIJKERMAN, A. "The coins of the Decapolis and provincia Arabia", Jerusalem 1978, pp.66-89, 282-283, pls.12-17.

STEVENSON, S.W. "A dictionary of Roman coins", London 1964 (rp), pp.133-134.

TIEPOLO, L. and F. "Musei Theupoli antiqua numismata..", Venetiis 1736, series 4, pp.726, 730, 741, 748; series 6, pp.831, 936.

VAILLANT, J. "Numismata aera imperatorum, augustarum et caesarum in coloniis, municipiis et urbibus..", Paris 1688, part II, pp.163-166, 186-187, 351-352 (Tyre).

VAILLANT, J. "Numismata imperatorum, augustarum et caesarum a populis Romanae ditionis Graece loquentibus..", Paris 1698, pp.76, 116, 233, 477.

WEBSTER, W. "List of inedited Greek coins - copper", NC, Ns 13, 1873, p.40.

WICZAY, C.M. "Musei Hedervarii numi antiqui..", Vindobonae 1814, part I, p.293, nos. 6273-6276.

Auction Catalogues and Price Lists

AGORA Tel-Aviv 1975 (2), nos. 226-229, pl.10.

BETTER Haifa 1972 (1), nos. 271-273.
Haifa 1972 (2), nos. 366-368.
Haifa 1973 (4), nos. 266-268.
Jaffo 1974 (7), nos. 268-276.
Haifa 1974 (8), nos. 176-182.

CAHN, A.E. Frankfurt 1931 (71), p.69, nos. 1120-1121.

EIDELSTEIN AND HOLLAND, (price list), Haifa, summer 1976, no. 167.

GANS, E. "Numismatic Fine Arts" (Stock cat.), New York 1943 (2), p.27, no. 6311.

GANS, E. "Numismatic Fine Arts", Berkeley CA, USA 1956 (20), pl.16, no. 4992.

BOSTRA

GLENDINING London, 10 March 1965, p.23, nos. 178-179, pl.6.

HESS, A. Frankfurt 1936 (224), p.59, no. 1752.

HOLZER, H. "The Thomas Ollive Mabbott collection", part I, New York 1969, p.111, nos. 2865-2870.

KRESS, K. München 1978 (172), p.35, no.841.

MALTER, J.L. "Journal of Numismatic Fine Arts", Encino CA, USA 1973 (2/2), p.37/B 62.

MONNAIES ET MÉDAILLES, Basel, 1966 (32), pp.50-51, nos. 498-506, pl.29.

MÜNZEN UND MEDAILLEN, Basel 1955 (152), p.12, no. 237.
1958 (176), p.4, no. 59.
1980 (424), pp.4 (no. 67), 17 (no. 207).
1981 (436), p.14, no. 160.

MÜNZZENTRUM KÖLN, 1981 (43), p.34, nos. 198-199.
1982 (47), p.44, nos. 257-258.
1984 (53), p.81, nos. 2042-2043.

NUMISMATIC FINE ARTS, Beverly Hills CA, USA 1976 (3), no. 167/2.

RAUCH, H.D. Wien 1985 (34), no. 204.

SALTON-SCHLESSINGER, M.M. (price list), New York 1958 (27), p.7, nos. 139-141.

SCHLESSINGER, F. (price list), Amsterdam 1938 (9), p.5, nos. 694-696.

SCHULMAN, H.M.F., New York, 6-7 Apr. 1971, p.50, no. 579.

SEABY, London 1957 (474), p.484, no. AG 972.
1957 (475), p.522, no. AG 1083.
1958 (481), p.244, no. AG 581.
1960 (509), p.423, no. A 874.
1961 (513), p.73, no. A 166.
1964 (554), p.261, no. A 482.
1969 (616), pp.438, 439, nos. A 1151, A 1179.
1970 (628), p.461, no. A 1059.
1972 (647), p.280, no. A 860.

SPINK AND SON, London 1930 (38/11), no. 1807.
1931 (39/1), no. 3453.
1931 (39/4), no. 6044.
1932 (40/1), nos. 12401-12408.
1934 (42/10), no. 36185.
1934 (42/12), nos. 37856-37857.
1979 (87/11), p.511, no. 10051.

STERNBERG, F. Zürich, 25-26 Nov. 1976, pp.73-74, nos.565-572, pl.23.
18-19 Nov. 1982 (12), p.74, no. 629, pl.24.

SUPERIOR STAMP AND COIN CO., Los-Angeles, June 1976, p.24, nos. 261-264.

TAMAR Tel-Aviv 1975 (9), p.8, nos. 170-175.
Tel-Aviv 1975 (10), p.10, no.163.
Ramat-Gan, Israel 1976 (11), p.11, nos. 145-146.
Ramat-Gan, Israel 1976 (12), p.53, nos. 883-884.

VECCHI, V.C. "Bonhams", London 1982 (8), p.19, no. 219, pl.10.

CAESAREA

ANONYMOUS — *CH* 1, 1975, p.34/124.

ANONYMOUS — "Caesarea coins hitherto unpublished", (L. Kadman), *INB* 2, 1962, p.57, pl.1/21-22. Heb ed. pp.50-51, pl.1/21-22.

ANONYMOUS — "Numismatic finds: Coin finds from Masada", (L. Kadman), *INB* 6-7, 1964, p.28 (Hebrew).

ANONYMOUS — "City-coins of ancient Israel" *JIN* 1 (2) 1966, p.50.

ARIEL, D.T. — "A survey of coin finds in Jerusalem", *LA* 32, 1982, pp.292, 295, 318.

ARRIGONI, O. — "Numismata quaedam cujuscunque formae..", Tarvisii, part II (1744), Numismata in coloniis cusa a J. Vaillant non relata, pls. 5/40; 6/57; 8/79; Numismata Imperatoria in graecis urbibus percusa a J. Vaillant non relata, pl.5/39.

BANKS, A.F. — "Coins of Bible days", New York 1955, p.104.

BARAG, D. — "The countermarks of the Legio Decima Fretensis", International numismatic convention in Jerusalem (1963), proceedings (A. Kindler, ed.), Tel-Aviv 1967, pp.119, 120, pls. 9/5-6; 10/7.

BARAG, D. — "Tyrian currency in Galilee", *INJ* 6-7, 1982/3, pp.10, 11, 12.

BARAMKI, D.C. — "The coins exhibited in the Archaeological Museum of the American University of Beirut", Beirut 1968, p.91/305-307, pl.8.

BARAMKI, D.C. "The coin collection of the American University of Beirut Museum. Palestine and Phoenicia", Beirut 1974, pp.6-16, pls. 1/14-18; 2; 3/1-2.

BARAMKI, J. "Coins in the Palestine Archaeological Museum, III", QDAP 8, 1939, p.79, pl.41/13.

BELLINGER, A.R. "Coins from Jerash", NNM 81, 1938, pp.9, 25, nos. 22-23, pl.1.

BELLINGER, A.R. "The Syrian tetradrachms of Caracalla and Macrinus", ANS NS 3, 1940, pp.11, 13, 15, 17, 18, 19, 20, 98-99, pls.24/17; 25/1-14.

BELLINGER, A.R. "The excavations at Dura-Europos. Final report VI. The coins", New Haven, USA 1949, pp.16/286-290; 18/348-351; 19/363-364; 89/1893; 165, 167, 175, 183.

BENTINCK, de "Catalogue d'une collection de médailles antiques", Amsterdam 1787, part II, p.1072; suppl., (1788), p.207.

BERMAN, A. "A numismatic survey in Yotapatha", INB 2, 1962, p.49. Heb. ed. p.43.

BERNHART, M. "Dionysos und seine Familie auf griechischen Münzen", JNG 1, 1949, p.112/842-843.

CARRADICE, I. "Coinage in Judaea in the Flavian period, AD 70-96", INJ 6-7, 1982/3, pp.17, 19.

CARSON, R.A.G. "The coins of Caesarea Maritima. Corpus Nummorum Palaestinensium, vol. II by Leo Kadman - Review", NCirc. 66 (4), 1958, p.93.

CARSON, R.A.G. "The inflation of the Third Century and its monetary influence in the Near East", International numismatic

CARSON, R.A.G. (con't) convention in Jerusalem (1963), proceedings (A. Kindler, ed.), Tel-Aviv 1967, pp.240, 242.

CHAIX, E. "Recherche des monnaies coloniales Romaines non decrites dans l'ouvrage de H. Cohen", ASFN 16, 1892, pp.204/25; 223/2.

CHEHAB, M. "Monnaies Gréco-Romaines et Phéniciennes du Musée National, Beyrouth, Liban", Paris 1977, p.77.

COHEN, H. "De la numismatique de Pescennius Niger", RN, Ns 13, 1868, p.435, pl.15/6.

COHEN, H. "Médailles Imperiales", Leipzig 1930 (rp), vol. II, pp.93/710-714; 242/1585-1589; 403/1243-1248; vol. III, pp.123-124/1205-1215; 167-168/309-310; 212-213/418-420; 225/108; 375/1184-1187; vol. IV, pp.96/935; 135/335; 236-237/907-914; 309-310/186-189; 318/49; 370/465-467; 475/713-714; vol. V, pp.85/564; 130/356-358; 177/139; 201-203/151-166; 214/45-46; 222/49-53; 234/76-80; 261/198-204; 286/192-198; 335/375.

ECKHEL, J. "Catalogus Musei Caesarei Vindobonensis numorum veterum..", Vindobonae 1779, part I, pp.246-247.

ECKHEL, J. "Doctrina numorum veterum..", Vienna, vol. III (1794), pp.361, 428-432, vol. V (1795), p.358.

FLESCH, M. "Group of city coins", in 'Collector's choice', Bezalel National Museum, Jerusalem 1964, p.15/78.

FORRER, L. "The Weber collection, vol. III, part 2: Greek coins", London 1929, pp.795-796, nos. 8105-8106, pl.299.

FROVA, A. "Scavi di Caesarea Maritima", Milano 1965, pp.229-230.

GERSHT, R. "The Tyche of Caesarea Maritima", PEQ 116, 1984, p.110.

GESSNER, J.J. "Numismata antiqua Imperatorum Romanorum latina et graeca..", Tiguri (Zürich), 18th cent., pls. 68/14; 79/66-68; 102/73; 111/52-53; 112/59-60; 118/44; 147/61; 155/10-12; 156/1; 158/30-31; 165/28.

GILMORE, P.M. "The formulae of Antioch and Tyre", NCirc. 86 (2), 1978, p.76.

GILMORE, P.M. "Syrian officinae under Caracalla and Macrinus", NCirc. 87 (6) 1979, p.288.

GILMORE, P.M. "Caracalla's silver mints in Syria", NCirc. 88 (3), 1980, p.88.

GROSE, S.W. "Catalogue of the McClean collection of Greek coins in the Fitzwilliam Museum", vol. III, Cambridge 1929, pp.379-380/9538-9540, pl.354/1-3.

HAMBURGER, A. "Gems from Caesarea Maritima", ATIQOT, Es 8, 1968, pp.7/15-17, 19-21; 14/102-106; 15-16/114; 16/116.

HAMBURGER, H. "Caesarea coin-finds and the history of the city", BJPES 15 (3-4), 1950, pp.78-82 (Hebrew).

HAMBURGER, H. "Minute coins from Caesarea", ATIQOT, Es 1, 1955, pp.115-138, pls.10-12. Heb. ed. pp.99-121, pls.10-12.

HAMBURGER, H. "A hoard of Syrian tetradrachms and Tyrian bronze coins from Gush Halav", in 'Recent studies and discoveries on ancient Jewish and Syrian coins', PINS 1, 1954, pp.67, 69, 79, 84. Same in IEJ 4 (3-4), 1954, pp.203, 205, 215, 220.

CAESAREA

HAMBURGER, H. "The coin issues of the Roman administration from the mint of Caesarea", _IEJ_ 20 (1-2), 1970, pp.81-91.

HAMBURGER, L. "Die beiden palästinensischen Münzstätten Nikopolis-Emmaus", (Sonder-Abdruck aus den Frankfurter Münzblättern 1, 1899, nos 8, 9), p.11.

HARDING, L. "Recent work on the Jerash Forum. The coins", _PEQ_ 1949, p.18.

HEAD, B.V. "Historia numorum", Oxford 1911, p.802.

HENDIN, D. "Guide to ancient Jewish coins", New York 1976, pp.103-104, pl.8/244, 246.

HEYMANN, H. "Roman legionary coins from Phoenicia", _INJ_ 1 (3), 1963, pp.49, 51 (note 16).

HILL, G.F. "Some Palestinian cults in the Graeco-Roman age", Proceedings of the British Academy, vol. V, London 1912, pp.412-414, pl./6.

HILL, G.F. BMC, Palestine, 1914, pp.xvi-xviii, pp.12-42, pls.2/8-15; 3; 4; 5/1-4.

HOWGEGO, C. "The behaviour and function of Greek Imperial countermarks", _INJ_ 6-7, 1982/3, pp.51, 52, pl.11/12, 19.

JONAS, R. "Mythology on Palestinian coins", internal circular no. 2, Israel Num. Society, Haifa branch, 1959, pp.3, 6.

KADMAN, L. "The coins of Caesarea Maritima", Corpus Nummorum Palaestinensium, vol. II, Jerusalem 1957.

KADMAN, L. "Notes on B. Lifshitz's article on 'Roman Legions in Palestine', BIES 24 (1), 1959, pp.63-65 (Hebrew).

KADMAN, L. "When was Aelia Capitolina named 'Commodiana' and by whom?" IEJ 9 (2), 1959, p.139 (note 20).

KADMAN, L. "Numismatic evidence of the architectonic revolution in the Second Century C.E.", INB 3-4, 1962, pp.71, 72, pl.1/13. Heb. ed. pp.63, 65, pl.1/13.

KADMAN, L. and KINDLER, A. "Coins in Palestine throughout the ages", Tel-Aviv 1963, pp.31-32, pl.14/15-22 (Hebrew).

KANITZ, L.E. "The countermark KOB on coins of Caesarea Maritima", SM 101, 1976, pp.2-6.

KANITZ, L.E. "The countermark KOB on coins of Caesarea Maritima", SAN 8 (1), 1976, pp.6-8.

KANITZ, L.E. "Divus Vespasian - Divus Titus, a new light on two coins of Domitian struck at Caesarea Maritima", SAN 8 (4), 1977, pp.60-61.

KINDLER, A. "Thesaurus of Judaean coins from the fourth century B.C. to the third century A.D.", Jerusalem 1958, no.33 (Hebrew).

KINDLER, A. "Two countermarks, one of Caesarea and other of the Tenth Legion on one and the same coin", ALON 2 (4), 1968, p.77 (Hebrew).

KINDLER, A. "A new coin-type of Caesarea", ALON 2 (4), 1968, pp.77-78, pl.4/2 (Hebrew).

KINDLER, A. "The coin issues of the Roman administration in the provincia Judaea during the reign of Domitian, ALON 3 (4), 1969, pp.91-92, 93, 94, 95, pl.6/15-17 (Hebrew).

CAESAREA

KINDLER, A. "New types of Palestinian city-coins", ALON 4 (2), 1969, p.21, pl.3/1 (Hebrew).

KINDLER, A. "Coins of the land of Israel. Bank of Israel collection", Jerusalem 1971, pp.137-138, no. 206 (Hebrew).

KINDLER, A. "Two remarks", CATHEDRA 8, 1978, p.67 (Hebrew).

KINDLER, A. "The 'DAMNATIO MEMORIAE' of Elagabal on city-coins of the Near East", SM 117, 1980, pp.5, 6, figs. 2-3.

KINDLER, A. "The status of cities in the Syro-Palestinian area as reflected by their coins", INJ 6-7, 1982/3, pp.81, 84.

KINDLER, A. "The coinage of Bostra", Warminster, England 1983, pp.30, 32, 33, 34, 49, 51, 52, 55, 61, 64, 65, 66, 79.

KIRKBRIDE, A.S. "Currencies in Transjordan", PEQ, 1939, p.156.

KLIMOWSKY, E.W. "The monetary function of city coins", International numismatic convention in Jerusalem (1963), proceedings (A. Kindler, ed.), Tel-Aviv 1967, pp.131, 146, 150, 151, 152, 153, 154, 155, 160, 162, 164, 168, 170, 172, 177.

KLIMOWSKY, E.W. "Roman imperial 'Virtutes' on contemporaneous city coins" in 'On ancient Palestinian and other coins, their symbolism and metrology', PINS 7, Tel-Aviv, 1974, pp.87, 95, 96, 97, pls. 5/8, 19; 6/21, 32; 7/54. Same in INJ 3, 1965/6, pp.15, 22, 23, 24, pls. 4/8; 5/19, 21; 6/32; 7/54.

KLIMOWSKY, E.W. "The origin and meaning of Marsyas in the Greek imperial coinage", INJ 6-7, 1982/3, p.98.

KRAFT, K. "Das System der kaiserzeitlichen Münzprägung in Kleinasien", Berlin 1972, pp.98, 101, pl.117/9.

KUBITSCHEK, W. "Zu Münzen von Caesarea in Samaria", NZ 44, 1911, pp.13-20.

KUBITSCHEK, W. "Zur Geschichte von Städten des römischen Kaiserreiches. Epigraphisch-numismatische Studien", heft 1, Wien 1916, pp.64, 67-73.

LAMBERT, C. "Coins in the Palestine Museum, II", QDAP 1, 1931/2, p.133, pl.54/13-14.

LEDERER, P. "Neue Beiträge zur antiken Münzkunde aus schweizerischen öffentlichen und privaten Sammlungen", SNR 30, 1943, p.82, pl.6/96.

LEVINE, L. "Some observations on the coins of Caesarea Maritima", IEJ 22 (2-3), 1972, pp.131-140.

MACDONALD, G. "Catalogue of Greek coins in the Hunterian collection", Glasgow 1905, vol. III, pp.275-277, pl.77/21-23.

MALTIEL-GERSTENFELD, J. "A portrait coin of Berenice sister of Agrippa II?", INJ 4, 1980, p.25.

MANNS, F. "Gemmes de l'époque Gréco-Romaine provenant de Palestine", LA 28, 1978, pp.155-156, 158, 159-160, 161, 169, pls.25/6-8; 26/17; 27/25-28; 28/32-33; 33/76.

MATSSON, G.O. "The gods, goddesses and heroes on the ancient coins of Bible Lands", Stockholm 1969, pp.12, 14, 72, 81, 168, 197, 215, 217, pls. 1/8a, 9; 4/56b, 59.

CAESAREA

MESHORER, Y. "A find of coins of Alexander Severus struck in Caesarea Maritima", INB 5, 1963, pp.20-21, pl.3. Heb. ed. pp.20-21, pl.3.

MESHORER, Y. "Coins from the excavations at Khorazin", EI 11, 1973, p.158, pl.29/4 (Hebrew).

MESHORER, Y. "Coins of the Ancient World", Minneapolis 1975, pp.76-77. Hebrew version (Jerusalem 1979), pp.56-57. Same in "Münzen, Zeugen der Vergangenheit", Zürich - Köln, 1979, pp.76-77.

MESHORER, Y. "The city coins of Eretz-Israel and the Decapolis in the Roman period", Jerusalem 1984, pp.19-21, 111 (Hebrew).

MIONNET, T.E. "Description de médailles antiques, grecques et romaines", Paris 1806-1837, vol. V, pp.486-497, vol. VIII, suppl., pp.334-343.

NARKISS, M. "Coins of Palestine, part 2: The coinage of the Gentiles, I", Jerusalem 1938, p.76 (Hebrew).

NEGEV, A. "The Mempsis (Kurnub) hoard of Roman and provincial silver. A preliminary note", INJ 3, 1965/6, p.29.

OESTREICHER, B. "A contemporary picture of Caesarea's ancient harbor", INB 2, 1962, pp.44-47, pl.1/17-19. Heb. ed. pp.39-41, pl.1/17-19.

OESTREICHER, B. "Attribution of a coin to Caesarea Maritima", INJ 1 (2), 1963, p.28.

OESTREICHER, B. "A Roman provincial coin", ALON 1 (2), 1966, pp.21-22, pl.A/1-2 (Hebrew).

PATIN, C. "Imperatorum Romanorum numismata ex aere mediae et minimae formae descripta et enarrata..", Amsterdam(?), 1671, pp.195-196, 200, 249, 255, 261.

PELLERIN, J. "Mélange de diverses médailles..", t.I, part 3, Paris 1764, p.286, pl.17/7; p.324, pl.21/12.

PLANT, R. "Greek coin types and their identification", London 1979, nos. 410, 449, 788, 1316, 2664.

PRICE, M.J. and TRELL, B.L. "Coins and their cities", London 1977, pp.164, 283, fig. 367.

RAHMANI, L.Y. "The coins from Nahal Scelim and Nahal Hardof", IEJ 11 (1-2), 1961, p.64.

RAHMANI, L. and SHARABANI, M. "List of coins", in 'Hammath Tiberias', by M. Dothan, Jerusalem 1983, p.72, pl.22/14.

RAYNOR, J. "Numismatic report of Nabratein, 1980" in 'Preliminary report on the 1980 excavations at En-Nabratein, Israel", BASOR 244, 1981, p.20, fig.11/5.

REICHARDT, H.C. "Unpublished Greek Imperial coins", NC, Ns 2, 1862, pp.109-110.

RESHEF, M. "A coin of Nysa-Scythopolis countermarked with the name of the city", ALON 1 (13), 1967, pp.41-42, pl.2/1-4 (Hebrew).

RIDER, G. le "Les ateliers monétaires de la côte Syrienne, Phénicienne, Palestinienne, Égyptienne and Cyrénéenne", Congresso Internazionale di numismatica (Roma 1961), vol. I, Relazioni, Roma 1961, pp.94, 96.

RINGEL, J. "The harbour god of Caesarea Maritima", SEFUNIM 4, 1972/75, pp.22-27, pl.2/3-7. Heb. ed. pp.19-23.

CAESAREA

RINGEL, J. "The Tyche of Caesarea and the Genius accompanying her", ALON 5 (4), 1976, pp.73-74, pl.6/12 (Hebrew).

ROSENBERGER, M. "City-coins of Palestine", vol. II, Jerusalem 1975, pp.1--28, 78.

ROSENBERGER, M. "City-coins of Palestine", vol III, Jerusalem 1977, pp.79-80.

ROSENBERGER, M. "The coinage of Eastern Palestine", Jerusalem 1978, p.84.

ROSENTHAL-HEGINBOTTOM, R. "The Mampsis hoard - A preliminary report", INJ 4, 1980, pp.42, 48.

SAULCY, F. de "Numismatique de la Terre Sainte", Paris 1874, pp.112-141, pl.7.

SCHONWALTER, R. "Numismatic evidence from the Dead Sea", NUMISMATIST 71 (7), 1958, p.796.

SEAR, D.R. "Greek imperial coins and their values", London 1982, nos. 629, 881, 1092, 1248, 1505, 1680, 1800, 1875, 1912, 2056, 2682-2683, 2967-2968, 3026, 3119, 3374, 3965, 4152, 4211, 4253, 4284, 4303, 4354, 4397, 5214.

SESTINI, D. "Descriptio numorum veterum..", Lipsiae 1796, p.543.

SESTINI, D. "Classes generales geographiae numismaticae sev monetae urbium, populorum et regum..", Lipsiae 1797, part I, p.70, part II, pp.102-103.

SESTINI, D. "Classes generales sev moneta vetus urbium, populorum et regum..", Florentiae 1821, pp.149-150.

SESTINI, D. "Descrizione d'alcune medaglie Greche del museo del Signore Carlo D'Ottavio Fontana", Firenze 1822, p.13.

SESTINI, D. "Descrizione delle medaglie antiche Greche del Museo Hedervariano", part 3, Firenze 1829, pp.105-106, pl.31/16.

SEYRIG, H. "Antiquités Syriennes, 10. Note sur le culte de Déméter en Palestine", SYRIA 13, 1932, pp.355-357.

SEYRIG, H. "Antiquités Syriennes, 11. Sur certains tétradrachmes provinciaux de Syrie", SYRIA 13, 1932, pp.360, 367.

SEYRIG, H. "Antiquités Syriennes, 100. Tyché de Césarée de Palestine", SYRIA 49, 1972, pp.114-115.

SEYRIG, H. "Notes on Syrian coins", NNM 119, 1950, p.32.

SHARABANI, M. "Coins" in 'The excavations of Kursi-Gergesa' by V. Tzaferis. ATIQOT, Es 16, 1983, p.39, pl.17/2.

SNG ANS part 6, "Palestine - South Arabia", 1981, pls.23-27, figs. 744-857.

SNG DNM "Palestine-Characene", 1961, pl.1/5-13.

SPANHEMIUS, E. "Dissertationes de praestantia et usu numismatum antiquorum", new ed., t.I, London 1706, p.527.

SPERBER, D. "Roman Palestine 200-400. Money and prices", Jerusalem 1974, pp.133, 143.

SPIJKERMAN, A. "Herodion III. Catalogo delle monete", Jerusalem 1972, pp.18/24; 99.

CAESAREA

SPIJKERMAN, A. "Cafarnao III. Catalogo delle monete della città", Jerusalem 1975, pp.24/124; 28/160; 41/322; 46/382; 50/424; pl.2/4.

SPIJKERMAN, A. and STARCKY, J. "Un nouveau lot de monnaies palestiniennes", RB 65, 1958, pp.568, 569, 570, 571-576, pls.18; 19/45, 48.

STAHL, Z. "The Flavian Emperors and their coins in Eretz-Israel", special brochure of Israel Num. Society, Tel-Aviv branch, 1976, p.7 (Hebrew).

STAHL, Z. "Roman coins of Palestinian cities issued during the Jewish War, 66-70 C.E.", special brochure of Israel Num. Society, Tel-Aviv branch, 1979, pp.12, 17-18, 25 (Hebrew).

STEVENSON, S.W. "A dictionary of Roman coins", London 1964 (rp), pp.162-163.

SUTHERLAND, C.H.V. "The pattern of monetary development in Phoenicia and Palestine during the Early Empire", International numismatic convention in Jerusalem (1963), proceedings (A. Kindler, ed.), Tel-Aviv 1967, pp.89, 90, 91, 94, 95, 96, 97, 98, 99, 100, 101.

TIEPOLO, L. and F. "Musei Theupoli antiqua numismata..", Venetiis 1736, series 4, pp.679-680, 682, 705, 719, 727, 741-742, 756, 760.

VAILLANT, J. "Numismata aera imperatorum, augustarum et caesarum in coloniis, municipiis et urbibus...", Paris 1688, part I, pp.194-195, 198-199, 213-214, 223-224, 241-242, 255-257, 281, 283-284, 301, 322; part II, pp.25-26, 40-41, 72-73, 91-92, 103-104, 112-113, 166, 279-282, 301, 318-319.

VAILLANT, J. "Numismata imperatorum, augustarum et caesarum a populis Romanae ditionis Graece loquentibus..", Paris 1698, pp.15, 238.

VAUX, R. de "Fouilles au Khirbet Qumrân, IV: Les monnaies", _RB_ 61, 1954, pp.230, 231.

VAUX, R. de "Fouilles de Khirbet Qumrân, V: Les monnaies et les dates d'occupation", _RB_ 63, 1956, pp.566, 567.

VLIET, N. van der "Monnaies inédites ou très rares du médaillier de Sainte-Anne de Jérusalem", _RB_ 57, 1950, pp.117-119, pl.2/14-17.

WAAGE, D.B. "Antioch on-the-Orontes, IV. Part two: Greek, Roman, Byzantine and Crusaders' coins", Princeton 1952, p.86/925, 926.

WALCHER de MOLTHEIN, L. "Catalogue de la collection des médailles grecques de M. Le Chevalier", Paris - Vienne, 1895, pp.268-269, nos. 3166-3167.

WICZAY, C.M. "Musei Hedervarii numi antiqui..", Vindobonae 1814, part I, pp.287-288, nos. 6189-6200.

ZURI, N. "A hoard of bronze and silver coins from Ain Hanaziv", _INB_ 1962 (3-4), p.105. Heb. ed. p.88.

Auction Catalogues and Price Lists

AGORA Tel-Aviv 1974 (1), p.21, no. 128, pl.7.
1975 (2), nos. 175-180, pls.7-8.

BETTER Haifa 1972 (1), nos. 155-170.
Haifa 1972 (2), nos. 256-271.
Haifa 1973 (3), nos. 272, 302-308.
Haifa 1973 (4), nos. 185-196A.

CAESAREA

BETTER (con't) Jaffo 1974 (5), nos. 140-149.
Jaffo 1974 (7), nos. 204-219A.
Haifa 1974 (8), nos. 115-130a.

BUTTON, E. (price list), Frankfurt 1938 (35), p.5, nos. 3047-3048.

CAHN, A.E. Frankfurt 1930 (68), p.95, nos. 1583-1585.
1931 (71), p.66, nos. 1087-1088, pl.32.

EIDELSTEIN AND HOLLAND, Haifa, 10 Nov. 1975, nos. 165-166.

EIDELSTEIN AND HOLLAND, (price list), Haifa, summer 1976, nos. 168-170.

GANS, E. "Numismatic Fine Arts" (Stock cat.), New York
1942 (1), p.33, no. 6099.
1943 (2), pp.16, (no. 7329), 19 (no. 6300).
1943 (3), p.9, nos. 7333, 6099, 7329, 6300, 8763, 7311.

GANS, E. "Numismatic Fine Arts" (mail bid sale), Berkeley CA, USA 1955 (15), p.23, no. 370.

GANS, E. "Numismatic Fine Arts", Berkeley CA, USA
1956 (18), p.1, nos. 4202-4206.
1956 (20), p.15, nos. 4952-4956.
1958 (24), p.12, no. 5831.

GLENDINING London, 19 July 1950, p.46, no. 334.
21-23 Feb. 1961, p.98, no. 3004.
30-31 Oct. 1963, p.32, no. 395.
10 March 1965, p.20, nos. 153-156, pl.6.

HESS, A. Frankfurt 1936 (224), p.58, no. 1734.

HOLZER, H. "The Thomas Ollive Mabbott collection", part I, New York 1969, p.104, nos. 2674-2680.

KRAUS, F.F. (price list), Braunschweig, Germany, 1928 (2), p.46, no. 1059.

MALTER, J.L. "Journal of Numismatic Fine Arts", Encino CA, USA 1973 (2/2), p.37/B 65.

MONNAIES ET MÉDAILLES, Basel
1962 (25), p.20, nos. 518-521, pl.8.
1966 (32), pp.40-41, nos. 328-349, pls.22-23.

MÜNZEN UND MEDAILLEN, Basel 1947 (65), p.2, no. 37.
1950 (96), p.2, nos. 22-23.
1951 (101), p.9, no. 204.
1952 (112), p.6, nos. 130-133.
1955 (151), p.12, nos. 232-239.
1958 (176), p.3, nos. 41-45.
1968 (293), p.4, nos. 42-43.
1972 (336), p.3, no. 48.
1980 (424), p.17, nos. 212-213.
1981 (436), p.14, nos. 153-155.
1983 (457), p.2, no. 26.
1984 (468), p.14, nos. 176-177.
1985 (475), p.2, no. 32.

MÜNZZENTRUM KÖLN (price list), 1970 (2), p.9, no. 184e.

MÜNZZENTRUM KÖLN, auctions 1979 (36), p.28, no. 182.
1980 (42), p.33, nos. 198-199.
1983 (48), p.32, no. 208.

MYERS, R.J. New York 1971 (1), no. 306.

NUMISMATIC FINE ARTS, Beverly Hills CA, USA 1979 (6), no. 406.

CAESAREA

RAUCH, H.D. Wien 1985 (34), nos. 205-227.

RIGO (price list), Nurnberg 1959 (40), p.14, no. 287.

SCHLESSINGER, F. (price list), Amsterdam 1938 (9), p.3, no. 646.

SCHULMAN, H.M.F., New York, 18-19 Nov. 1955, p.71, nos. 1937, 1941.
26-28 May 1970, p.11, nos. 212-213.
7-9 July 1970, p.19, nos. 392-393.
6-8 Oct. 1970, p.19, no. 230.
14-15 Dec. 1970, p.18, nos. 960-962.
6-7 Apr. 1971, p.24, nos. 438-440.

SEABY, London 1949 (378), p.536, nos. AM 335-337.
1959 (494), p.268, no. A 668-669.
1965 (567), p.317, nos. A 761-762.
1968 (593), p.29, no. A 72.
1968 (604), p.433, no. A 947.
1969 (616), p.439, no. A 1178.
1971 (637), p.336, nos. A 851-856.

SIMONETTI, L. "Bollettino numismatico", Firenze 1964 (1/1), p.13, no. 71.

SPINK AND SON London, 1905 (13/153), nos. 18162-18177.
1925 (33/11-12), nos. 45405-45406.
1930 (38/9), no. 115.
1930 (38/10), nos. 963-964.
1930 (38/11), nos. 1761, 1798-1799.
1931 (39/4), nos. 6008-6009.
1931 (39/9), nos. 10024- 10030.
1934 (42/7), no. 34223.
1934 (42/8-9), nos. 35037-35040.
1934 (42/10), no. 36191.
1934 (42/12), nos. 37859-37866, 37882.
1936 (44/1), nos. 48004-48018.
1939 (47/3), nos. 78590-78600.

SPINK AND SON (con't) 1971 (79/7-8), p.290, no. 7372.
1977 (85/7-8), p.318, no. 6648.
1981 (89/6), p.205, nos. 4526-4527.
1984 (92/3), p.83, no. 1824.

STACK'S New York, 4-7 May 1960, p.19, nos. 244-246.

STERNBERG, F. Zürich, 25-26 Nov. 1976, pp.74-75, nos. 573-586, pls.23-24.

SUPERIOR STAMP AND COIN CO., Los-Angeles, June 1976, pp.24-25, nos. 265-272.

TAMAR Tel-Aviv 1975 (9), pp.6-7, nos. 126-139.
Tel-Aviv 1975 (10), p.9, nos. 130-139.
Ramat-Gan, Israel 1976 (11), p.10 (nos. 114-123), p.14 (no. 209).
Ramat-Gan, Israel 1976 (12), p.51, nos. 840-848.

VECCHI, V.C. "Bonhams", London 1982 (8), p.18, no. 213, pl.9.

VINCHON, J. "Monnaies Juives", Paris, 13 Fév. 1970, nos. 78-84.

CANATHA

BENTINCK de "Catalogue d'une collection de médailles antiques", Amsterdam 1788, suppl., p.208.

BERNHART, M. "Dionysos und seine Familie auf Griechischen Münzen", JNG 1, 1949, p.71 no. 312.

CARRADICE, I. "Coinage in Judaea in the Flavian period, AD 70-96", INJ 6-7, 1982/3, p.17.

ECKHEL, J. "Catalogus Musei Caesarei Vindobonensis numorum veterum..", Vindobonae 1779, pars I, p.251.

ECKHEL, J. "Doctrina numorum veterum..", vol. III, Vienna 1794, p.347.

HEAD, B.V. "Historia numorum", Oxford 1911, p.786.

KADMAN, L. and KINDLER, A. "Coins in Palestine throughout the ages", Tel-Aviv 1963, p.40, pl.18/6 (Hebrew).

KINDLER, A. "The status of cities in the Syro-Palestinian area as reflected by their coins", INJ 6-7, 1982/3, p.85 (note 49).

KINDLER, A. "The coinage of Bostra", Warminster, England, 1983, pp.16, 38, 53, 58, 143.

KLIMOWSKY, E.W. "The monetary function of city coins", International numismatic convention in Jerusalem (1963), proceedings (A. Kindler, ed.), Tel-Aviv 1967, pp.164, 172.

MESHORER, Y. "The city coins of Eretz-Israel and the Decapolis in the Roman period", Jerusalem 1984, pp.76, 119 (Hebrew).

MIONNET, T.E. "Description de médailles antiques, grecques et romaines", Paris 1806-1837, vol. V, p.321, vol. VIII, suppl., p.225.

REICHARDT, H.C. "Die Münzen Canatha's Dekapolis", NZ 12, 1880, pp.68-73, pl.1.

RIDER, G. le "Les ateliers monétaires de la côte Syrienne, Phénicienne, Palestinienne, Égyptienne et Cyrénéene", Congresso Internazionale di numismatica (Roma 1961), vol. I, Relazioni, Roma 1961, p.96.

ROSENBERGER, M. "The coinage of Eastern Palestine", Jerusalem 1978, pp.17-18.

SAULCY, F. de "Numismatique de la Terre Sainte", Paris 1874, pp.399-401, pl.23/8-10.

SEAR, D.R. "Greek imperial coins and their values", London 1982, nos. 398, 474, 877, 2049, 3105.

SESTINI, D. "Descriptio numorum veterum..", Lipsiae 1796, p.531.

SESTINI, D. "Classes generales geographiae numismaticae sev monetae urbium, populorum et regum..", Lipsiae 1797, part I, p.67, part II, pp.100, 103.

SESTINI, D. "Classes generales sev moneta vetus urbium, populorum et regum..", Florentiae 1821, p.143.

SESTINI, D. "Descrizione d'alcune medaglie Greche del museo del Signore Carlo D'Ottavio Fontana", Firenze 1822, p.13.

SESTINI, D. "Descrizione delle medaglie antiche Greche del Museo Hedervariano", part 3, Firenze 1829, pp.73-74, pl.31/3.

CANATHA

SNG ANS part 6, "Palestine - South Arabia", 1981, pl.43/1257-1269.

SNG DNM "Syria, Cities", 1959, pl.12/448.

SNG FM vol. IV, part 8, "Syria-Nabathaea", 1971, pl.132/5980.

SPIJKERMAN, A. and STARCKY, J. "Un nouveau lot de monnaies palestiniennes", RB 65, 1958, pp.569, 584.

SPIJKERMAN, A. "An unknown coin-type of Pella Decapoleos", LA 20, 1970, p.355.

SPIJKERMAN, A. "The coins of the Decapolis and provincia Arabia", Jerusalem 1978, pp.90-95, 284, pl.18.

VAILLANT, J. "Numismata imperatorum, augustarum et caesarum a populis Romanae ditionis Graece loquentibus..", Paris 1698, pp.22, 239, 356.

WAAGE, D.B. "Antioch on-the-Orontes, IV. Part 2: Greek, Roman, Byzantine and Crusaders' coins", Princeton 1952, p.83/890-891.

WICZAY, C.M. "Musei Hedervarii numi antiqui..", Vindobonae 1814, part I, p.278/6029.

WROTH, W. BMC, Galatia, Cappadocia and Syria, 1899, pp.lxxxiv-lxxxv, p.302, pl.38/2, 3.

<u>Auction Catalogues and Price Lists</u>

AGORA Tel-Aviv 1974 (1), p.27, no. 168, pl.10.
1975 (2), no. 218, pl.9.

BETTER Haifa 1972 (1), no. 242.

HOLZER, H. "The Thomas Ollive Mabbott collection", part I, New York 1969, p.102, nos. 2628-2630.

MALTER, J.L. "Journal of Numismatic Fine Arts", Encino, CA, USA 1973 (2/2), p.37/B 66.

MÜNZEN UND MEDAILLEN, Basel 1969 (305), p.3, no. 43.
1984 (464), p.15, no. 191.

NUMISMATIC FINE ARTS, Beverly Hills, CA, USA 1976 (3), no. 165/4.

SPINK AND SON London 1902 (10/116), nos. 85064-85065.
1971 (79/6), no. 6611.

STACK'S New York, 10-11 June 1970, p.36, no. 443.

STERNBERG, F. Zürich, 25-26 Nov. 1976, p.75, no. 587, pl.24.

SUPERIOR STAMP AND COIN CO., Los-Angeles, June 1976, p.25, nos.273-274.

TAMAR Ramat-Gan, Israel 1976 (12), p.52, no. 876.

CAPITOLIAS

BELLINGER, A.R. "The Syrian tetradrachms of Caracalla and Macrinus", ANS NS 3, 1940, p.14.

ECKHEL, J. "Catalogus Musei Caesarei Vindobonensis numorum veterum..", Vindobonae 1779, pars I, p.236.

ECKHEL, J. "Doctrina numorum veterum..", vol. III, Vienna 1794, pp.328-329.

GESSNER, J.J. "Numismata antiqua Imperatorum Romanorum latina et graeca..", Tiguri (Zürich), 18th cent., pl.134/35-36.

HEAD, B.V. "Historia numorum", Oxford 1911, p.787.

KADMAN, L. "Numismatic evidence of the architectonic revolution in the Second Century C.E.", INB 1962 (3-4), p.72. Heb. ed. p.65.

KADMAN, L. and KINDLER, A. "Coins in Palestine throughout the ages", Tel-Aviv 1963, p.40, pl.18/9 (Hebrew).

KELLNER, W. "Commodus-Münzen aus der Dekapolis", SM 77, 1970, pp.1, 2, 3.

KINDLER, A. "The status of cities in the Syro-Palestinian area as reflected by their coins", INJ 6-7, 1982/3, pp.80, 82.

KLIMOWSKY, E.W. "The monetary function of city coins", International numismatic convention in Jerusalem (1963), proceedings (A. Kindler, ed.), Tel-Aviv 1967, pp.164, 172.

LIEBE, C.S. "Gotha numaria, sistens Thesauri Fridericiani numismata antiqua..", Amsterdam 1730, pp.321-323.

MATSSON, G.O. "The gods, goddesses and heroes on the ancient coins of Bible Lands", Stockholm 1969, p.243, pl.8/115c.

MESHORER, Y. "The city coins of Eretz-Israel and the Decapolis in the Roman period", Jerusalem 1984, pp.86, 120 (Hebrew).

MIONNET, T.E. "Description de médailles antiques, grecques et romaines", Paris 1806-1837, vol. V, pp.281-283; vol. VII (Notes et obs.), p.109; vol. VIII, suppl., p.192.

PRICE, M.J. and TRELL, B.L. "Coins and their cities", London 1977, pp.34, 164, 282, fig. 285.

REICHARDT, H.C. "Unpublished Greek Imperial coins", NC, Ns 2, 1862, p.104.

RIDER, G. le "Les ateliers monétaires de la côte Syrienne, Phénicienne, Palestinienne, Égyptienne et Cyrénéene", Congresso Internazionale di numismatica (Roma 1961), vol. I, Relazioni, Roma 1961, p.87.

ROSENBERGER, M. "The coinage of Eastern Palestine", Jerusalem 1978, pp.19-22.

SAULCY, F. de "Numismatique de la Terre Sainte", Paris 1874, pp.304-307, pl.16/9.

SEAR, D.R. "Greek imperial coins and their values", London 1982, nos. 1675, 1873, 1910, 2050, 2666, 2897, 2957, 3106.

SESTINI, D. "Descriptio numorum veterum..", Lipsiae 1796, p.527.

SESTINI, D. "Classes generales geographiae numismaticae sev monetae urbium, populorum et regum..", Lipsiae 1797, part I, p.66; part II, p.99.

CAPITOLIAS

SESTINI, D. "Classes generales sev moneta vetus urbium, populorum et regum..", Florentiae 1821, p.141.

SEYRIG, H. "Antiquités Syriennes, 73. Temples, cultes et souvenirs historiques de la Décapole", SYRIA 36, 1959, pp.62-66, 76-77, 192 (erratum), pl.12/6-14.

SEYRIG, H. "Antiquités Syriennes, 87. Alexandre le Grand, fondateur de Gérasa", SYRIA 42, 1965, pp.26, 27.

SNG ANS part 6, "Palestine - South Arabia", 1981, pl.43/1270-1276.

SNG FM vol. IV, part 8, "Syria-Nabathaea", 1971, pl.132/5981.

SPIJKERMAN, A. "An unknown coin-type of Pella Decapoleos", LA 20, 1970, p.356.

SPIJKERMAN, A. "The coins of the Decapolis and provincia Arabia", Jerusalem 1978, pp.96-107, 285, 317, pls. 19-21.

VAILLANT, J. "Numismata imperatorum, augustarum et caesarum a populis Romanae ditionis Graece loquentibus..", Paris 1698, pp.56, 71, 73, 78, 95, 121, 239, 261, 356-357.

WROTH, W. BMC, Galatia, Cappadocia and Syria, 1899, pp.lxxiii, 278, pl.33/9.

Auction Catalogues and Price Lists

AGORA Tel-Aviv 1974 (1), p.27, no. 169, pl.10.

MALTER, J.L. "Journal of Numismatic Fine Arts", Encino, CA, USA 1973 (2/2), p.37/B 67.

MONNAIES ET MÉDAILLES, Basel 1966 (32), p.48, nos. 461-462, pl.28.
1970 (41), p.77, nos. 608-609, pl.38.

MÜNZEN AND MEDAILLEN, Basel 1977 (386), p.16, no. 237.
1978 (398), p.1, no. 4.

NUMISMATIC FINE ARTS, Beverly Hills, CA, USA 1976 (3), no. 161.

SPINK AND SON London 1931 (39/8), nos. 9251-9252.
1934 (42/12), nos. 37868-37869.
1939 (47/3), no. 78516.

VECCHI, V.C. "Bonhams", London 1982 (2), p.9, no. 214, pl.10.

VINCHON, J. "Monnaies Juives", Paris, 13 Fév. 1970, nos. 90-92.

CHARACHMOBA

BABELON, E. "Characmoba", RN, 4th ser. 3, 1899, pp.274-277.

HEAD, B.V. "Historia numorum", Oxford 1911, p.812.

HILL, G.F. BMC, Arabia, Mesopotamia and Persia, 1922, pp.xxx-xxxi, p.27, pl.4/14.

KINDLER, A. "The status of cities in the Syro-Palestinian area as reflected by their coins", INJ 6-7, 1982/3, p.82.

KINDLER, A. "The coinage of Bostra", Warminster, England 1983, pp.16, 37, 38, 53, 59, 81, 82, 83, 86.

MATSSON, G.O. "The gods, goddesses and heroes on the ancient coins of Bible Lands", Stockholm 1969, p.73.

MESHORER, Y. "The city coins of Eretz-Israel and the Decapolis in the Roman period", Jerusalem 1984, pp.104, 122 (Hebrew).

NEGEV, A. "Seal impressions from Tomb 107 at Kurnub (Mampsis)", IEJ 19 (2), 1969, pp.91, 94.

PATRICH, J. "Prohibition of a graven-image among the Nabateans - the testimony of the Massebot-cult", CATHEDRA 26, 1982, pp.62, 65, fig. 13 (Hebrew).

PRICE, M.J. and TRELL, B.L. "Coins and their cities", London 1977, p.285.

ROSENBERGER, M. "The coinage of Eastern Palestine", Jerusalem 1978, p.22.

SEAR, D.R. "Greek imperial coins and their values", London 1982, no. 3132.

SPIJKERMAN, A. "The coins of the Decapolis and provincia Arabia", Jerusalem 1978, pp.108-115, 276, 286, pls.22-23.

Auction Catalogues and Price Lists

GLENDINING London, 10 March 1965, p.23, no. 180, pl.6.

MALTER, J.L. "Journal of Numismatic Fine Arts", Encino, CA, USA 1973 (2/2), p.37/B 68.

DIOSPOLIS

ANONYMOUS "City coins of ancient Israel", JIN 1 (3), 1966, pp.78-79.

BARAMKI, D.C. "The coins exhibited in the Archaeological Museum of the American University of Beirut", Beirut 1968, p.92, nos. 308-309, pl.8.

BARAMKI, D.C. "The coin collection of the American University of Beirut Museum. Palestine and Phoenicia", Beirut 1974, pp.17-18, pl.3/3-6.

BELLINGER, A.R. "The Syrian tetradrachms of Caracalla and Macrinus", ANS NS 3, 1940, p.13.

ECKHEL, J. "Doctrina numorum veterum..", vol. III, Vienna 1794, pp.432-433.

HEAD, B.V. "Historia numorum", Oxford 1911, p.802.

HENDIN, D. "Guide to ancient Jewish coins", New York 1976, p.112.

HILL, G.F. BMC, Palestine, 1914, p.xxiii, p.43, pl.5/5-6.

KADMAN, L. "Numismatic evidence of the architectonic revolution in the Second Century C.E.", INB 1962 (3-4), p.72. Heb. ed. p.65.

KADMAN, L. and KINDLER, A. "Coins in Palestine throughout the ages", Tel-Aviv 1963, p.38, pl.17/5-6 (Hebrew).

KINDLER, A. "Thesaurus of Judaean coins from the fourth century B.C. to the third century A.D.", Jerusalem 1958, no. 25 (Hebrew).

KINDLER, A. "The status of cities in the Syro-Palestinian area as reflected by their coins", INJ 6-7, 1982/3, pp.81, 85 (note 45), 87.

KINDLER, A. "The coinage of Bostra", Warminster, England 1983, pp.37, 61.

KLIMOWSKY, E.W. "The monetary function of city coins", International numismatic convention in Jerusalem (1963), proceedings (A. Kindler, ed.), Tel-Aviv 1967, pp.166, 172.

KUBITSCHEK, W. "Zur Geschichte von Städten des römischen Kaiserreiches. Epigraphisch-numismatische Studien", heft 1, Wien 1916, pp.9, 16-17.

LAMBERT, C. "Coins in the Palestine Museum, II, QDAP 1, 1931/2, pp.133-134, pl.55/15-16.

MATSSON, G.O. "The gods, goddesses and heroes on the ancient coins of Bible Lands", Stockholm 1969, pp.172, 207, 237, pls.2/37; 7/105a.

MESHORER, Y. "The city coins of Eretz-Israel and the Decapolis in the Roman period", Jerusalem 1984, pp.55, 116 (Hebrew).

MIONNET, T.E. "Description de médailles antiques, grecques et romaines", Paris 1806-1837, vol. V, pp.497-498, vol. VIII, suppl., p.344.

PRICE, M.J. and TRELL, B.L. "Coins and their cities", London 1977, p.283.

ROSENBERGER, M. "City-coins of Palestine", vol. II, Jerusalem 1975, pp.28-31.

DIOSPOLIS

ROSENBERGER, M. "City-coins of Palestine", vol. III, Jerusalem 1977, p.80.

SAULCY, F. de "Numismatique de la Terre Sainte", Paris 1874, pp.170-171, pl.9/1-2.

SEAR, D.R. "Greek imperial coins and their values", London 1982, nos. 2459, 2684, 3120.

SESTINI, D. "Descriptio numorum veterum..", Lipsiae 1796, p.543.

SESTINI, D. "Classes generales geographiae numismaticae sev monetae urbium, populorum et regum..", Lipsiae 1797, part I, p.70.

SESTINI, D. "Classes generales sev moneta vetus urbium, populorum et regum..", Florentiae 1821, p.150.

SEYRIG, H. "Antiquités Syriennes, 10. Note sur le culte de Déméter en Palestine", SYRIA 13, 1932, p.357.

SNG ANS part 6, "Palestine - South Arabia", 1981, pl.28/889-890.

STAHL, Z. "The city of Ludd and her coins", special brochure of Israel Num. Society, Tel-Aviv branch, 1973 (Hebrew).

SUTHERLAND, C.H.V. "The pattern of monetary development in Phoenicia and Palestine during the Early Empire", International numismatic convention in Jerusalem (1963), proceedings (A. Kindler, ed.), Tel-Aviv 1967, p.96.

VAILLANT, J. "Numismata imperatorum, augustarum et caesarum a populis Romanae ditionis Graece loquentibus..", Paris 1698, pp.105, 235, 349-350.

WICZAY, C.M. "Musei Hedervarii numi antiqui..", Vindobonae 1814, part I, p.288/6201.

Auction Catalogues and Price Lists

MONNAIES ET MÉDAILLES, Basel 1966 (32), p.41, no. 351, pl.23.

NUMISMATIC FINE ARTS, Beverly Hills, CA, USA 1973 (1), p.23, no. 233.

SCHLESSINGER, F. (price list), Amsterdam 1938 (9), p.3. no. 647.

SUPERIOR STAMP AND COIN CO., Los-Angeles, June 1976, p.25, no. 276.

DIUM

ANONYMOUS — CH 1, 1975, p.34/123.

BABELON, E. — "Le cabinet des Médailles pendant la guerre", RN, 4th ser. 23, 1920, pp.116-117.

BARAG, D. — "Tyrian currency in Galilee", INJ 6-7, 1982/3, p.10.

ECKHEL, J. — "Doctrina numorum veterum..", vol. III, Vienna 1794, pp.347-348.

HEAD, B.V. — "Historia numorum", Oxford 1911, p.787.

HILL, G.F. — BMC, Arabia, Mesopotamia and Persia, 1922, pp.xxxi-xxxii, p.28, pl.4/15-16.

KADMAN, L. — "Numismatic evidence of the architectonic revolution in the Second Century C.E.", INB 1962 (3-4), p.72. Heb. ed. p.65.

KADMAN, L. and KINDLER, A. "Coins in Palestine throughout the ages", Tel-Aviv 1963, p.40, pl.18/2 (Hebrew).

KINDLER, A. — "The coinage of Bostra", Warminster, England 1983, pp.16, 37, 38, 56, 58, 143.

KLIMOWSKY, E.W. "The monetary function of city coins", International numismatic convention in Jerusalem (1963), proceedings (A. Kindler, ed.), Tel-Aviv 1967, pp.164, 172.

MATSSON, G.O. — "The gods, goddesses and heroes on the ancient coins of Bible Lands", Stockholm 1969, pp.38, 204, 216, 245, pls. 2/29b; 4/56b.

MESHORER, Y. — "A hoard of coins from Migdal", ATIQOT, Es 11, 1976, pp.56, 70-71, pl.15/151.

MESHORER, Y. "The city coins of Eretz-Israel and the Decapolis in the Roman period", Jerusalem 1984, pp.90, 121 (Hebrew).

MIONNET, T.E. "Description de médailles antiques, grecques et romaines", Paris 1806-1837, vol. V, p.322, vol. VIII, suppl., p.226.

PRICE, M.J. and TRELL, B.L. "Coins and their cities", London 1977, pp.166, 282, fig. 374.

RIDER, G. le "Les ateliers monétaires de la côte Syrienne, Phénicienne, Palestinienne, Égyptienne et Cyrénéenne", Congresso Internazionale di numismatica (Roma 1961), vol. I, Relazioni, Roma 1961, pp.87, 96.

RIDER, G. le "Monnaies grecques récemment acquises par le cabines des médailles", RN, 6th ser., 3, 1961, p.23, pl.2/B.

ROSENBERGER, M. "The coinage of Eastern Palestine", Jerusalem 1978, pp.33-34.

SAULCY, F. de "Numismatique de la Terre Sainte", Paris 1874, pp.378-383, pl.19/8-9.

SEAR, D.R. "Greek imperial coins and their values", London 1982, nos. 2465, 2695, 2905, 3133.

SESTINI, D. "Descriptio numorum veterum..", Lipsiae 1796, p.531.

SESTINI, D. "Classes generales geographiae numismaticae sev monetae urbium, populorum et regum..", Lipsiae 1797, part I, p.67.

SESTINI, D. "Classes generales sev moneta vetus urbium, populorum et regum..", Florentiae 1821, p.144.

DIUM

SESTINI, D. "Descrizione delle medaglie antiche Greche del Museo Hedervariano", part 3, Firenze 1829, p.74, pl.31/4.

SEYRIG, H. "Antiquités Syriennes, 73. Temples, cultes and souvenirs historique de la Décapole", SYRIA 36, 1959, pp.68, 77, pl.13/15-17.

SNG ANS part 6, "Palestine - South Arabia", 1981, pl.43/1277-1282.

SNG DNM "Syria, Cities", 1959, pl.12/449.

SNG FM vol. IV, part 8, "Syria-Nabathaea", 1971, pl.132/5982.

SPIJKERMAN, A. "The coins of the Decapolis and provincia Arabia", Jerusalem 1978, pp.116-121, 287, pl.24.

SPIJKERMAN, A. and STARCKY, J. "Un nouveau lot de monnaies palestiniennes", RB 65, 1958, p.583.

WROTH, W. BMC, Galatia, Cappadocia and Syria, 1899, pp.lxxxv-lxxxvi, p.303, pl.38/4.

Auction Catalogues and Price Lists

AGORA Tel-Aviv 1974 (1), p.26, no. 167, pl.9.

BETTER Jaffo 1974 (7), nos. 277, 277 A.

MALTER, J.L. "Journal of Numismatic Fine Arts", Encino, CA, USA 1973 (2/2), p.37/B 69.

MONNAIES ET MÉDAILLES, Basel 1966 (32), p.48, no. 464, pl.28.

MÜNZEN UND MEDAILLEN, Basel 1969 (305), p.3, no. 41.
1981 (436), p.14, no. 149.

STERNBERG, F. Zürich, 25-26 Nov. 1976, pp.76-77, nos. 595-596, pl.24.

SUPERIOR STAMP AND COIN CO., Los-Angeles, June 1976, p.25, no. 277.

TAMAR Ramat-Gan, Israel 1976 (11), p.12, no. 168.

DORA

ARIEL, D.T. "A survey of coin finds in Jerusalem", *LA* 32, 1982, pp.292, 317.

BABELON, E. "Les Rois de Syrie, d'Arménie et de Commagène", Paris 1890, pp.cxxxix-cxl.

BABELON, E. "Les Perses Achéménides ... Cypre & Phenicie", Paris 1893, pp.205-207, pl.26/23-28.

BARAG, D. "The countermarks of the Legio Decima Fretensis", International numismatic convention in Jerusalem (1963), proceedings (A. Kindler, ed.), Tel-Aviv 1967, p.120.

BARAG, D. "Tyrian currency in Galilee", *INJ* 6-7, 1982/3, p.11.

BARAMKI, D.C. "The coin collection of the American University of Beirut Museum. Palestine and Phoenicia", Beirut 1974, pp.160-161, pl.20/1-4.

BELLINGER, A.R. "The Syrian tetradrachms of Caracalla and Macrinus", *ANS NS* 3, 1940, p.13.

DECLOEDT, A. "Monnaies de Syrie (Dora, Philadelphie, Nabateenne, moules araméen et arabe)", *RN,* 4th ser. 15, 1911, pp.366-367.

DECLOEDT, A. "Monnaies inédites ou peu connues du médaillier de Sainte-Anne-de-Jérusalem", *RN,* 4th ser. 16, 1912, pp.461-463, pl.13/1-3.

ECKHEL, J. "Doctrina numorum veterum..", vol. III, Vienna 1794, pp.362-363.

FLESCH, M. "Group of city coins", in 'Collector's choice", Bezalel National Museum, Jerusalem 1964, p.15/75.

FLUSSER, D. "Gods, personifications and sea-monsters", SEFUNIM 3, 1969/71, pp.40, 41, pl.7/10, 12. Heb. ed. pp.38, 39.

FRANCESCO DE DOMINICIS, "Repertorio numismatico..", Napoli 1827, tom II, pp.99-100.

HEAD, B.V. "Historia numorum", Oxford 1911, p.792.

HENDIN, D. "Guide to ancient Jewish coins", New York 1976, p.102.

HENDIN, D. "Coins of ancient Israel", SHEKEL 10 (6), 1977, pp.21, 32.

HILL, G.F. BMC, Phoenicia, 1910, pp.lxxiv-lxxvi, pp.113-118, pl.14.

JANIS, E. "The other coin cities of Israel", SHEKEL 3 (3), 1970, p.15.

JONAS, R. "Mythology on Palestinian coins", internal circular no. 2, Israel Num. Society, Haifa branch, 1959, p.5.

KADMAN, L. "Numismatic evidence of the architectonic revolution in the Second Century C.E.", INB 1962 (3-4), p.72. Heb. ed. p.65.

KADMAN, L. and KINDLER, A. "Coins in Palestine throughout the ages", Tel-Aviv 1963, pp.30-31, pl.14/12-14 (Hebrew).

KINDLER, A. "Thesaurus of Judaean coins from the fourth century B.C. to the third century A.D.", Jerusalem 1958, no. 37 (Hebrew).

DORA

KINDLER, A. "Coins of the Land of Israel. Bank of Israel collection", Jerusalem 1971, p.131, no. 200 (Hebrew).

KINDLER, A. "Two remarks", CATHEDRA 8, 1978, p.67 (Hebrew).

KINDLER, A. "The status of cities in Syro-Palestinian area as reflected by their coins", INJ 6-7, 1982/3, pp.80, 82.

KLAWANS, Z.H. "An outline of ancient Greek coins", Wisconsin, USA 1959, p.87.

KLIMOWSKY, E.W. "The monetary function of city coins", International numismatic convention in Jerusalem (1963), proceedings (A. Kindler, ed.), Tel-Aviv 1967, pp.158, 160, 162, 164, 166, 170, 172.

LAMBERT, C. "Coins in the Palestine Museum, II", QDAP 1, 1931/2, p.135, pl.55/21.

MACDONALD, G. "Catalogue of Greek coins in the Hunterian collection", Glasgow 1905, vol. III, p.245.

MATSSON, G.O. "The gods, goddesses and heroes on the ancient coins of Bible Lands", Stockholm 1969, pp.66, 213, pl.3/50.

MESHORER, Y. "Coins of the Ancient World", Jerusalem 1979, p.56 (Hebrew).

MESHORER, Y. "The city coins of Eretz-Israel and the Decapolis in the Roman period", Jerusalem 1984, pp.16, 110 (Hebrew).

MIONNET, T.E. "Description de médailles antiques, grecques et romaines", Paris 1806-1837, vol. V, pp.359-362, vol. VIII, suppl., pp.258-260.

PICCIRILLO, M. "Le moneta della Fortezza di Macheronte", LA 30, 1980, pp.410-411, pl.103/92.

PRICE, M.J. and TRELL, B.L. "Coins and their cities", London 1977, p.280.

QEDAR, S. "A new coin-type of the city of Dora", ALON 5 (4), 1976, p.75, pl.6/13 (Hebrew).

RIDER, G. le "Les ateliers monétaires de la côte Syrienne, Phénicienne, Palestinienne, Égyptienne et Cyrénéenne", Congresso Internazionale di numismatica (Roma 1961), vol. I, Relazioni, Roma 1961, p.88.

ROSENBERGER, M. "City-coins of Palestine", vol. II, Jerusalem 1975, pp.31-37.

ROSENBERGER, M. "City-coins of Palestine", vol. III, Jerusalem 1977, pp.80-81.

ROUVIER, J. "Numismatique des villes de la Phénicie", JIAN 4, 1901, pp.125-131, nos. 752-776, pl.Z.

SAULCY, F. de "Numismatique de la Terre Sainte", Paris 1874, pp.142-148, 405, pl.6/6-12.

SCHONWALTER, R. "Numismatic evidence from the Dead Sea", NUMISMATIST 71 (7), 1958, p.796.

SEAR, D.R. "Greek imperial coins and their values", London 1982, nos. 739, 782, 1085, 1243, 5200.

SEGUIN, P. "Selecta numismata antiqua..", Paris 1684, p.309.

SESTINI, D. "Descriptio numorum veterum..", Lipsiae 1796, p.534.

DORA

SESTINI, D. "Classes generales geographiae numismaticae sev monetae urbium, populorum et regum..", Lipsiae 1797, part I, p.68.

SESTINI, D. "Lettere e dissertazioni numismatiche..", vol. IX, Firenze 1820, p.96.

SESTINI, D. "Classes generales sev moneta vetus urbium, populorum et regum..", Florentiae 1821, p.145.

SEYRIG, H. "Notes on Syrian coins", NNM 119, 1950, p.31.

SEYRIG, H. "Antiquités Syriennes, 43. Démétrias de Phénicie", SYRIA 27, 1950, pp.51-52, fig. 3/e.

SNG DNM "Phoenicia", 1961, pl.4/154-156.

SNG FM vol. IV, part 8, "Syria-Nabathaea", 1971, pl.134/6036.

SPIJKERMAN, A. "Herodion III. Catalogo delle monete", Jerusalem 1972, p.98.

SPIJKERMAN, A. "Cafarnao III. Catalogo delle monete della città", Jerusalem 1975, p.37, no. 281.

STAHL, Z. "The Flavian Emperors and their coins in Eretz-Israel", special brochure of Israel Num. Society, Tel-Aviv branch, 1976, p.7 (Hebrew).

STAHL, Z. "Roman coins of Palestine cities issued during the Jewish War, 66-70 C.E.", special brochure of Israel Num. Society, Tel-Aviv branch, 1979, pp.12, 15-17, 25 (Hebrew).

STERN, E. and BEIT-ARIEH, I. "Excavation at Tel-Kedesh (Tel Abu-Qudeis)", TEL-AVIV 6 (1-2), 1979, p.11.

SUTHERLAND, C.H.V. "The pattern of monetary development in Phoenicia and Palestine during the Early Empire", International numismatic convention in Jerusalem (1963), proceedings (A. Kindler, ed.), Tel-Aviv 1967, pp.90, 94, 95.

TIEPOLO, L. and F. "Musei Theupoli antiqua numismata..", Venetiis 1736, series 6, p.864.

VAILLANT, J. "Numismata imperatorum, augustarum et caesarum a populis Romanae ditionis Graece loquentibus..", Paris 1698, pp.27, 33, 235, 261, 264, 350-351.

VAUX, R. de "Fouilles au Khirbet Qumrân, IV. Les monnaies", _RB_ 61, 1954, pp.230, 231.

VAUX, R. de "Fouilles de Khirbet Qumrân, V. Monnaies et les dates d'occupation", _RB_ 63, 1956, p.566.

VLIET, N. van der "Monnaies inédites ou très rares du médaillier de Sainte-Anne de Jérusalem", _RB_ 57, 1950, pp.431-432, pl.6/2.

WICZAY, C.M. "Musei Hedervarii numi antiqui..", Vindobonae 1814, part I, p.281, nos. 6069-6070.

ZURI, N. "A hoard of bronze and silver coins from Ain Hanaziv", _INB_ 1962 (3-4), p.105. Heb. ed. p.88.

Auction Catalogues and Price Lists

AGORA Tel-Aviv 1974 (1), p.24, nos. 146-148, pl.8.
1975 (2), nos. 170-173, pl.7.

BETTER Haifa 1972 (1), nos. 171-172.
Haifa 1972 (2), nos. 252-255.
Haifa 1973 (3), nos. 352-353.
Haifa 1973 (4), nos. 197-198.

DORA

BETTER (con't) Jaffo 1974 (5), nos. 150, 150A.
Jaffo 1974 (7), nos. 220-221.
Haifa 1974 (8), no. 131.

CAHN, A.E. Frankfurt 1931 (71), p.65, no. 1063, pl.32.

EIDELSTEIN AND HOLLAND, (Summer price list), Haifa 1976, no. 173.

GANS, E. "Numismatic Fine Arts", Berkeley CA, USA 1956 (20), p.15, nos. 4979-4980.

GLENDINING London, 10 March 1965, pp.21-22, nos. 166-168, pl.6.

HOLZER, H. "The Thomas Ollive Mabbott collection", part I, New York 1969, p.105, no. 2698.

KRAUS, F.F. (price list), Braunschweig, Germany,
1928 (2), p.46, nos. 1051-1052.
1929 (1-2), p.50, nos. 1149-1151.

MALTER, J.L. "Journal of Numismatic Fine Arts", Encino CA, USA
1973 (2/2), p.37/B 70.
1977 (6/1), p.13/S 60-61.

MONNAIES ET MÉDAILLES, Basel 1966 (32), p.41, nos. 352-354, pl.23.

MÜNZEN UND MEDAILLEN, Basel 1954 (131), p.5, no. 79.
1969 (305), p.3, no. 42.
1980 (424), p.17, no. 205.

SCHLESSINGER, F. (price list), Amsterdam 1938 (9), p.2, nos. 638-640.

SEABY London 1960 (502), p.107, no. A 281.
1961 (512), p.25, no. A 77.

SPINK AND SON London 1905 (13/150), nos. 15002-15007.
1927 (35/3), no. 65435.

STERNBERG, F. Zürich, 25-26 Nov. 1976, p.77, nos. 597-598, pl.24.

SUPERIOR STAMP AND COIN CO., Los-Angeles, June 1976, p.25,
nos. 278-279.

TAMAR Tel-Aviv 1975 (9), pl.7 no. 140.
Tel-Aviv 1975 (10), p.9, no. 140.
Ramat-Gan, Israel 1976 (12), p.51, nos. 838-839.

ELEUTHEROPOLIS

ANONYMOUS *CH* 1, 1975, p.34/124.

ARIEL, D.T. "A survey of coin finds in Jerusalem", *LA* 32, 1982, p.318.

BARAMKI, D.C. "The coin collection of the American University of Beirut Museum. Palestine and Phoenicia", Beirut 1974, p.58, pl.9/11.

BELLINGER, A.R. "The Syrian tetradrachms of Caracalla and Macrinus", *ANS NS* 3, 1940, p.13.

ECKHEL, J. "Doctrina numorum veterum.", vol. III, Vienna 1794, p.448.

FLESCH, M. "Group of city coins", in 'Collector's choice', Bezalel National Museum, Jerusalem 1964, p.15/74.

HAMBURGER, A. "Gems from Caesarea Maritima", *ATIQOT,* Es 8, 1968, pp.6-7, no. 14.

HEAD, B.V. "Historia numorum", Oxford 1911, p.804.

HENDIN, D. "Guide to ancient Jewish coins", New York 1976, p.117, pl.9/271.

HILL, G.F. BMC, Palestine, 1914, pp.lxv-lxvi, pp.141-142, pl.14/17-20.

IMHOOF-BLUMER, F. "Zur syrischen Münzkunde", *NZ* 33, 1901, pp.13-14.

JANIS, E. "The other coin cities of Israel", *SHEKEL* 3 (3), 1970, p.15.

JONAS, R. "Mythology on Palestinian coins", internal circular no. 2, Israel Num. Society, Haifa branch, 1959, pp.3-4.

KADMAN, L. "Numismatic evidence of the architectonic revolution in the Second Century C.E.", INB 1962 (3-4), p.72. Heb. ed. p.65.

KADMAN, L. and KINDLER, A. "Coins in Palestine throughout the ages", Tel-Aviv 1963, p.39, pl.16/18-19 (Hebrew).

KINDLER, A. "Thesaurus of Judaean coins from the fourth century B.C. to the third century A.D.", Jerusalem 1958, no. 26 (Hebrew).

KINDLER, A. "The status of cities in the Syro-Palestinian area as reflected by their coins", INJ 6-7, 1982/3, pp.81, 85 (note 45), 87.

KINDLER, A. "The coinage of Bostra", Warminster, England 1983, pp.27, 37.

KLAWANS, Z.H. "An outline of ancient Greek coins", Wisconsin, USA 1959, p.90.

KLIMOWSKY, E.W. "The monetary function of city coins", International numismatic convention in Jerusalem (1963), proceedings (A. Kindler, ed.), Tel-Aviv 1967, pp.166, 172.

KUBITSCHEK, W. "Zur Geschichte von Städten des römischen Kaiserreiches. Epigraphisch-numismatische Studien", heft 1, Wien 1916, pp.9, 16, 17.

LAMBERT, C. "Coins in the Palestine Museum, II", QDAP 1, 1931/2, p.131, pl.54/8.

ELEUTHEROPOLIS

MATSSON, G.O. "The gods, goddesses and heroes on the ancient coins of Bible Lands", Stockholm 1969, pp.168, 172, 193, 237, pl.7/105b.

MESHORER, Y. "The city coins of Eretz-Israel and the Decapolis in the Roman period", Jerusalem 1984, pp.64, 117 (Hebrew).

MIONNET, T.E. "Description de médailles antiques, grecques et romaines", Paris 1806-1837, vol. V, pp.534-535, vol. VIII, suppl., pp.370-371.

PRICE, M.J. and TRELL, B.L. "Coins and their cities", London 1977, p.284.

ROSENBERGER, M. "City-coins of Palestine", vol. II, Jerusalem 1975, pp.37-43.

ROSENBERGER, M. "City-coins of Palestine", vol. III, Jerusalem 1977, p.81.

SAULCY, F. de "Numismatique de la Terre Sainte", Paris 1874, pp.241-243, pl.12/5-6.

SEAR, D.R. "Greek imperial coins and their values", London 1982, nos. 2275, 2691, 2983, 3029, 3126.

SESTINI, D. "Classes generales geographiae numismaticae sev monetae urbium, populorum et regum..", Lipsiae 1797, part I, p.71.

SESTINI, D. "Classes generales sev moneta vetus urbium, populorum et regum..", Florentiae 1821, p.152.

SNG ANS part 6, "Palestine - South Arabia", 1981, pl.29/891-897.

SNG FM vol. IV, part 8, "Syria-Nabathaea", 1971, pl.136/6107-6108.

SPIJKERMAN, A. "The coins of Eleutheropolis Iudaeae", LA 22, 1972, pp.369-384, pls.1-4.

STAHL, Z. "The city of Ludd and her coins", special brochure of Israel Num. Society, Tel-Aviv branch, 1973, p.14 (Hebrew).

WEBSTER, W. "List of inedited Greek coins - copper", NC, Ns 13, 1873, p.40.

Auction Catalogues and Price Lists

AGORA Tel-Aviv 1974 (1), p.25, no. 154, pl.9.

BETTER Haifa 1972 (1), nos. 173-174.
Haifa 1973 (4), no. 199.
Jaffo 1974 (5), no. 151.
Jaffo 1974 (7), no. 222.

CAHN, A.E. Frankfurt 1931 (71), p.68, nos. 1108-1109, pl.33.

GANS, E. "Numismatic Fine Arts", Berkeley, CA, USA 1956 (20), p.15, nos. 4967-4968.

HOLZER, H. "The Thomas Ollive Mabbott collection", part I, New York 1969, p.106, no. 2722.

MALTER, J.L. "Journal of Numismatic Fine Arts", Encino, CA, USA 1973 (2/2), p.37/B71, pl.10.

MONNAIES ET MÉDAILLES, Basel 1966 (32), p.41, nos. 355-358, pls.23-24.

RAUCH, H.D. Wien 1985 (34), no. 228.

ELEUTHEROPOLIS

SCHLESSINGER, F. (price list), Amsterdam 1938 (9), p.4, nos. 679-682.

STERNBERG, F. Zürich, 25-26 Nov. 1976, p.77, no. 599, pl.24.

SUPERIOR STAMP AND COIN CO., Los-Angeles, June 1976, pp.25-26, nos. 280-281.

TAMAR Tel-Aviv 1975 (9), p.7, no. 141.
Tel-Aviv 1975 (10), p.9, no. 141.
Ramat-Gan, Israel 1976 (11), p.10, no. 124.

VECCHI, V.C. "Bonhams", London 1982 (8), p.19, no. 215, pl.10.

ESBUS

BELLINGER, A.R. "Coins from Jerash 1928-1934", NNM 81, 1938, pp.9, 31, no.49, pl.3.

BEN-DAVID, A. "'Dinarei Arba' and silver coins called 'Harubim'", ALON 5 (2), 1974, p.28 (Hebrew).

ECKHEL, J. "Doctrina numorum veterum..", vol. III, Vienna 1794, p.503.

HARDUIN, J. "Nummi antiqui populorum et urbium illustrati", Parisiis 1684, p.158.

HEAD, B.V. "Historia numorum", Oxford 1911, p.812.

HILL, G.F. BMC, Arabia, Mesopotamia and Persia, 1922, p.xxxiii, pp.29-30, pl.5/1-3.

HILL, G.F. "Some Palestinian cults in the Graeco-Roman age", Proceedings of the British Academy, vol. 5, London 1912, p.413.

HORN, H.S. "Tell Hesbân", RB 82, 1975, p.104.

KADMAN, L. "Numismatic evidence of the architectonic revolution in the Second Century C.E.", INB 1962 (3-4), p.73. Heb. ed. p.65.

KINDLER, A. "The coinage of Bostra", Warminster, England 1983, pp.16, 37, 38.

KIRKBRIDE, A.S. "Currencies in Transjordan", PEQ 1939, p.155.

MACDONALD, G. "Catalogue of Greek coins in the Hunterian collection", Glasgow 1905, vol. III, p.300, pl.78/22.

ESBUS

MATSSON, G.O. "The gods, goddesses and heroes on the ancient coins of Bible Lands", Stockholm 1969, pp.133, 138, 225, 226, pl.5/80, 83a.

MESHORER, Y. "Was there a mint at Eboda?", SM 106, 1977, pp.33-34.

MESHORER, Y. "The city coins of Eretz-Israel and the Decapolis in the Roman period", Jerusalem 1984, pp.98, 122 (Hebrew).

MIONNET, T.E. "Description de médailles antiques, grecques et romaines", Paris 1806-1837, vol. V, pp.585-586, vol. VIII, suppl., p.387.

PRICE, M.J. and TRELL, B.L. "Coins and their cities", London 1977, p.285.

ROSENBERGER, M. "The coinage of Eastern Palestine", Jerusalem 1978, p.35.

SAULCY, F. de "Numismatique de la Terre Sainte", Paris 1874, pp.393-394, pl.23/5-7.

SEAR, D.R. "Greek imperial coins and their values", London 1982, no. 3134.

SESTINI, D. "Classes generales geographiae numismaticae sev monetae urbium, populorum et regum..", Lipsiae 1797, part I, p.73.

SESTINI, D. "Classes generales sev moneta vetus urbium, populorum et regum..", Florentiae 1821, p.156.

SNG ANS part 6, "Palestine - South Arabia", 1981, pl.44/1283-1286.

SPIJKERMAN, A. "The coins of the Decapolis and provincia Arabia", Jerusalem 1978, pp.122-125, 287, pl.25.

VAILLANT, J. "Numismata imperatorum, augustarum et caesarum a populis Romanae ditionis Graece loquentibus..", Paris 1968, pp.118, 236, 477.

WALCHER de MOLTHEIN, L. "Catalogue de la collection des medailles grecques de M. Le Chevalier", Paris - Vienne, 1895, p.280, no. 3279.

Auction Catalogues and Price Lists

AGORA Tel-Aviv 1975 (2), no. 233, pl.10.

MALTER, J.L. "Journal of Numismatic Fine Arts", Encino, CA, USA 1973 (2/2), p.37/B 72.

SUPERIOR STAMP AND COIN CO., Los-Angeles, June 1976, p.26, no. 282.

GABA

ANONYMOUS — CH 1, 1975, p.34/123.

BARAG, D. — "Tyrian currency in Galilee", INJ 6-7, 1982/3, pp.10, 11.

BARAMKI, D. — "The coins exhibited in the Archaeological Museum of the American University of Beirut", Beirut 1968, p.75, nos. 252-254, pl.7.

BELLINGER, A.R. — "The Syrian tetradrachms of Caracalla and Macrinus", ANS NS 3, 1940, p.13.

CARRADICE, I. — "Coinage in Judaea in the Flavian period, AD 70-96", INJ 6-7, 1982/3, p.17.

ECKHEL, J. — "Doctrina numorum veterum..", vol. III, Vienna 1794, pp.344-345, 352-353.

ECKHEL, J. — "Catalogus Musei Caesarei Vindobonensis numorum veterum", Vindobonae 1779, part I, p.246.

FROELICH, E. — "Quatuor tentamina in re numaria vetere", 2nd ed., Viennae 1737, pp.167-168, 169.

HARDUIN, J. — "Nummi antiqui populorum et urbium illustrati", Parisiis 1684, pp.173-174.

HEAD, B.V. — "Historia numorum", Oxford 1911, p.786.

KADMAN, L. — "Numismatic evidence of the architectonic revolution in the Second Century C.E.", INB 1962 (3-4), pp.71, 72. Heb. ed. pp.63, 65.

KINDLER, A. "Thesaurus of Judaean coins from the fourth century B.C. to the third century A.D.", Jerusalem 1958, no. 39 (Hebrew).

KINDLER, A. "The status of cities in the Syro-Palestinian area as reflected by their coins", INJ 6-7, 1982/3, p.84.

KINDLER, A. "The coinage of Bostra", Warminster, England 1983, p.37.

KIRKBRIDE, A. "Currencies in Transjordan", PEQ 1939, p.156.

KLAWANS, Z.H. "An outline of ancient Greek coins", Wisconsin, USA 1959, p.92.

KLIMOWSKY, E.W. "The monetary function of city coins", International numismatic convention in Jerusalem (1963), proceedings (A. Kindler, ed.), Tel-Aviv 1967, p.164, 172.

KLIMOWSKY, E.W. "On ancient Palestinian and other coins, their symbolism and metrology", PINS 7, Tel-Aviv 1974, pl.7/55. Same in INJ 3, 1965/6, pl.7/55.

MATSSON, G.O. "The gods, goddesses and heroes on the ancient coins of Bible Lands", Stockholm 1969, p.133.

MESHORER, Y. "A hoard of coins from Migdal", ATIQOT, Es 11, 1976, pp.55, 56, 70, pl.15/149.

MESHORER, Y. "Was there a mint at Eboda?" SM 106, 1977, pp.33-36.

MESHORER, Y. "The city coins of Eretz-Israel and the Decapolis in the Roman period", Jerusalem 1984, pp.38, 114 (Hebrew).

GABA

MIONNET, T.E. "Description de médailles antiques, grecques et romaines", Paris 1806-1837, vol. V, pp.316-318, vol. VIII, suppl., pp.220-222.

PELLERIN, J. "Second supplément aux six volumes de recueils des médailles..", Paris 1766, p.1 (vignette), p.iv (explication des médailles..).

PRICE, M.J. and TRELL, B.L. "Coins and their cities", London 1977, p.283.

ROSENBERGER, M. "City-coins of Palestine", vol. II, Jerusalem 1975, pp.43-47, 79.

ROSENBERGER, M. "City-coins of Palestine", vol. III, Jerusalem 1977, pp.81-82.

ROSENBERGER, M. "A new type of Gaba and a coin prepared for a Bar Kokhba overstriking", INJ 4, 1980, p.55, pl.16/1, 2.

SAULCY, F. de "Numismatique de la Terre Sainte", Paris 1874, pp.339-343, pl.19/1-7.

SEAR, D.R. "Greek imperial coins and their values", London 1982, nos. 473, 875, 1112, 1241, 1316, 1499, 1696.

SESTINI, D. "Descriptio numorum veterum..", Lipsiae 1796, p.530.

SESTINI, D. "Classes generales geographiae numismaticae sev monetae urbium, populorum et regum..", Lipsiae 1797, part I, p.67, part II, p.100.

SESTINI, D. "Classes generales sev moneta vetus urbium, populorum et regum..", Florentiae 1821, p.143.

SESTINI, D. "Descrizione delle medaglie antiche Greche del Museo Hedervariano", part 3, Firenze 1829, p.73.

SHAHAF, N. "Numismatists in search for the ruins of Gaba - the city 'of horsemen'", internal circular no. 1, Israel Num. Society, Haifa branch, 1958 (Hebrew).

SNG ANS part 6, "Palestine - South Arabia", 1981, pl.29/898-904.

SNG FM vol. IV, part 8, "Syria-Nabathaea", 1971, pl.132/5975-5976.

SPIJKERMAN, A. "Cafarnao III. Catalogo delle monete della città", Jerusalem 1975, p.23, no. 120, pl.1/5.

STAHL, Z. "The Flavian Emperors and their coins in Eretz-Israel", special brochure of Israel Num. Society, Tel-Aviv branch, 1976, p.7 (Hebrew).

TIEPOLO, L. and F. "Musei Theupoli antiqua numismata..", Venetiis 1736, series 6, p.877.

VAILLANT, J. "Numismata imperatorum, augustarum et caesarum a populis Romanae ditionis Graece loquentibus..", Paris 1698, pp.31, 33, 43, 234, 339-340.

WROTH, W. BMC, Galatia, Cappadocia and Syria, 1899, pp.lxxxii-lxxxiii, p.300, pl.37/8-9.

<u>Auction Catalogues and Price Lists</u>

AGORA Tel-Aviv 1974 (1), pp.22-23, nos. 134-140, pl.8.
1975 (2), no. 174, pl.7.

BETTER Haifa 1972 (2), nos. 350-352.
Haifa 1973 (4), no. 283.

CAHN, A.E. Frankfurt 1931 (71), p.64, no. 1055, pl.32.

GABA

GLENDINING London, 19 July 1980, p.45, no. 332.

HOLZER, H. "The Thomas Ollive Mabbott collection", part I, New York 1969, p.102, nos. 2624-2625.

MALTER, J.L. "Journal of Numismatic Fine Arts", Encino, CA, USA 1973 (2/2), p.37/B 73, pl.10.

MONNAIES ET MÉDAILLES, Basel 1966 (32), p.48, no. 465, pl.28.

SCHLESSINGER, F. (price list), Amsterdam 1938 (9), p.1, nos. 613-614.

SPINK AND SON London 1930 (38/11), no. 1784.
1931 (39/8), nos. 9256-9257.
1934 (42/12), no. 37853.

STERNBERG, F. Zürich, 25-26 Nov. 1976, p.77, no. 602, pl.25.

SUPERIOR STAMP AND COIN CO., Los-Angeles, June 1976, p.26, no. 283.

VECCHI, V.C. "Bonhams", London 1982 (8), p.19, no. 216, pl.10.

GADARA

AKERMAN, J.Y. "Numismatic illustrations of the narrative portions of the New Testament", NC 8, 1846, p.148.

ANONYMOUS CH 1, 1975, p.34/123.

ARIEL, D.T. "A survey of coin finds in Jerusalem", LA 32, 1982, p.317.

ARRIGONI, O. "Numismata quaedam cujuscunque formae..", Tarvisii, part I (1741), Numismata Imperatoria in graecis urbibus percussa a J. Vaillant non edita, pls. 3/28; 5/70; 10/148.

BARAG, D. "The countermarks of the Legio Decima Fretensis", International numismatic convention in Jerusalem (1963), proceedings (A. Kindler, ed.), Tel-Aviv 1967, p.120.

BARAG, D. "Tyrian currency in Galilee", INJ 6-7, 1982/3, pp.10, 11.

BARAMKI, D.C. "The coins exhibited in the Archaeological Museum of the American University of Beirut", Beirut 1968, pp.73-74, nos. 246-248, pl.7.

BELLINGER, A.R. "The Syrian tetradrachms of Caracalla and Macrinus", ANS NS 3, 1940, pp.11, 14, 15, 17, 18, 20, 90-92, pls.22/14-15; 23/1-8.

BELLINGER, A.R. "The excavations at Dura-Europos. Final report VI. The coins", New Haven, USA 1949, pp.15-16/278-280; 18/342-346; 165, 171, 175, 176, 183, pls.8, 10.

BENTINCK, de "Catalogue d'une collection de médailles antiques", Amsterdam 1788, suppl., p.96.

GADARA

CARRADICE, I. "Coinage in Judaea in the Flavian period, AD 70-96", <u>INJ</u> 6-7, 1982/3, p.17.

CAVEDONI, D.C. "Biblische Numismatik", vol. I, Hannover 1855 (Italienisches Original: Appendice alla Numismatica, Modena 1855), p.111.

ECKHEL, J. "Numi veteres anecdoti ex museis Caesareo Vindobonensi, Florentino Magni Ducis Etruriae,..", Viennae 1775, pp.276-277.

ECKHEL, J. "Catalogus Musei Caesarei Vindobonensis numorum veterum..", Vindobonae 1779, part I, p.251.

ECKHEL, J. "Doctrina numorum veterum..", vol. III, Vienna 1794, pp.348-350.

FROELICH, E. "Quatuor tentamina in re numaria vetere", 2nd ed., Viennae 1737, pp.256-257.

GESSNER, J.J. "Numismata antiqua imperatorum Romanorum latina et graeca..", Tiguri (Zürich), 18th cent., pls.48/19, 20; 102/12; 145/45; 148/65; 158/1; 159/3.

GILMORE, P.M. "The formulae of Antioch and Tyre", <u>NCirc</u> 86 (2), 1978, p.76.

GILMORE, P.M. "Syrian officinae under Caracalla and Macrinus", <u>NCirc</u> 87 (6), 1979, p.287.

GILMORE, P.M. "Caracalla's silver mints in Syria", <u>NCirc</u> 88, 1980, pp.89, 90.

GILMORE, P.M. "A fresh look at Caracalla's Syrian silver", <u>NCirc</u> 92 (2), 1984, pp.41, 42.

GROSE, S.W. "Catalogue of the McClean collection of Greek coins in the Fitzwilliam Museum", vol. III, Cambridge 1929, p.362/9442, pl.348/15.

HAMBURGER, H. "A hoard of Syrian tetradrachms and Tyrian bronze coins from Gush Halav", IEJ 4 (3-4), 1954, pp.203, 215, pl.19/58. Same in 'Recent studies and discoveries on ancient Jewish and Syrian coins', PINS 1, Jerusalem 1954, pp.67, 79, pl.19/58.

HAMBURGER, H. "An unknown Syrian tetradrachm of Caracalla", IEJ 6 (3), 1956, pp.188-190, pl.28.

HANSON, R.S. "Meiron coins: 1974-75", AASOR 43, 1976, pp.100, 101, no. R75258.

HARDUIN, J. "Nummi antiqui populorum et urbium illustrati", Parisiis 1684, pp.175-176.

HEAD, B.V. "Historia numorum", Oxford 1911, p.787.

HEYMANN, H. "Roman legionary coins from Phoenicia", INJ 1963 (3), p.49.

KADMAN, L. "Numismatic evidence of the architectonic revolution in the Second Century C.E.", INB 1962 (3-4), p.72. Heb. ed. p.65.

KADMAN, L. and KINDLER, A. "Coins in Palestine throughout the ages", Tel-Aviv 1963, p.40, pl.18/3 (Hebrew).

KINDLER, A. "Thesaurus of Judaean coins from the fourth century B.C. to the third century A.D.", Jerusalem 1958, no. 41 (Hebrew).

KINDLER, A. "Two remarks", CATHEDRA 8, 1978, p.67 (Hebrew).

GADARA

KINDLER, A. "The status of cities in the Syro-Palestinian area as reflected by their coins", INJ 6-7, 1982/3, pp.80, 82.

KINDLER, A. "The coinage of Bostra", Warminster, England 1983, p.58.

KLAWANS, Z.H. "An outline of ancient Greek coins", Wisconsin, USA 1959, p.93.

KLIMOWSKY, E.W. "The monetary function of city coins", International numismatic convention in Jerusalem (1963), proceedings (A. Kindler, ed.), Tel-Aviv 1967, pp.147, 150, 154, 158, 160, 162, 164, 168, 170, 172, 177.

KUBITSCHEK, W. "Eine Münze der Stadt Gadara", NZ 49, 1916, p.174.

LAMBERT, C. "Coins in the Palestine Museum, II", QDAP 1, 1931/2, p.137, pl.56/28-31.

MATSSON, G.O. "The gods, goddesses and heroes on the ancient coins of Bible Lands", Stockholm 1969, pp.218, 244, pls.4/61c; 8/118c.

MESHORER, Y. "Coins of the city of Gadara struck in commemoration of a local 'naumachia'", SEFUNIM 1, 1966, pp.28-31, pl.2/1-2. Heb. ed. pp.25-27.

MESHORER, Y. "A hoard of coins from Migdal", ATIQOT, Es 11, 1976, pp.54, 56, 62-64, pl.12/75-91.

MESHORER, Y. "A ring from Gadara", IEJ 29 (3-4), 1979, pp.221-222, pl.25.

MESHORER, Y. "The city coins of Eretz-Israel and the Decapolis in the Roman period", Jerusalem 1984, pp.80-83, 119-120 (Hebrew).

MEYSHAN, J. "A find of coins of Agrippa II - together with coins of Sidon in Lower Galilee", NCirc 67 (4), 1959, pp.74, 75. Same in 'Essays in Jewish numismatics', Jerusalem 1968, pp.153-154.

MIONNET, T.E. "Description de médailles antiques, grecques et romaines", Paris 1806-1837, vol. V, pp.323-328, vol. VII (Notes et observ.), p.109, vol. VIII, suppl., pp.227-230.

PATIN, C. "Imperatorum Romanorum numismata ex aere mediae et minimae formae descripta et enarrata..", Amsterdam(?), 1671, pp.229, 306, 334.

PELLERIN, J. "Recueil de médailles de peuples et de villes", part 6, suppl., Paris 1763, vignette (title page).

PELLERIN, J. "Mélange de diverses médailles..", t.II, Paris 1765, pp.124, pl.28/7; p.174, pl.29/3.

PLANT, R. "Greek coin types and their identification", London 1979, no. 2047.

PRICE, M.J. and TRELL, B.L. "Coins and their cities", London 1977, p.282.

RAHMANI, L. and SHARABANI, M. "List of coins", in 'Hammath Tiberias' by M. Dothan, Jerusalem 1983, p.72, pl.22/15.

REICHARDT, H.C. "Remarks on some Jewish coins, and on some inedited coins of Phoenicia, Judaea, etc.", NC, Ns 4, 1864, p.185.

RIDER, G. le "Les ateliers monétaires de la côte Syrienne, Phénicienne, Palestinienne, Égyptienne et Cyrénéenne", Congresso Internazionale di numismatica (Roma 1961), vol. I, Relazioni, Roma 1961, pp.83, 87, 96.

GADARA

RIDER, G. le "Deux grands bronzes de Gadara", _Bulletin de la Société Française de numismatique_ 16 (1), 1961, p.5.

ROGERS, E. "A handy guide to Jewish coins", London 1914, p.79.

ROSENBERGER, M. "The coinage of Eastern Palestine", Jerusalem 1978, pp.36-50.

ROSENTHAL-HEGINBOTTOM, R. "The Mampsis hoard - A preliminary report", _INJ_ 4, 1980, p.48.

SAULCY, F. de "Numismatique de la Terre Sainte", Paris 1874, pp.294-303, pl.15.

SEAR, D.R. "Greek imperial coins and their values", London 1982, nos. 113, 294, 399, 475, 624, 738, 780, 1500, 1676, 1709, 1798, 1874, 2051, 2098, 2267, 2454, 2667-2668, 2728, 2958, 3107, 3781.

SEGUIN, P. "Selecta numismata antiqua", Paris 1684, p.312.

SESTINI, D. "Descriptio numorum veterum..", Lipsiae 1796, p.531.

SESTINI, D. "Classes generales geographiae numismaticae sev monetae urbium, populorum et regum..", Lipsiae 1797, part I, pp.67-68, part II, p.100.

SESTINI, D. "Descrizione delle medaglie Greche e Romane del Fu Benkowitz", Berlino, 1809, p.33.

SESTINI, D. "Lettere e dissertazione numismatiche..", Firenze 1820, vol. IX, pp.86-89.

SESTINI, D. "Classes generales sev moneta vetus urbium, populorum et regum..", Florentiae 1821, p.144.

SESTINI, D. "Descrizione d'alcune medaglie Greche del museo del Signore Carlo D'Ottavio Fontana", Firenze 1822, p.13.

SESTINI, D. "Descrizione delle medaglie antiche Greche del Museo Hedervariano", part 3, Firenze 1829, pp.74-75, pl.31/5-6.

SEYRIG, H. "Notes on Syrian coins", NNM 119, 1950, p.32.

SEYRIG, H. "Antiquités Syriennes, 73. Temples, cultes et souvenirs historiques de la Décapole", SYRIA 36, 1959, pp.71-75, fig. 4.

SNG ANS part 6, "Palestine - South Arabia", 1981, pls. 44-46, figs. 1287-1341.

SNG DNM "Syria, Cities", 1959, pl.12/450.

SNG FM vol. IV, part 8, "Syria-Nabathaea", 1971, pl.132/5983-5984.

SPIJKERMAN, A. "Moneta della sinagoga di Cafarnao", LA 20, 1970, p.155, no. 116.

SPIJKERMAN, A. "An unknown coin-type of Pella Decapoleos", LA 20, 1970, p.355.

SPIJKERMAN, A. "Cafarnao III. Catalogo delle monete della città", Jerusalem 1975, p.47, no. 393, pl.2/1.

SPIJKERMAN, A. "The coins of the Decapolis and provincia Arabia", Jerusalem 1978, pp.126-155, 288-289, pls.26-32, suppl., I, 34a, 45a, 66a, 72a, 76a.

SPIJKERMAN, A. and STARCKY, J. "Un nouveau lot de monnaies palestiniennes", RB 65, 1958, p.583.

GADARA

TIEPOLO, L. and F. "Musei Theupoli antiqua numismata..", Venetiis 1736, series 6, pp.846, 916, 1046.

VAILLANT, J. "Numismata imperatorum, augustarum et caesarum a populis Romanae ditionis Graece loquentibus..", Paris 1698, pp.2, 8, 15, 21, 26, 43, 54, 70, 76, 153, 180, 234, 340-343, 477.

VLIET, N. van der "Monnaies inédites ou très rares du médaillier de Sainte-Anne de Jérusalem", RB 57, 1950, pp.244-250, pls.4/2-7; 5/8.

WICZAY, C.M. "Musei Hedervarii numi antiqui..", Vidobonae 1814, part I, p.279, nos. 6030-6033, pl.26/566.

WROTH, W. BMC, Galatia, Cappadocia and Syria, 1899, pp.lxxxvi-lxxxviii, pp.304-305, pl.38/5-8.

Auction Catalogues and Price Lists

AGORA Tel-Aviv 1974 (1), p.26, nos. 163-165, pl.9.
1975 (2), nos. 220-224, pl.9.

BETTER Haifa 1972 (1), nos. 237-241.
Haifa 1972 (2), nos. 354-356.
Haifa 1973 (3), no. 356.
Haifa 1973 (4), nos. 285-286.
Jaffo 1974 (7), nos. 285-290.
Haifa 1974 (8), nos. 168-174.

CAHN, A.E. Frankfurt 1931 (71), p.65, nos. 1058-1059, pl.32.

COIN GALLERIES (price list), New York 1959 (17), p.16, no. A 235.

EIDELSTEIN AND HOLLAND, Haifa, 10 Nov. 1975, no. 167.

GANS, E. "Numismatic Fine Arts" (Stock cat.), New York
1942 (1), p.29, no. 7314.
1943 (3), pp.9, 18, nos. 6314, 7314.

GANS, E. "Numismatic Fine Arts", Berkeley CA, USA
1956 (20), p.16, nos. 4987-4989.
1962 (28), p.18, no. 7012.

GLENDINING 19 July 1950, p.45, no. 332.
10 March 1965, p.22, nos. 170-174, pl.6.

HESS-LEU Luzern 1965 (28), p.42, nos. 299-300, pl.13.

HOLZER, H. "The Thomas Ollive Mabbott collection", part I,
New York 1969, pp.102-103, nos. 2631-2647.

KRESS, K. München 1976 (167), p.58, no. 1371.

MALTER, J.L. "Journal of Numismatic Fine Arts", Encino CA, USA
1973 (2/2), p.37/B 74, pl.10.
1975 (4/1), p.25/C 31.
1977 (6/1), p.13/S 40-47.

MONNAIES ET MÉDAILLES, Basel 1966 (32), pp.48-49, nos. 467-476, pl.28.

MÜNZEN AND MEDAILLEN, Basel
1955 (151), p.12, no. 230.
1968 (293), p.4, no. 44.
1978 (398), p.1, no. 3.
1979 (417), p.23, no. 343.
1980 (424), p.4, no. 61, p.17, no. 209.
1982 (448), p.1, no. 14.
1983 (453), p.6, no. 58.

MÜNZZENTRUM KÖLN 1979 (36), p.28, nos. 183-185.
1980 (39), p.12, no. 636.

GADARA

SALTON-SCHLESSINGER, M.M. (price list), New York 1958 (27), p.7, no. 135.

SCHLESSINGER, F. (price list), Amsterdam 1938 (9), p.2, nos. 616-625.

SCHULMAN, H.M.F., New York, 6-7 Apr. 1971, p.24, nos. 442-443.

SEABY London 1960 (510), p.461, no. A.960.
1966 (570), p.28, no. A 58.
1971 (637), p.337, no. A 866.
1973 (658), pp.215, 217, nos. A 602, A 638.

SPINK AND SON London 1902 (10/116), nos. 85066-85072.
1905 (13/149), nos. 13826-13831.
1927 (35/3), no. 65410.
1931 (39/4), nos. 6025-6026.
1931 (39/8), nos. 9259-9262.
1971 (79/6), p.252, no. 6610.
1977 (85/7-8), p.318, no. 6646.
1984 (92/5), p.157, no. 3516.

STERNBERG, F. Zürich, 25-26 Nov. 1976, pp.78-79, nos.604-611, pl.25.

SUPERIOR STAMP AND COIN CO., Los-Angeles, June 1976, p.26, nos. 284-285.

TAMAR Tel-Aviv 1975 (9), p.8, nos. 160-169.
Tel-Aviv 1975 (10), p.10, nos. 158-162.
Ramat-Gan, Israel 1976 (11), p.12, nos. 155-167.
Ramat-Gan, Israel 1976 (12), pp.53-54, nos. 878-882, 901.

GAZA

ANONYMOUS — *CH* 1, 1975, p.34/124.

ARIEL, D.T. — "A survey of coin finds in Jerusalem", *LA* 32, 1982, pp.292, 318.

BABELON, J. — "Catalogue de la collection de Luynes", vol. IV, Paris 1936, p.48/3478, pl.129.

BARAG, D. — "Tyrian currency in Galilee", *INJ* 6-7, 1982/3, pp.9, 11.

BARAMKI, D.C. — "The coins exhibited in the Archaeological Museum of the American University of Beirut", Beirut 1968, pp.96-97, nos. 320-322, pl.8.

BARAMKI, D.C. — "The coin collection of the American University of Beirut Museum. Palestine and Phoenicia", Beirut 1974, pp.59-67, pls.9/12-15; 10/1-9.

BARAMKI, J. — "Coins in the Palestine Archaeological Museum, III", *QDAP* 8, 1939, pp.78-79, pl.41/9-11.

BELLINGER, A.R. — "The Syrian tetradrachms of Caracalla and Macrinus", *ANS NS* 3, 1940, pp.11, 13, 15, 17, 18, 19, 20, 102-103, pl.26/1-7.

BELLINGER, A.R. — "The excavations at Dura-Europos. Final report VI. The coins", New Haven, USA 1949, pp.16 (nos. 292-293), 183, pl.9.

BENTINCK, de — "Catalogue d'une collection de médailles antiques", Amsterdam 1787, part II, p.1071.

CARRADICE, I. — "Coinage in Judaea in the Flavian period, AD 70-96", *INJ* 6-7, 1982/3, p.17.

GAZA

CARSON, R.A.G. "The inflation of the Third Century and its monetary influence in the Near East", International numismatic convention in Jerusalem (1963), proceedings (A. Kindler, ed.), Tel-Aviv 1967, p.242.

DOWLING, T.E. "Notes on Gaza coins", PEQ 44, 1912, pp.98-100.

ECKHEL, J. "Catalogus Musei Caesarei Vindobonensis numorum veterum..", Vindobonae 1779, part I, pp.250-251, pl.4/15.

ECKHEL, J. "Doctrina numorum veterum..", vol.III, Vienna 1794, pp.448-454.

FLESCH, M. "Group of city coins", in 'Collector's choice', Bezalel National Museum, Jerusalem 1964, p.15/76.

FORRER, L. "Weber collection, vol. III, part 2: Greek coins", London 1929, pp.798-800, nos. 8117-8122, pl.299.

FRANCESCO DE DOMINICIS "Repertorio numismatico", Napoli, t.I (1826), pp.510, 549, t.II (1827), pp.101, 178, 253.

FROELICH, E. "Quatuor tentamina in re numaria vetere", 2nd end., Viennae 1737, p.249.

GESSNER, J.J. "Numismata antiqua Imperatorum Romanorum latina et graeca", Tiguri (Zürich), 18th cent., pls.102/13; 112/5; 126/64, 65; 136/6; 151/5.

GILMORE, P.M. "The formulae of Antioch and Tyre", NCirc 86 (2), 1978, p.76.

GILMORE, P.M. "Syrian officinae under Caracalla and Macrinus", NCirc 87 (6), 1979, pp.288, 289.

GILMORE, P.M. "Caracalla's silver mints in Syria", NCirc 88 (3), 1980, p.88.

HAMBURGER, H. "A hoard of Syrian tetradrachms and Tyrian bronze coins from Gush Halav", IEJ 4 (3-4), 1954, pp.203, 215. Same in "Recent studies and discoveries on ancient Jewish and Syrian coins", PINS 1, Jerusalem 1954, pp.67, 79.

HANSON, R.S. "Tyrian influence in the Upper Galilee", Cambridge 1980, p.52.

HARDUIN, J. "Nummi antiqui populorum et urbium illustrati", Parisiis 1684, pp.177-178.

HEAD, B.V. "Historia numorum", Oxford 1911, p.805.

HENDIN, D. "Guide to ancient Jewish coins", New York 1976, pp.119-120.

HILL, G.F. "Some Palestinian cults in the Graeco-Roman age", Proceedings of the British Academy, vol. V, London 1912, pp.423-427, pl./19-20.

HILL, G.F. BMC, Palestine, 1914, pp.lxvi-lxxix, pp.143-168, pls.15, 16, 17/1-9.

HOWGEGO, C. "The behaviour and function of Greek Imperial countermarks", INJ 6-7, 1982/3, p.57, pl.14/11-14.

IMHOOF-BLUMER, F. "Zur griechischen Münzkunde", SNR 8, 1898, p.44.

JANIS, E. "The other coin cities of Israel", SHEKEL 3 (3), 1970, p.15.

GAZA

JONAS, R. "Mythology on Palestinian coins", internal circular no. 2, Israel Num. Society, Haifa branch, 1959, pp.2, 4, 6, 7.

KADMAN, L. "Numismatic evidence of the architectonic revolution in the Second Century C.E.", INB 1962 (3-4), p.72. Heb. ed. p.65.

KADMAN, L. and KINDLER, A. "Coins in Palestine throughout the ages", Tel-Aviv 1963, p.34, pl.15/14-20 (Hebrew).

KASHER, A. "Milestones in the history of Gaza in the Second Temple times", CATHEDRA 15, 1980, pp.33-35 (Hebrew).

KINDLER, A. "Thesaurus of Judaean coins from the fourth century B.C. to the third century A.D.", Jerusalem 1958, no. 29 (Hebrew).

KINDLER, A. "Ein Münzpalimpsest aus dem Bar-Kochba-Krieg", SNR 42, 1962/3, pp.16-19, pl.2.

KINDLER, A. "Imperial portraits on coins of Ascalon", MHB 5, 1963, pp.46-47. Heb. ed. pp.43-44.

KINDLER, A. "A hoard of coins of Ascalon from the area of Hebron", ALON 2 (4), 1968, pp.67, 68, 71, 72, pl.5/79 (Hebrew).

KINDLER, A. "New types of Palestinian city-coins", ALON 3 (2), 1968, pp.47-49, pl.2/7 (Hebrew).

KINDLER, A. "A hoard of coins of Ascalon and Gaza", ALON 3 (2), 1968, p.55 (Hebrew).

KINDLER, A. "Coins of the land of Israel. Bank of Israel collection", Jerusalem 1971, p.134/203 (Hebrew).

KINDLER, A. "Numismatic documentation of Hadrian's visit to Gaza", MHB 17/18, 1975, pp.61-67, pl.12 (Hebrew).

KINDLER, A. "Akko, a city of many names", BASOR 231, 1978, p.51.

KINDLER, A. "The coinage of Bostra", Warminster, England 1983, pp.28, 42, 144.

KIRKBRIDE, A.S. "Currencies in Transjordan", PEQ 1939, p.156.

KLAWANS, Z.H. "An outline of ancient Greek coins", Wisconsin, USA 1959, p.93.

KLIMOWSKY, E.W. "The monetary function of city coins", International numismatic convention in Jerusalem (1963), proceedings (A. Kindler, ed.), Tel-Aviv 1967, pp.147, 150, 153, 160, 162, 164, 166, 168, 170, 172, 177.

KLIMOWSKY, E.W. "On ancient Palestinian and other coins, their symbolism and metrology", PINS 7, Tel-Aviv 1974, pp.87, 96, 97, pls.6/25; 7/39. Same in INJ 3, 1965/6, pp.15, 23, 24, pls.5/25; 6/39.

KUBITSCHEK, W. "Zur Geschichte von Städten des römischen Kaiserreiches. Epigraphisch-numismatische Studien", heft 1, Wien 1916, pp.29-33.

LAMBERT, C. "Coins in the Palestine Museum, II", QDAP 1, 1931/2, p.132, pl.54/9.

LIEBE, C.S. "Gotha numaria, sistens Thesauri Fridericiani..", Amsterdam 1730, pp.304-305.

MACDONALD, G. "Catalogue of Greek coins in the Hunterian collection", Glasgow 1905, vol. III, pp.282-284, pls.77/30-31; 78/2-3.

GAZA

MANNS, F. "Gemmes de l'époque Gréco-Romaine provenant de Palestine", LA 28, 1978, p.160, pl.28/29.

MATSSON, G.O. "The gods, goddesses and heroes on the ancient coins of Bible Lands", Stockholm 1969, pp.24, 42, 48, 53, 116, 117, 127, 137, 147, 191-192, 193, 199, 206, 207, 221, 223, 226, 230, 239; pls.1/15; 2/34b, 38a, b; 5/68b, 82; 6/96b, 98b-f.

MESHORER, Y. "Coins from the excavations at Khorazin", EI 11, 1973, p.158, pl.29/1 (Hebrew).

MESHORER, Y. "Three Gaza coins from the Persian period", IMN 12, 1977, p.78, fig. 2.

MESHORER, Y. "Was there a mint at Eboda?", SM 106, 1977, p.34.

MESHORER, Y. "Coins of the Ancient World", Jerusalem 1979, pp.57-58 (Hebrew).

MESHORER, Y. "The city coins of Eretz-Israel and the Decapolis in the Roman period", Jerusalem 1984, pp.29-30, 112 (Hebrew).

MILDENBERG, L. "Numismatische Evidenz zur Chronologie der Bar Kochba - Erhebung", SNR 34, 1948/9, pp.22-23, 24-25, pl.3/4-9.

MIONNET, T.E. "Description de médailles antiques, grecques et romaines", Paris 1806-1837, vol. V, pp.535-549, vol. VIII, suppl., pp.371-375.

PATIN, C. "Imperatorum Romanorum numismata ex aere mediae et minimae formae descripta et enarrata..", Amsterdam(?), 1671, pp.200, 246, 313.

PELLERIN, J. "Second supplément aux six volumes de recueils des médailles..", Paris 1766, p.54, pl.2/11.

PLANT, R. "Greek coin types and their identification", London 1979, nos. 28, 1238, 1627, 2058.

PRICE, M.J. and TRELL, B.L. "Coins and their cities", London 1977, p.284.

REICHARDT, H.C. "Unpublished Greek Imperial coins", NC, Ns 2, 1862, pp.120-122.

RIDER, G. le "Les ateliers monétaires de la côte Syrienne, Phénicienne, Palestinienne, Égyptienne et Cyrénéenne", Congresso Internazionale di numismatica (Roma 1961), vol. I, Relazioni, Roma 1961, p.96.

ROSENBERGER, M. "City-coins of Palestine", vol. II, Jerusalem 1975, pp.47-75, 79.

ROSENBERGER, M. "City-coins of Palestine", vol. III, Jerusalem 1977, pp.82-85.

ROSENBERGER, M. "The coinage of Eastern Palestine", Jerusalem 1978, pp.83, 84.

ROSENTHAL-HEGINBOTTOM, R. "The Mampsis hoard - A preliminary report", INJ 4, 1980, p.48.

SAULCY, F. de "Numismatique de la Terre Sainte", Paris 1874, pp.209-233, pl.11.

SEAR, D.R. "Greek imperial coins and their values", London 1982, nos. 120, 741, 1251, 1509, 1684, 1713, 1809, 1878, 2060, 2276, 2463, 2692-2693, 2729, 2904, 3030, 3127, 3182, 3258, 3786, 5217.

GAZA

SESTINI, D. "Descriptio numorum veterum..", Lipsiae 1796, p.546.

SESTINI, D. "Classes generales geographiae numismaticae sev monetae urbium, populorum et regum..", Lipsiae 1797, part I, p.71; part II, p.103.

SESTINI, D. "Classes generales sev moneta vetus urbium, populorum et regum..", Florentiae 1821, p.152.

SESTINI, D. "Descrizione d'alcune medaglie Greche del museo del Signore Carlo D'Ottavio Fontana", Firenze 1822, p.13.

SESTINI, D. "Descrizione delle medaglie antiche Greche del Museo Hedervariano", part 3, Firenze 1829, pp.114-116, pl.31/17-18.

SEYRIG, H. "Antiquités Syriennes, 11. Sur certains tétradrachmes provinciaux de Syrie", SYRIA 13, 1932, p.367.

SEYRIG, H. "Notes on Syrian coins", NNM 119, 1950, p.32.

SNG ANS part 6, "Palestine - South Arabia", 1981, pls.29-31, figs. 905-960.

SNG DNM "Palestine-Characene", 1961, pl.2/43-54.

SNG FM vol. IV, part 8, "Syria-Nabathaea", 1971, pl.136/6109-6111.

SPERBER, D. "Roman Palestine 200-400. Money and prices", Jerusalem 1974, p.143.

SPIJKERMAN, A. "Cafarnao III. Catalogo delle monete della città", Jerusalem 1975, p.14/12, pl.1/11.

SPIJKERMAN, A. and STARCKY, J. "Un nouveau lot de monnaies palestiniennes", RB 65, 1958, pp.569, 570, 582, pl.20/88.

STAHL, Z. "The Flavian Emperors and their coins in Eretz-Israel", special brochure of Israel Num. Society, Tel-Aviv branch, 1976, p.7 (Hebrew).

STAHL, Z. "Roman coins of Palestinian cities issued during the Jewish War, 66-70 C.E.", special brochure of Israel Num. Society, Tel-Aviv branch, 1979, pp.12, 23-24, 25 (Hebrew).

SUTHERLAND, C.H.V. "The pattern of monetary development in Phoenicia and Palestine during the Early Empire", International numismatic convention in Jerusalem (1963), proceedings (A. Kindler, ed.) Tel-Aviv 1967, pp.89, 90, 95, 96, 97.

TIEPOLO, L. and F. "Musei Theupoli antiqua numismata..", Venetiis 1736, series 6, pp.877, 890.

VAILLANT, J. "Numismata imperatorum, augustarum et caesarum a populis Romanae ditionis Graece loquentibus..", Paris 1698, pp.20, 33, 43, 54, 70, 76, 117, 138, 153, 234, 343-348, 387, 403.

WALCHER de MOLTHEIN, L. "Catalogue de la collection des medailles grecques de M. Le Chevalier", Paris - Vienne, 1895, pp.271-272, nos. 3200-3208.

WICZAY, C.M. "Musei Hedervarii numi antiqui..", Vindobonae 1814, part I, p.290, nos. 6228-6234.

Auction Catalogues and Price Lists

AGORA Tel-Aviv 1974 (1), p.25, nos. 155-159, pl.9.
1975 (2), no. 213, pl.9.

GAZA

BETTER	Haifa 1972 (1), nos. 175-189. Haifa 1972 (2), nos. 271A-281. Haifa 1973 (3), nos. 309-313. Haifa 1973 (4), nos. 200-208A. Jaffo 1974 (5), nos. 152-154. Jaffo 1974 (7), nos. 223-243. Haifa 1974 (8), nos. 132-136.
BUTTON, E.	(price list), Frankfurt 1938 (35), p.5, no. 3058.
CAHN, A.E.	Frankfurt 1930 (68), p.96, nos.1593-1594. 1931 (71), p.68, nos.1110-1116, pls.32-33, 22.
COIN GALLERIES	(mail bid sale), New York, 13 July 1954, nos. 1197-1198.
GANS, E.	"Numismatic Fine Arts", (Stock cat.), New York 1943 (2), pp.15 (no.7326), 17 (no.7321), 21 (no.7327) 25 (no.7309). 1943 (3), p.10, nos. 7309, 7321, 7326, 7327.
GANS, E.	"Numismatic Fine Arts", Berkeley CA, USA 1956 (20), p.15, no. 4969.
GLENDINING	London, 10 March 1965, p.21, no. 165, pl.6.
HAMBURGER, L.	Frankfurt 1932 (96), p.10, nos. 179-182, pl.6.
KRAUS, F.F.	(price list), Braunschweig, Germany 1928 (2), pp.47-48, nos. 1087-1088. 1929 (1-2), p.54, nos. 1247-1250.
MALTER, J.L.	"Journal of Numismatic Fine Arts", Encino CA, USA 1973 (2/2), p.37/B 75, pl.10.

MONNAIES ET MÉDAILLES, Basel
1954 (13), p.72, no. 937, pl.33.
1962 (25), pp.20-21, nos. 522-532, pls.8-9.
1966 (32), pp.41-43, nos. 359-380, pl.24.

MÜNZEN UND MEDAILLEN, Basel 1950 (96), p.2, no. 25.
1955 (152), p.12, nos. 235-236.
1958 (176), p.4, no. 57.
1968 (293), p.4, nos. 45-46.
1979 (417), p.23, no. 347.
1980 (424), p.17, nos. 226-229.
1981 (435), p.21, no. 235.
1983 (457), p.2, nos. 27, 30, 33.
1984 (468), p.14, nos. 184-187.
1984 (469), p.7, no. 66.

MÜNZZENTRUM KÖLN (auc.), 1979 (36), p.28, no. 186.
1981 (43), p.36, nos. 215-216.
1983 (48), p.32, no. 206.
1984 (53), p.79, nos. 2025-2027.

MYERS, R.J. New York 1973 (5), no. 271.

NUMISMATIC FINE ARTS, Beverly Hills, CA, USA, 1976 (3), no. 162.
1979 (6), no. 409.
1983 (12), nos. 106-109.

RAUCH, H.D. Wien 1985 (34), nos. 229-238.

SCHLESSINGER, F. (price list), Amsterdam 1938 (9), p.4, nos. 683-688.

SCHULMAN, H.M.F., New York, 14-15 Dec. 1970, p.18, nos. 964-965.
6-7 Apr. 1971, p.24, no. 444.

SEABY London 1949 (373), p.288, nos. A 1656-1657.
1962 (526), p.122, nos. A 169-171.
1963 (542), p.247, no. A 591.

SEABY (con't) 1969 (616), p.437, no. A 1145.
1971 (637), pp.336-337, nos. A 861-865.

SPINK AND SON London 1905 (13/154), nos. 19052-19061.
1925 (33/3-4), nos. 37849-37851.
1925 (33/11-12), nos. 45425, 45439-45440.
1930 (38/11), nos. 1787-1789, 1800, 1813.
1931 (39/1), no. 3409.
1931 (39/10), nos. 10801-10820.
1934 (42/10), nos. 36192-36197.
1934 (42/11), nos. 37009-37018.
1934 (42/12), nos. 37870-37871, 37883.
1936 (44/1), nos. 48082-48100.
1936 (44/2), nos. 48851-48860.
1939 (47/4), nos. 79444-79458.
1952 (60/4), p.214, nos. 3383-3386.
1977 (85/7-8), p.318, nos. 6653-6656.
1981 (89/6), p.205, no. 4530.

STERNBERG, F. Zürich, 25-26 Nov. 1976, pp.79-80, nos. 612-622, pls.25-26.

STERNBERG, F. Zürich 1982 (12), pp.71 (no.600), 73 (no.613), pl.24.

SUPERIOR STAMP AND COIN CO., Los-Angeles, June 1976, pp.26-27, nos. 287-297.

TAMAR Tel-Aviv 1975 (9), p.7, nos. 142-146.
Tel-Aviv 1975 (10), p.9, nos. 142-148.
Ramat-Gan, Israel 1976 (11), p.10, nos. 125-129.
Ramat-Gan, Israel 1976 (12), p.52, nos. 872-875.

GERASA

BELLINGER, A.R. "Coins from Jerash 1928-1934", NNM 81, 1938, pp.9, 29-31, nos. 40-47, pls.2-3.

BELLINGER, A.R. "The excavations at Dura-Europos. Final report VI. The coins", New Haven, USA 1949, p.87/1855.

ECKHEL, J. "Numi veteres anecdoti ex museis Caesareo Vindobonensi..", Viennae 1775, p.277.

ECKHEL, J. "Doctrina numorum veterum..", vol. III, Vienna 1794, p.350.

HARDING, L. "Recent work on the Jerash Forum. The coins", PEQ 1949, p.18.

HEAD, B.V. "Historia numorum", Oxford 1911, p.787.

HILL, G.F. BMC, Arabia, Mesopotamia and Persia, 1922, pp.xxxiii-xxxv, pp.31-32, pl.5/4-6.

HILL, G.F. "Greek coins acquired by the British Museum in 1922", NC, 5th ser. 3, 1923, pp.238-239.

IMHOOF-BLUMER, F. "Fluss- und Meergötter auf griechischen und römischen Münzen", SNR 23, 1923, p.370, pl.15/16-17.

IMHOOF-BLUMER, F. "Zur griechischen Münzkunde", SNR 8, 1898, pp.47-48.

KADMAN, L. and KINDLER, A. "Coins in Palestine throughout the ages", Tel-Aviv 1963, p.40, pl.18/4 (Hebrew).

KINDLER, A. "Akko, a city of many names", BASOR 231, 1978, p.52.

GERASA

KINDLER, A. "The coinage of Bostra", Warminster, England 1983, pp.28, 36, 37, 38, 39, 53, 77, 144.

KIRKBRIDE, A.S. "Currencies in Transjordan", PEQ 1939, p.155.

KIRKBRIDE, A.S. "Some rare coins from Transjordan", BASOR 106, 1947, p.5, fig. 2.

KLIMOWSKY, E.W. "The monetary function of city coins", International numismatic convention in Jerusalem (1963), proceedings (A.Kindler, ed.), Tel-Aviv 1967 pp.162, 164, 170, 172.

MANNS, F. "Gemmes de l'époque Gréco-Romaine provenant de Palestine", LA 28, 1978, pp.155-156, pl.25/7, 8.

MATSSON, G.O. "The gods, goddesses and heroes on the ancient coins of Bible Lands", Stockholm 1969, pp.25, 47, 184, 199-200, 210, 241-242, pl.1/16a, b.

McCOWN, C.C. "The goddesses of Gerasa", AASOR 13, 1931/2, pp.131-134, 136, 137, 138, 164.

MESHORER, Y. "The city coins of Eretz-Israel and the Decapolis in the Roman period", Jerusalem 1984, pp.94, 121 (Hebrew).

MIONNET, T.E. "Description de médailles antiques, grecques et romaines", Paris 1806-1837, vol. V, p.329, vol. VIII, suppl., pp.230-231.

NEGEV, A. "Seal impressions from Tomb 107 at Kurnub (Mampsis)", IEJ 19 (2), 1969, p.95.

RIDER, G. le "Les ateliers monétaires de la côte Syrienne, Phénicienne, Palestinienne, Égyptienne et Cyrénéenne", Congresso Internazionale di numismatica (Roma 1961), vol. I, Relazioni, Roma 1961, pp.87, 96.

ROSENBERGER, M. "The coinage of Eastern Palestine", Jerusalem 1978, pp.50-56.

SAULCY, F. de "Numismatique de la Terre Sainte", Paris 1874, pp.384-385, pl.22/1-2.

SCOTT, W.H. "Unpublished varieties of Greek, colonial, imperial and Roman coins", NC 14, 1852, p.122.

SEAR, D.R. "Greek imperial coins and their values", London 1982, nos. 1253, 1687, 1804, 1879, 1914, 2064, 2099, 2279, 2696, 3135, 5219.

SESTINI, D. "Classes generales geographiae numismaticae sev monetae urbium, populorum et regum..", Lipsiae 1797, part I, p.68, part II, p.100.

SESTINI, D. "Lettere e dissertazioni numismatiche..", vol. V, Firenze 1818, pp.108-110.

SESTINI, D. "Lettere e dissertazioni numismatiche..", vol. VI, Firenze 1819, p.102, pl.2/10.

SESTINI, D. "Classes generales sev moneta vetus urbium, populorum et regum..", Florentiae 1821, p.144.

SESTINI, D. "Descrizione delle medaglie antiche Greche del Museo Hedervariano", part 3, Firenze 1829, p.75.

SEYRIG, H. "Notes on Syrian coins", NNM 119, 1950, p.32.

SEYRIG, H. "Antiquités Syriennes, 87. Alexandre le Grand, fondateur de Gerasa", SYRIA 42, 1965, pp.25-28.

SNG ANS part 6, "Palestine - South Arabia", 1981, pl.46/1342-1350.

GERASA

SNG FM vol. IV, part 8, "Syria-Nabathaea", 1971, pl.132/5985.

SPIJKERMAN, A. "An unknown coin-type of Pella Decapoleos", LA 20, 1970, p.355.

SPIJKERMAN, A. "A list of the coins of Gerasa Dacapoleos", LA 25, 1975, pp.73-84, pls.41-44.

SPIJKERMAN, A. "The coins of the Decapolis and provincia Arabia", Jerusalem 1978, pp.156-167, 290, pls.33-35.

SPIJKERMAN, A. and STARCKY, J. "Un noveau lot de monnaies palestiniennes", RB 65, 1958, p.583, pl.20/89.

VAILLANT, J. "Numismata imperatorum, augustarum et caesarum a populis Romanae ditionis Graece loquentibus..", Paris 1698, pp.33, 87, 234, 389.

VLIET, N. van der "Monnaies inédites ou très rares du médaillier de Sainte-Anne de Jérusalem", RB 57, 1950, pp.250-252, pl.5/9, 10.

WROTH, W. BMC, Galatia, Cappadocia and Syria, 1899, pp.lxxxviii-lxxxix.

WROTH, W. "Greek coins acquired by British Museum in 1900", NC, 3rd ser. 20, 1900, p.295.

ZURI, N. "A hoard of bronze and silver coins from Ain Hanaziv", INB 1962 (3-4), p.105. Heb. ed. p.88.

Auction Catalogues and Price Lists

AGORA Tel-Aviv 1974 (1), p.26, no. 166, pl.9.
1975 (2), no. 230, pl.10.

BETTER Haifa 1972 (1), nos. 274-275.
Haifa 1972 (2), nos. 369-370.
Haifa 1973 (4), no. 269.
Jaffo 1974 (7), no. 278.
Jaffo 1974 (8), no. 183.

GLENDINING London, 19 July 1950, p.45, no. 332.
10 March 1965, p.22 (no.175) 26 (no.219), pl.8.

HOLZER, H. "The Thomas Ollive Mabbott collection", part I, New York 1969, pp.103-104, nos. 2660-2665.

MALTER, J.L. "Journal of Numismatic Fine Arts", Encino CA, USA
1973 (2/2), p.37/B 76, pl.10.
1977 (6/1), p.13/S 48.

MONNAIES ET MÉDAILLES, Basel 1966 (32), p.51, nos. 507-510, pl.30.

MÜNZEN UND MEDAILLEN, Basel 1969 (305), p.3, nos. 44-45.
1980 (424), pp.4 (no.62) 17 (nos.210-211).
1981 (436), p.14, no. 148.
1984 (464), p.15, no. 190.
1984 (468), p.14, no. 174.

SCHULMAN, H.M.F., New York, 6-7 April 1971, p.24, no. 445.

SEABY London 1961 (523), p.476, no. A 1169.
1969 (616), p.438, no. A 1152.

SPINK AND SON London 1932 (40/1), nos. 12409-12410.

STERNBERG, F. Zürich, 25-26 Nov. 1976, p.80, nos. 623-624, pl.26.

SUPERIOR STAMP AND COIN CO., Los-Angeles, June 1976, p.27, nos.298-299.

TAMAR Tel-Aviv 1975 (9), p.8, nos. 176-177.
Ramat-Gan, Israel 1976 (12), p.53, nos. 885-888.

HIPPOS

ANONYMOUS CH 1, 1975, p.34/123.

BARAG, D. "Tyrian currency in Galilee", INJ 6-7, 1982/3, p.10.

BARAMKI, D.C. "The coins exhibited in the Archaeological Museum of the American University of Beirut", Beirut 1968, pp.75-76, nos. 255-257, pl.7.

BELLINGER, A.R. "The Syrian tetradrachms of Caracalla and Macrinus", ANS NS 3, 1940, p.13.

CARRADICE, I. "Coinage in Judaea in the Flavian period, AD 70-96", INJ 6-7, 1982/3, p.17.

ECKHEL, J. "Catalogus Musei Caesarei Vindobonensis numorum veterum..", Vindobonae 1779, part I, p.236.

ECKHEL, J. "Doctrina numorum veterum..", vol. III, Vienna 1794, pp.346-347.

HARDUIN, J. "Nummi antiqui populorum et urbium illustrati", Parisiis 1684.

HEAD, B.V. "Historia numorum", Oxford 1911, p.786.

HENDIN, D. "Coins of ancient Israel", SHEKEL 11 (6), 1978, pp.28, 30.

IMHOOF-BLUMER, F. "Griechische Münzen aus dem Museum in Klagenfurt und anderen Sammlungen", NZ 16, 1884, p.293.

KADMAN, L. and KINDLER, A. "Coins in Palestine throughout the ages", Tel-Aviv 1963, p.40, pl.18/5 (Hebrew).

KINDLER, A. "Thesaurus of Judaean coins from the fourth century B.C. to the third century A.D.", Jerusalem 1958, no. 42 (Hebrew).

KINDLER, A. "Akko, a city of many names", BASOR 231, 1978, p.52.

KINDLER, A. "The status of cities in the Syro-Palestinian area as reflected by their coins", INJ 6-7, 1982/3, pp.80, 82.

KINDLER, A. "The coinage of Bostra", Warminster, England 1983, pp.37, 144.

KLIMOWSKY, E.W. "The monetary functions of city coins", International numismatic convention in Jerusalem (1963), proceedings (A. Kindler, ed.), Tel-Aviv 1967, pp.162-164, 166, 170, 172.

MATSSON, G.O. "The gods, goddesses and heroes on the ancient coins of Bible Lands", Stockholm 1969, pp.184, 231, 242, pls. 6/49b; 8/115a, b.

MESHORER, Y. "Coins from the excavations at Khorazin", EI 11, 1973, p.158, pl.29/5 (Hebrew).

MESHORER, Y. "A hoard of coins from Migdal", ATIQOT, Es 11, 1976, pp.55, 56, 68-69, pls.14/132-138; 15/139.

MESHORER, Y. "The city coins of Eretz-Israel and the Decapolis in the Roman period", Jerusalem 1984, pp.72-75, 118-119 (Hebrew).

MIONNET, T.E. "Description de médailles antiques, grecques et romaines", Paris 1806-1837, vol. V, pp.319-320; vol. VIII, suppl., p.224.

PELLERIN, J. "Mélange de diverses médailles...", t.II, Paris 1765, p.124, pl.28/1.

HIPPOS

PLANT, R. "Greek coin types and their identification", London 1979, no. 1163.

PRICE, M.J. and TRELL, B.L. "Coins and their cities", London 1977, p.282.

REICHARDT, H.C. "Unpublished Greek Imperial coins", NC, Ns 2, 1862, p.104.

RIDER, G. le "Les ateliers monétaires de la côte Syrienne, Phénicienne, Palestinienne, Égyptienne et Cyrénéenne", Congresso Internazionale di numismatica (Roma 1961), vol. I, Relazioni, Roma 1961, pp.87, 96.

ROSENBERGER, M. "City-coins of Palestine", vol. III, Jerusalem 1977, pp.1-4.

SAULCY, F. de "Numismatique de la Terre Sainte", Paris 1874, pp.344-347, pl.19/10-15.

SEAR, D.R. "Greek imperial coins and their values", London 1982, nos. 623, 779, 876, 1674, 2048, 3108.

SESTINI, D. "Descriptio numorum veterum..", Lipsiae 1796, p.531, pl.12/4.

SESTINI, D. "Classes generales geographiae numismaticae sev monetae urbium, populorum et regum..", Lipsiae 1797, part I, p.67.

SESTINI, D. "Classes generales sev moneta vetus urbium, populorum et regum..", Florentiae 1821, p.143.

SEYRIG, H. "Antiquités Syriennes, 73. Temples, cultes et souvenirs historiques de la Decapole", SYRIA 36, 1959, pp.70-71, 77-78, pl.13/18-21.

SNG FM vol. IV, part 8, "Syria-Nabathaea", 1971, pl.132/5978-5979.

SPIJKERMAN, A. "An unknown coin-type of Pella Decapoleos", LA 20, 1970, p.355.

SPIJKERMAN, A. "The coins of the Decapolis and provincia Arabia", Jerusalem 1978, pp.168-179, 291, pls.36-38.

SPIJKERMAN, A. and STARCKY, J. "Un noveau lot de monnaies palestiniennes", RB 65, 1958, p.583, no. 91.

VAILLANT, J. "Numismata imperatorum, augustarum et caesarum a populis Romanae ditionis Graece loquentibus..", Paris 1698, pp.53, 69, 75, 231, 260, 326-327.

WROTH, W. BMC, Galatia, Cappadocia and Syria, 1899, pp.lxxxiii-lxxxiv, p.301, pl.38/1.

Auction Catalogues and Price Lists

AGORA Tel-Aviv 1974 (1), p.25, no. 160, pl.9.
1975 (2), nos. 216-217, pl.9.

BETTER Haifa 1972 (1), no. 233.
Haifa 1973 (3), nos. 354-355.
Haifa 1973 (4), no. 281.
Haifa 1974 (8), nos. 161-167.

CAHN, A.E. Frankfurt 1931 (71), p.64, no. 1057.

GANS, E. "Numismatic Fine Arts", Berkeley, CA, USA 1956 (20), p.16, no. 4986.

GLENDINING London, 30-31 Oct. 1963, p.32, no. 395.

HIPPOS

HESS-LEU Luzern 1965 (28), p.41, no. 298, pl.13.

HOLZER, H. "The Thomas Ollive Mabbott collection", part I, New York 1969, p.103, nos. 2648-2659.

MALTER, J.L. "Journal of Numismatic Fine Arts", Encino, CA, USA 1973 (2/2), p.37/B 77, pl.11.

MONNAIES ET MÉDAILLES, Basel 1966 (32), p.47, no. 457, pl.28.

MÜNZEN UND MEDAILLEN, Basel 1969 (305), p.3, no. 38.

SALTON-SCHLESSINGER, M.M. (price list), New York 1958 (27), p.7, no. 134.

SCHLESSINGER, F. (price list), Amsterdam 1938 (9), p.2, no. 615.

SCHULMAN, H.M.F., New York, 14-15 Dec. 1970, p.18, no. 966.
6-7 Apr. 1971, p.24, no. 447.

SPINK AND SON London 1930 (38/9), no. 114.
1931 (39/8), no. 9258.
1934 (42/7), no. 34224.
1934 (42/12), no. 37855.

STERNBERG, F. Zürich, 25-26 Nov. 1976, p.82, nos. 635-637, pl.26.

SUPERIOR STAMP AND COIN CO., Los-Angeles, June 1976, p.27, nos. 300-301.

TAMAR Tel-Aviv 1975 (9), p.8, no. 185.
Ramat-Gan, Israel 1976 (11), p.12, nos. 152-154.

JOPPE

ANONYMOUS CH 1, 1975, p.34/124.

ANONYMOUS "City-coins of ancient Israel", JIN 1 (4), 1966, p.116.

BELLINGER, A.R. "The Syrian tetradrachms of Caracalla and Macrinus", ANS NS 3, 1940, p.13.

ECKHEL, J. "Doctrina numorum veterum..", vol. III, Vienna 1794, p.433.

FRANCESCO DE DOMINICIS, "Repertorio numismatico", Napoli 1827, t.II, p.299.

HAMBURGER, L. "The beiden palästinensischen Münzstätten Nikopolis-Emmaus", (Sonder-Abdruck aus den Frankfurter Münzblättern 1, 1899, nos. 8-9), p.9, pl.7/14.

HEAD, B.V. "Historia numorum", Oxford 1911, p.803.

HENDIN, D. "Guide to ancient Jewish coins", New York 1976, p.111.

HILL, G.F. BMC, Palestine, 1914, pp.xxiv-xxv, p.44, pl.5/7.

JONAS, R. "Mythology on Palestinian coins", internal circular no. 2, Israel Num. Society, Haifa branch, 1959, p.3.

KADMAN, L. and KINDLER, A. "Coins in Palestine throughout the ages", Tel-Aviv 1963, p.32, pls.15/1-2; 18/12-13 (Hebrew).

KINDLER, A. "Thesaurus of Judaean coins from the fourth century B.C. to the third century A.D.", Jerusalem 1958, no. 27 (Hebrew).

KINDLER, A. "New coin-types of the city of Jaffa", ALON 2 (4), 1968, pp.78-79, pl.4/3-4.

JOPPE

KINDLER, A. "The status of cities in the Syro-Palestinian area as reflected by their coins", INJ 6-7, 1982/3, p.84.

KINDLER, A. "Coinage of Joppe", MHY 20-21, 1985/6, pp.21-30 (Hebrew).

KLIMOWSKY, E.W. The monetary function of city coins", International numismatic convention in Jerusalem (1963), proceedings (A. Kindler, ed.), Tel-Aviv 1967, pp.166, 172.

LEDERER, P. "Neue Beiträge zur antiken Münzkunde aus schweizerischen öffentlichen und privaten Sammlungen", SNR 30, 1943, p.82, pl.6/97.

MATSSON, G.O. "The gods, goddesses and heroes on the ancient coins of Bible Lands", Stockholm 1969, pp.142, 196, 227, pl.1/5.

MESHORER, Y. "Coins of the Ancient World", Minneapolis 1975, p.77. Hebrew version (Jerusalem 1979), p.56. Same in "Münzen, Zeugen der Vergangenheit", Zürich - Köln, 1979, p.77.

MESHORER, Y. "The city coins of Eretz-Israel and the Decapolis in the Roman period", Jerusalem 1984, pp.24, 111 (Hebrew).

MIONNET, T.E. "Description de médailles antiques, grecques et romaines", Paris 1806-1837, vol. V, p.499.

REICHARDT, H.C. "Unpublished Greek Imperial coins", NC, Ns 2, 1862, p.111.

ROSENBERGER, M. "City-coins of Palestine", vol. II, Jerusalem 1975, pp.76-78.

SAULCY, F. de "Numismatique de la Terre Sainte", Paris 1874, pp.176-177, pl.9/3-4, pp.331-332, pl.17/8 (Dabora).

SCHUMAN, E. "Tel-Aviv's older sister", SHEKEL 11 (3), 1978, pp.34-35.

SEAR, D.R. "Greek imperial coins and their values", London 1982, no.3121.

SESTINI, D. "Classes generales geographiae numismaticae sev monetae urbium, populorum et regum", Lipsiae 1797, part I, p.70.

SESTINI, D. "Classes generales sev moneta vetus urbium, populorum et regum..", Florentiae 1821, p.150.

SUTHERLAND, C.H.V. "The pattern of monetary development in Phoenicia and Palestine during the Early Empire", International numismatic convention in Jerusalem (1963), proceedings (A. Kindler, ed.), Tel-Aviv 1967, p.96.

TOLKOWSKY, S. "The gateway of Palestine. A history of Jaffa", London 1924, pp.58, 71. Heb. version, Tel-Aviv 1926, pp.36-38, 46-47, 56-57.

WALCHER de MOLTHEIN, L. "Catalogue de la collection des médailles grecques de M. Le Chevalier", Paris - Vienne 1895, p.269, no. 3168.

Auction Catalogues and Price Lists

HOLZER, H. "The Thomas Ollive Mabbott collection", part I, New York 1969, p.104, no. 2681.

MONNAIES ET MÉDAILLES, Basel 1954 (13), p.72, no. 932, pl.33.

MEDABA

BEN-DAVID, A. "'Dinarei Arba' and the silver coins called 'Harubim'", ALON 5 (2), 1974, p.28 (Hebrew).

DECLOEDT, A. "Une nouvelle monnaie de Médaba en Moabitide (Arabie)", RN, 4th ser. 14, 1910, pp.532-533.

HEAD, B.V. "Historia numorum", Oxford 1911, p.812.

HILL, G.F. "Some Palestinian cults in the Graeco-Roman age", Proceedings of the British Academy, vol. V, London 1912, p.413.

HILL, G.F. BMC, Arabia, Mesopotamia and Persia, 1922, pp.xxxv-xxxvi, p.33, pl.5/7-9.

KINDLER, A. "The coinage of Bostra", Warminster, England 1983, pp.16, 37, 38, 53, 54, 58, 78, 81, 82, 83, 86-87, 142, 144.

MESHORER, Y. "The city coins of Eretz-Israel and the Decapolis in the Roman period", Jerusalem 1984, pp.100, 122 (Hebrew).

MESHORER, Y. and SPAER, A. "Some additional apparently unpublished city coins", INJ 3, 1965/6, pp.75-76, pl.15/1.

PATRICH, J. "Prohibition of a graven-image among the Nabateans - the testimony of the Massebot-cult", CATHEDRA 26, 1982, pp.62, 65, 66, fig. 14 (Hebrew).

REED, W.L. "The excavations at Dibon (Dhibān) in Moab. The second campaign, 1952. The coins", AASOR 36-37, 1964, p.61.

ROSENBERGER, M. "The coinage of Eastern Palestine", Jerusalem 1978, pp.56-58.

SEAR, D.R. "Greek imperial coins and their values", London 1982, nos. 2280, 2697, 3136.

SEYRIG, H. "Antiquités Syriennes, 21. Sur quelques sculptures palmyréniennes", SYRIA 18, 1937, p.45, fig. 27.

SNG ANS part 6, "Palestine - South Arabia", 1981, pl.46/1351-1352.

SPIJKERMAN, A. "The coins of the Decapolis and provincia Arabia", Jerusalem 1978, pp.180-185, 292, pls.39-40.

VLIET, N. van der "Monnaies inédites ou très rares du médaillier de Sainte-Anne de Jérusalem", RB 57, 1950, pp.126-127, pl.3/27.

Auction Catalogues and Price Lists

AGORA Tel-Aviv 1975 (2), no. 234, pl.10.

MONNAIES ET MÉDAILLES, Basel 1966 (32), p.51, no. 511, pl.30.

RAUCH, H.D. Wien 1985 (34), no. 239.

STERNBERG, F. Zürich, 25-26 Nov. 1976, p.84, no. 646, pl.27.

SUPERIOR STAMP AND COIN CO., Los-Angeles, June 1976, p.27, nos. 302-304.

NEAPOLIS

AKERMAN, J.Y. "Numismatic illustrations of the New Testament", Chicago 1966 (rp), pp.29-30.

ANONYMOUS "Ancient rarity described", JIN 1 (5), 1966, pp.152-153.

ANONYMOUS SHEKEL 7 (1), 1974, p.7.

ARIEL, D.T. "A survey of coin finds in Jerusalem", LA 32, 1982, pp.295, 318.

BANKS, F.A. "Coins of Bible days", New York 1955, p.140.

BARAG, D. "The countermarks of the Legio Decima Fretensis", International numismatic convention in Jerusalem (1963), proceedings (A. Kindler, ed.), Tel-Aviv 1967, pp.117, 118.

BARAG, D. "Tyrian currency in Galilee", INJ 6-7, 1982/3, p.11.

BARAMKI, D.C. "Note on a cemetery at Karm al-Shaikh, Jerusalem. Summary of coins found", QDAP 1, 1931/2, p.7.

BARAMKI, D.C. "The coins exhibited in the Archaeological Museum of the American University of Beirut", Beirut 1968, pp.92-93, nos. 310-311, pl.8.

BARAMKI, D.C. "The coin collection of the American University of Beirut Museum. Palestine and Phoenicia", Beirut 1974, pp.19-29, pls.3/7-12; 4; 5; 6/1.

BARAMKI, J. "Coins in the Palestine Archaeological Museum, III", QDAP 8, 1939, p.79, pl.41/14.

BELLINGER, A.R. "Coins from Jerash 1928-1934", NNM 81, 1938, pp.9, 26, nos. 25-28, pl.1.

BELLINGER, A.R. "The Syrian tetradrachms of Caracalla and Macrinus", ANS NS 3, 1940, pp.7, 11, 13, 15, 17, 18, 19, 93-94, pl.23/9-16.

BELLINGER, A.R. "The excavations at Dura-Europos. Final report VI. The coins", New Haven, USA 1949, pp.16/281-282; 89/1894, pl.8; pp.183, 193, 203.

BEN-DOR, S. "Two coins of Shechem (Neapolis)", BIES 12, 1945/6, pp.160-162, pl.7/2.

BEN-DOR, S. "Quelques rémarques à propos d'une monnaie de Néapolis", RB 59, 1952, pp.251-252, pl.9/1.

BENTINCK, de "Catalogue d'une collection de médailles antiques", Amsterdam 1787, part II, p.1073.

BERNHART, M. "Dionysos und seine Familie auf griechischen Münzen", JNG 1, 1949, p.167, nos. 1448-1454, pl.10/35, 41.

BULL, R.J. and CAMPBELL, E.F. jr. "The sixth campaign at Balatah (Shechem)", BASOR 190, 1968, pp.4, 5, 15-16, 20, 21.

CARNIG, P. "Mount Gerizim", SAN 2 (3-4), 1971, pp.44-45.

CARRADICE, I. "Coinage in Judaea in the Flavian period, AD 70-96", INJ 6-7, 1982/3, p.17, pl.2/10.

CARSON, R.A.G. "The inflation of the third century and its monetary influence in the Near East" International numismatic convention in Jerusalem (1963), proceedings (A. Kindler, ed.), Tel-Aviv 1967, pp.240, 242.

NEAPOLIS

CHAIX, E. "Recherche des monnaies coloniales Romaines non décrites dans l'ouvrage de H. Cohen", ASFN 16, 1892, pp.232/16; 233/5; 233-234/4-9; ASFN 17, 1893, pp.25/3-4; 27/5.

CHÉHAB, M. "Monnaies Gréco-Romaines et Phéniciennes du Musée National, Beyrouth, Liban", Paris 1977, p.77.

COHEN, H. "Médailles Imperiales", Leipzig 1930 (rp), vol. V, pp.131-132/359-371; 142-143/13-17; 157/117-121; 261-262/205.

DONALDSON, T.L. "Architectura Numismatica", London 1859, pp.116-121.

ECKHEL, J. "Doctrina numorum veterum..", vol. III, Vienna 1794, pp.433-438.

ECKHEL, J. "Numi veteres anecdoti ex museis Caesareo Vindobonensi, Florentino Magni Ducis Etruriae..", Viennae 1775, pp.282-288, pl.15/13.

ECKHEL, J. "Catalogus Musei Caesarei Vindobonensis numorum veterum..", Vindobonae 1779, part I, p.247.

FLESCH, M. "Group of city coins", in 'Collector's choice', Bezalel National Museum, Jerusalem 1964, p.15/77.

FORRER, L. "Weber collection, vol. III, part 2: Greek coins", London 1929, p.796/8107-8108, pl.299.

FROELICH, E. "Quatuor tentamina in re numaria vetere", 2nd ed., Viennae 1737, pp.346-347.

GESSNER, J.J. "Numismata antiqua Imperatorum Romanorum latina et graeca..", Tiguri (Zürich), 18th cent., pls.62/34; 70/20; 82/26; 97/24; 112/31, 32, 49; 115/68, 69;

GESSNER, J.J. (con't) 146/14, 15; 154/27; 155/41; 156/16; 180/33-35; 181/31, 32; 182/38; 183/26.

GILMORE, P.M. "The formulae of Antioch and Tyre", NCirc 86 (2), 1978, p.76.

GILMORE, P.M. "Syrian officinae under Caracalla and Macrinus", NCirc 87 (6), 1979, pp.287, 289.

GILMORE, P.M. "Caracalla's silver mints in Syria", NCirc 88 (3), 1980, pp.88, 90.

GROSE, S.W. "Catalogue of the McClean collection of Greek coins in the Fitzwilliam Museum", vol. III, Cambridge 1929, p.380/9541-9542, pl.354/4-5.

HAMBURGER, A. "Gems from Caesarea Maritima", ATIQOT, Es 8, 1968, pp.6/14; 12/85-90.

HAMBURGER, H. "A hoard of Syrian tetradrachms and Tyrian bronze coins from Gush Halav", IEJ 4 (3-4), 1954, pp.203, 207. Same in 'Recent studies and discoveries on ancient Jewish and Syrian coins", PINS 1, Jerusalem 1954, pp.67, 71.

HARDING, L. "Recent work on the Jerash Forum", PEQ 1949, p.18.

HARDUIN, J. "Nummi antiqui populorum et urbium illustrati", Parisiis 1684, pp.340-343.

HARL, K.W. "The coinage of Neapolis in Samaria, A.D.244-53", ANS MN 29, 1984, pp.61-97, pls.6-15.

HEAD, B.V. "Historia numorum", Oxford 1911, p.803.

HENDIN, D. "Guide to ancient Jewish coins", New York 1976, pp.108-109, pls.8/254; 9/256-257.

NEAPOLIS

HEYMANN, H. "Roman legionary coins from Phoenicia", INJ 1963 (3), pp.47, 48, 49, 51 (note 7).

HILL, G.F "Some Palestinian cults in the Graeco-Roman age", Proceedings of the British Academy, vol. V, London 1912, pp.413, 414, 415-418, pl./7-8.

HILL, G.F. BMC, Palestine, 1914, pp.xxv-xxxix, pp.45-74, pls.5/8-16; 6-7.

IMHOOF-BLUMER, F. "Zur syrischen Münzkunde", NZ 33, 1901, p.14.

IMHOOF-BLUMER, F. "Zur griechischen und römischen Münzkunde, II", SNR 14, 1908, p.129.

JANIS, E. "The other coin cities of Israel", SHEKEL 3 (3), 1970, p.14.

JONAS, R. "Mythology on Palestinian coins", internal circular no. 2, Israel Num. Society, Haifa branch, 1959, pp.4-5, 6.

KADMAN, L. "Numismatic evidence of the architectonic revolution in the Second Century C.E.", INB 1962 (3-4), p.72. Heb. ed. p.65.

KADMAN, L. and KINDLER, A. "Coins in Palestine throughout the ages", Tel-Aviv 1963, pp.37-38, pl.16/16-22 (Hebrew).

KANITZ, L.E. "The story of a coin", SAN 2 (3-4), 1971, pp.42-43, 62.

KINDLER, A. "Thesaurus of Judaean coins from the fourth century B.C. to the third century A.D., Jerusalem 1958, no. 32 (Hebrew).

KINDLER, A. "The coin issues of the Roman administration in the provincia Judaea during the reign of Domitian", ALON 3 (4), 1969, p.92, pl.6/20 (Hebrew).

KINDLER, A. "Coins of the land of Israel, Bank of Israel collection", Jerusalem 1971, p.132/201 (Hebrew).

KINDLER, A. "The coins of the city of Neapolis", in 'Shomron, collected articles and sources', published by the section of geography in the Kibbutz movement, Tel-Aviv, 1971, pp.33-39 (Hebrew).

KINDLER, A. "The 'Damnatio memoriae' of Elagabal on city-coins of the Near East", SM 117, 1980, pp.3, 5, 6, figs, 1, 4, 13, 14.

KINDLER, A. "Was there a detachment of the Third Legion Cyrenaica at Neapolis in A.D. 151-153?" INJ 4, 1980, pp.56-58, pl.16/5-6.

KINDLER, A. "The status of cities in the Syro-Palestinian area as reflected by their coins", INJ 6-7, 1982/3, pp.80, 81, 84, 85 (note 48).

KINDLER, A. "The coinage of Bostra", Warminster, England 1983, pp.28, 30, 31, 32, 33, 34, 37, 40, 51, 58, 61, 63, 64, 66, 79, 92, 153.

KIRKBRIDE, A.S. "Currencies in Transjordan", PEQ 1939, p.156.

KLAWANS, Z.H. "An outline of ancient Greek coins", Wisconsin, USA 1959, p.118.

KLIMOWSKY, E.W. "The monetary function of city coins", International numismatic convention in Jerusalem (1963), proceedings (A. Kindler, ed.), Tel-Aviv 1967, pp.132, 143, 153, 154, 164, 168, 172, 177.

NEAPOLIS

KLIMOWSKY, E.W. "Roman imperial 'Virtutes' on contemporaneous city coins", INJ 3, 1965/6, pp.18, 21, 22, 25, pls.4/9; 5/13, 15, 17, 22, 26; 6/45, 49. Same in 'On ancient Palestinian and other coins, their symbolism and metrology", PINS 7, Tel-Aviv, 1974, pp.92, 94, 95, 98, pls.5/9, 13, 15, 17; 6/22, 26; 7/45, 49.

KLIMOWSKY, E.W. "The origin and meaning of Marsyas in the Greek Imperial coinage", INJ 6-7, 1982/3, pp.89, 95, 96, 98, 101, pl.17.

KRAFT, T.K. "Das System der kaiserzeitlichen Münzprägung in Kleinasien", Berlin 1972, pp.98, 101, pl.117/10.

KUBITSCHEK, W. "Zur Geschichte von Städten des römischen Kaiserreiches. Epigraphisch-numismatische Studien", heft 1, Wien 1916, pp.3-15.

MACDONALD, G. "Catalogue of Greek coins in the Hunterian collection", Glasgow 1905, vol. III, pp.277-280, pl.77/24-27.

MANNS, F. "Gemmes de l'époque Gréco-Romaine provenant de Palestine", LA 28, 1978, p.154, 169, pls.25/3-4; 33/76.

MATSSON, G.O. "The gods, goddesses and heroes on the ancient coins of Bible Lands", Stockholm 1969, pp.24, 73, 128, 129, 178, 193, 196, 199, 200, 215, 223, 238, 246, pls.1/6, 13, 19a, b; 5/76; 6/109a; 8/125.

MESHORER, Y. "Coins of the Ancient World", Minneapolis 1975, pp.66-68. Hebrew version (Jerusalem 1979), pp.54-55. Same in "Münzen, Zeugen der Vergangenheit", Zürich - Köln, 1979, pp.66-68.

MESHORER, Y. "Jewish symbols on Roman coins struck in Eretz Israel", IMN 14, 1978, pp.62, 63, nos. 11-16.

MESHORER, Y. "The city coins of Eretz-Israel and the Decapolis in the Roman period", Jerusalem 1984, pp.46-52, 115-116 (Hebrew).

MEYSHAN, J. "Asclepios on the coins of Neapolis", ALON 5 (1), 1973, pp.8-9 (Hebrew).

MIONNET, T.E. "Description de médailles antiques, grecques et romaines", Paris 1806-1837, vol. V, pp.499-511, vol. VIII, suppl., pp.344-355, pl.18/2.

NARKISS, M. "From the numismatic collection", OMANUTH, Quarterly of the Bezalel Museum, Jerusalem, vol. I (3), 1940, pp.56-57.

PATIN, C. "Imperatorum Romanorum numismata ex aere mediae et minimae formae descripta et enarrata..", Amsterdam(?), 1671, pp.151, 241, 253, 323, 327, 400.

PELLERIN, J. "Mélange de diverses médailles..", t.I, part 3, Paris 1764, p.324, pl.21/2-3.

PLANT, R. "Greek coin types and their identification", London 1979, nos. 458, 1881, 2000.

PRICE, M. "Coins and the Bible", London 1975, pp.7-8, fig. 5.

PRICE, M.J. and TRELL, B.L. "Coins and their cities", London 1977, pp.39, 165, 172-175, 283, figs. 55, 292, 302, 303, 422.

REICHARDT, H.C. "Unpublished Greek Imperial coins", NC, Ns 2, 1862, pp.111-112.

NEAPOLIS

REINACH, T. "Jewish coins", London 1903, p.60, pl.10/3.

RIDER, G. le "Les ateliers monétaires de la côte Syrienne, Phénicienne, Palestinienne, Égyptienne et Cyrénéenne", Congresso Internazionale di numismatica (Roma 1961), vol. I, Relazioni, Roma 1961, p.96.

RIDER, G. le "Monnaies grecques récemment acquises par le cabinet des médailles", RN 6th ser. 3, 1961, p.23, pl.2/E.

ROSENBERGER, M. "City-coins of Palestine", vol. III, Jerusalem 1977, pp.5-26, 85.

ROSENTHAL-HEGINBOTTOM, R. "The Mampsis hoard - A preliminary report", INJ 4, 1980, pp.42, 48.

SAULCY, F. de "Numismatique de la Terre Sainte", Paris 1874, pp.244-274, pls.12/10-12; 13/1-10; 14/1-3.

SEAR, D.R. "Greek imperial coins and their values", London 1982, nos. 882, 1506, 1681, 1801, 1876, 2057, 2460, 2685, 2969, 3027, 3122, 3217, 3256, 3375, 3481, 3966, 3979, 4062, 4153, 4355, 4398, 4399.

SESTINI, D. "Descriptio numorum veterum..", Lipsiae 1796, p.544.

SESTINI, D. "Classes generales geographiae numismaticae sev monetae urbium, populorum et regum..", Lipsiae 1797, part I, pp.70-71, part II, p.103.

SESTINI, D. "Descriptio selectiorum numismatum in aere maximi moduli e museo olim Abbatis De Camps..", Berolini 1808, p.44.

SESTINI, D. "Lettere e dissertazioni numismatiche..", t.IX, Firenze 1820, pp.102-108.

SESTINI, D. "Classes generales sev moneta vetus urbium, populorum et regum..", Florentiae 1821, p.150.

SESTINI, D. "Descrizione d'alcune medaglie Greche del museo del Signore Carlo D'Ottavio Fontana", Firenze 1822, p.13.

SESTINI, D. "Descrizione delle medaglie antiche greche del Museo Hedervariano", part 3, Firenze 1829, pp.107-110.

SEYRIG, H. "Antiquités Syriennes, 10. Note sur le culte de Déméter en Palestine", SYRIA 13, 1932, p.357.

SEYRIG, H. "Notes on Syrian coins", NNM 119, 1950, p.32.

SNG ANS part 6, "Palestine - South Arabia", 1981, pls.31-34, figs. 961-1042.

SNG DNM "Palestine-Characene", 1961, pl.1/14-21.

SNG FM vol. IV, part 8, "Syria-Nabathaea", 1971, pl.136/6104-6105.

SPAER, A. "A noted collector of ancient coins reveals his secrets", SHEKEL 6 (4), 1973, p.21.

SPERBER, D. "Roman Palestine 200-400. Money and prices", Jerusalem 1974, p.143.

SPIJKERMAN, A. and STARCKY, J. "Un nouveau lot de monnaies palestiniennes", RB 65, 1958, pp.568, 569, 570, 577-580, nos. 51-76, pls.19/52-69; 20/76.

STEVENSON, S.W. "A dictionary of Roman coins", London 1964 (rp), pp.567-568.

SUTHERLAND, C.H.V. "The pattern of monetary development in Phoenicia and Palestine during the Early Empire", International

SUTHERLAND, C.H.V. (con't) numismatic convention in Jerusalem (1963), proceedings (A. Kindler, ed.), Tel-Aviv 1967, p.94, 95, 96, 98.

TIEPOLO, L. and F. "Musei Theupoli antiqua numismata..", Venetiis 1736, series 4, p.749; series 6, pp.910-911, 973, 1019.

VAILLANT, J. "Numismata aera imperatorum, augustarum et caesarum in coloniis, municipiis et urbibus..", Paris 1688, part II, pp.244-248, 263, 272-273, 310-311, 321-322.

VAILLANT, J. "Numismata imperatorum, augustarum et caesarum a populis Romanae ditionis Graece loquentibus..", Paris 1698, pp.20, 22, 46, 58, 67, 80, 125, 148, 151, 156, 175, 244, 362-363, 477.

VLIET, N. van der "Monnaies inédites ou très rares du médaillier de Sainte-Anne de Jérusalem", RB 57, 1950, pp.121-125, pls.2/19-22; 3/23-25.

WAAGE, D.B. "Antioch on-the-Orontes, IV. Part 2: Greek, Roman, Byzantine and Crusaders' coins", Princeton 1952, p.86/927-928.

WALCHER de MOLTHEIN, L. "Catalogue de la collection des medailles grecques de M. Le Chevalier", Paris - Vienne 1895, p.269, nos. 3169-3170.

WICZAY, C.M. "Musei Hedervarii numi antiqui..", Vindobonae 1814, part I, p.288, nos. 6202-6209, pl.26/573.

Auction Catalogues and Price Lists

AGORA Tel-Aviv 1974 (1), p.22, nos. 129-131, pls.7-8.
1975 (2), nos. 186-190, pl.8.

BETTER Haifa 1972 (1), nos. 214-223.
Haifa 1972 (2), nos. 291-300.
Haifa 1973 (3), nos. 273-274, 330-331, 347.
Haifa 1973 (4), nos. 209-214, 237.
Jaffo 1974 (5), nos. 155-156.
Jaffo 1974 (7), nos. 244-255.
Haifa 1974 (8), nos. 137-152.

BUTTON, E. (price list), Frankfurt 1938 (35), p.5, no. 3049.

CAHN, A.E. Frankfurt 1930 (68), p.95, nos. 1586-1587.
1931 (71), p.66, nos. 1089-1091, pl.33.
1933 (80), p.26, no. 397.

COIN GALLERIES (mail bid sale), New York, 13 July 1954, no. 1192.

COIN GALLERIES (price list), New York 1959 (17), p.16, nos. A 239-240.

EIDELSTEIN AND HOLLAND, Haifa, 10 Nov. 1975, nos. 169-171.

GANS, E. "Numismatic Fine Arts", (Stock cat.), New York
1973 (2), pp.19 (nos 7318, 7353), 20 (nos.7312, 6103).
1973 (3), p.10, nos. 6301, 7343, 7318, 7353, 6302, 6103b.

GANS, E. "Numismatic Fine Arts", (mail bid sale), Berkeley CA, USA 1955 (15), p.23, nos. 371-372, pl.8.

GANS, E. "Numismatic Fine Arts", Berkeley CA, USA
1956 (18), p.1, nos. 4207-4208.
1956 (20), p.15, nos. 4957-4958.

GLENDINING London, 19 July 1950, p.46, no. 334.
21-23 Feb. 1961, p.98, no. 3004.
30-31 Oct. 1963, p.32, no. 395.

NEAPOLIS

GLENDINING (con't) 10 March 1965, pp.21 (nos. 157-159, pl.6), 27 (no. 221, pl.8).

HAMBURGER, L. Frankfurt 1932 (96), p.9, no. 175, pl.6.

HESS, A. Frankfurt 1936 (224), p.58, no. 1735.

HIRSCH, G. München 1963 (37), p.28, no. 554.

HOLZER, H. "The Thomas Ollive Mabbott collection", part I, New York 1969, pp.104-105, nos. 2682-2696.

KRAUS, F.F. (price list), Braunschweig, Germany 1929 (1-2), p.54, no. 1251.

KRESS, K. München 1983 (185), p.46, no. 913.

MALTER, J.L. "Journal of Numismatic Fine Arts", Encino CA, USA 1973 (2/2), p.37/B 78.

MONNAIES ET MÉDAILLES, Basel

1954 (13), p.72, no. 933, pl.33.
1962 (25), p.22, nos. 540-542, pl.9.
1966 (32), pp.44-45, nos. 408-434, pls.25-27.

MÜNZEN UND MEDAILLEN, Basel

1952 (112), p.6, no. 134.
1955 (151), p.12, nos. 240-242.
1958 (176), p.3, nos. 46-50.
1968 (293), p.4, nos. 48-50.
1978 (398), p.2, no. 7.
1980 (422), p.13, no. 166.
1980 (424), pp.4 (no. 70), 17 (nos. 214-217).
1981 (436), p.14, no. 156.
1984 (468), p.14, no. 178.
1984 (469), p.7, no. 64.
1985 (480), p.3, no. 24.

MÜNZZENTRUM KÖLN, 1979 (36), p.29, nos. 188-189.

NUMISMATICA WIEN, 1975 (9), p.23, no. 128.

NUMISMATIC FINE ARTS, Beverly Hills, CA, USA 1976 (3), no. 167/3.
1978 (5), nos. 341-342.

NUMISMATIC FINE ARTS (Winter mail bid sale), Beverly Hills, CA, USA, Jan. 1982, no. 265.

PEUS Frankfurt 1973 (37), p.5, no. 56.

RAUCH, H.D. Wien 1985 (34), nos. 240-254.

SCHLESSINGER, F. (price list), Amsterdam 1938 (9), p.3, nos. 648-665.

SCHULMAN, H.M.F., New York, 18-19 Nov. 1955, p.71, nos. 1935, 1942.
6-8 Oct. 1970, p.19, no. 231.
6-7 Apr. 1971, p.45, nos. 449-450.

SEABY London 1956 (453), p.65, no. AG 197.
1965 (567), p.317, nos. A 763-765.
1968 (598), p.220, no. A 480.
1969 (609), p.171, no. A 421.
1969 (615), p.396, no. A 999.

SPINK AND SON London 1905 (13/153), nos. 18178-18198.
1925 (33/11-12), nos. 45380-45381, 45448.
1930 (38/10), nos. 933-934.
1930 (38/11), nos. 1796-1797, 1801-1802.
1931 (39/1), nos. 3433, 3450-3451.
1931 (39/4), no. 6042.
1931 (39/9), nos. 10031-10042.
1934 (42/8-9), nos. 35008-35009.
1934 (42/12), nos. 37858, 37884-37886.
1936 (44/1), nos. 48019-48036.

NEAPOLIS

SPINK AND SON (con't) 1939 (47/4), nos. 79401-79412.
1939 (47/10-12), no. 840096.
1960 (68/1), pl.12, nos. 13-15.
1972 (80/9), p.328, no. 8146.
1977 (85/7-8), p.318, no. 6649.
1977 (85/12), p.553, no. 13058.
1978 (86/12), p.591, no. 14078.

STACK'S New York, 10-11 June 1970, p.36, no. 456.

STERNBERG, F. Zürich, 25-26 Nov. 1976, pp.84-86, nos. 647-671, pls.27-28.

SUPERIOR STAMP AND COIN CO., Los-Angeles, June 1976, pp.27-28, nos. 305-312.

TAMAR Tel-Aviv 1975 (9), p.7, nos. 147-154.
Tel-Aviv 1975 (10), p.9, nos. 149-150A.
Ramat-Gan, Israel 1976 (11), pp.10-11, nos. 130-136.
Ramat-Gan, Israel 1976 (12), pp.51-52, nos. 853-862.

VINCHON, J. "Monnaies Juives", Paris, 13 Fév. 1970, nos. 87-89.

NICOPOLIS

ARRIGONI, O. "Numismata quaedam cujuscunque formae..", Tarvisii, part I (1741), Num. Imperatoria in graecis urbibus percussa a J. Vaillant non edita, pl.4/55.

BELLINGER, A.R. "The Syrian tetradrachms of Caracalla and Macrinus", ANS NS 3, 1940, p.13.

ECKHEL, J. "Doctrina numorum veterum..", vol. III, Vienna 1794, p.454.

HAMBURGER, L. "Die beiden palästinensischen Münzstätten Nikopolis-Emmaus", (Sonder-Abdruck aus den Frankfurter Münzblättern 1, 1899, nos. 8, 9), pp.1-14, pl.7.

HEAD, B.V. "Historia numorum", Oxford 1911, pp.805-806.

HENDIN, D. "Guide to ancient Jewish coins", New York 1976, p.113.

HILL, G.F. BMC, Palestine, 1914, pp.lxxix-lxxxi, pp.169-170, pl.17/10-15.

IMHOOF-BLUMER, F. "Zur syrischen Münzkunde", NZ 33, 1901, pp.13-14.

JANIS, E. "The other coin cities of Israel", SHEKEL 3 (3), 1970, p.15.

KADMAN, L. "Numismatic evidence of the architectonic revolution in the Second Century C.E.", INB 1962 (3-4), p.72. Heb. ed. p.65.

KADMAN, L. and KINDLER, A. "Coins in Palestine throughout the ages", Tel-Aviv 1963, p.38, pl.17/3-4 (Hebrew).

NICOPOLIS

KINDLER, A. "Thesaurus of Judaean coins from the fourth century B.C. to the third century A.D.", Jerusalem 1958, no 24 (Hebrew).

KINDLER, A. "The status of cities in the Syro-Palestinian area as reflected by their coins", INJ 6-7, 1982/3, p.81.

KINDLER, A. "The coinage of Bostra", Warminster, England 1983, p.108.

KLIMOWSKY, E.W. "The monetary function of city coins", International numismatic convention in Jerusalem (1963), proceedings (A. Kindler, ed.), Tel-Aviv 1967, pp.164, 166, 172.

MACDONALD, G. "Catalogue of Greek coins in the Hunterian collection", Glasgow 1905, vol. III, p.284, pl.78/1.

MESHORER, Y. "The city coins of Eretz-Israel and the Decapolis in the Roman period", Jerusalem 1984, pp.56, 116-117 (Hebrew).

MIONNET, T.E. "Description de médailles antiques, grecques et romaines", Paris 1806-1837, vol. V, pp.550-551, vol. VIII, suppl., p.376.

PRICE, M.J. and TRELL, B.L. "Coins and their cities", London 1977, p.284.

ROSENBERGER, M. "City-coins of Palestine", vol. III, Jerusalem 1977, pp.26-27.

SAULCY, F. de "Numismatique de la Terre Sainte", Paris 1874, pp.172-175, 406, pl.6/3-5.

SEAR, D.R. "Greek imperial coins and their values", London 1982, nos. 1538, 3128.

SESTINI, D. "Classes generales geographiae numismaticae sev monetae urbium, populorum et regum..", Lipsiae 1797, part I, p.71.

SESTINI, D. "Classes generales sev moneta vetus urbium, populorum et regum..", Florentiae 1821, p.152.

SNG ANS part 6, "Palestine - South Arabia", 1981, pl.35/1043-1044.

SUTHERLAND, C.H.V. "The pattern of monetary development in Phoenicia and Palestine during the Early Empire", International numismatic convention in Jerusalem (1963), proceedings (A. Kindler, ed.), Tel-Aviv 1967, p.96.

VLIET, N. van der "Monnaies inédites ou très rares du médaillier de Sainte-Anne de Jérusalem", RB 57, 1950, pp.119-120, pl.2/18, 18bis.

Auction Catalogues and Price Lists

KRAUS, F.F. (price list), Braunschweig, Germany 1928 (2), p.48, no. 1089.

MONNAIES ET MÉDAILLES, Basel 1966 (32), p.46, no. 435.

SCHLESSINGER, F. (price list), Amsterdam 1938 (9), p.4, nos. 689-690.

VECCHI, V.C. "Bonhams", London 1982 (8), p.19, no. 217, pl.10.

NYSA-SCYTHOPOLIS

ANONYMOUS — CH 1, 1975, p.34/123.

ANONYMOUS — "City-coins of ancient Israel", JIN 1 (3), 1966, p.78.

ANONYMOUS — SHEKEL 13 (3), 1980, p.31.

ARIEL, D.T. — "A survey of coin finds in Jerusalem", LA 32, 1982, p.318.

BABELON, E. — "Le cabinet des médailles pendant la guerre", RN, 4th ser. 23, 1920, pp.117-118.

BARAG, D. — "Tyrian currency in Galilee", INJ 6-7, 1982/3, pp.10, 11.

BARAMKI, D.C. — "The coin collection of the American University of Beirut Museum. Palestine and Phoenicia", Beirut 1974, pp.30-31, pl.6/2-6.

BARAMKI, J. — "Coins in the Palestine Archaeological Museum, III", QDAP 8, 1939, p.80, pl.41/18-19.

BELLINGER, A.R. — "The Syrian tetradrachms of Caracalla and Macrinus", ANS NS 3, 1940, p.13.

BEN-DOR, S. — "Concerning the era of Nysa-Scythopolis", PEQ 1944, pp.152-156, pl.5.

BEN-DOR, S. — "Two new coins of Nysa-Scythopolis", PEQ 1945, pp.47-48, pl.6.

BENTINCK, de — "Catalogue d'une collection de médailles antiques", Amsterdam 1787, part II, p.1071.

BERNHART , M. — "Dionysos und seine Familie auf griechischen Münzen", JNG 1, 1949, pp.64/208; 105/758.

CARSON, R.A.G. "The inflation of Third Century and its monetary influence in the Near East", International numismatic convention in Jerusalem (1963), proceedings (A. Kindler, ed.), Tel-Aviv 1967, p.242.

ECKHEL, J. "Doctrina numorum veterum..", vol. III, Vienna 1794, pp.438-440.

FUKS, G. "Scythopolis", CATHEDRA 17, 1980, pp.26-27, 30, 31 (Hebrew).

HARDUIN, J. "Nummi antiqui populorum et urbium illustrati", Parisiis 1684, p.366.

HEAD, B.V. "Historia numorum", Oxford 1911, p.803.

HENDIN, D. "Guide to ancient Jewish coins", New York, 1976, pp.105-106, pl.8/249.

HILL, G.F. "Some Palestinian cults in the Graeco-Roman age", Proceedings of the British Academy, vol. V, London 1912, pp.413, 414-415, pl./5.

HILL, G.F. BMC, Palestine, 1914, pp.xxxiv-xxxvii, pp.75-77, pl.8/1-7.

HOWGEGO, C. "The behaviour and function of Greek Imperial countermarks", INJ 6-7, 1982/3, p.51, pl.11/13.

IMHOOF-BLUMER, F. "Nymphen und Chariten auf griechischen Münzen", JIAN 11, 1908, p.158.

JONAS, R. "Mythology on Palestinian coins", internal circular no. 2, Israel Num. Society, Haifa branch, 1959, pp.2, 5.

NYSA-SCYTHOPOLIS

JONAS, R. "The Winged Dionysos", internal circular no. 3, Israel Num. Society, Haifa branch, 1960, pp.2-3, 6 (note 18).

KADMAN, L. and KINDLER, A. "Coins in Palestine throughout the ages", Tel-Aviv 1963, p.40, pl.18/7 (Hebrew).

KINDLER, A. "Thesaurus of Judaean coins from the fourth century B.C. to the third century A.D.", Jerusalem 1958, no. 40 (Hebrew).

KINDLER, A. "An unpublished coin type of Nysa-Scythopolis and the problem of the eras of the city", *INJ* 1963 (3), pp.55-56, pl.3/4-5.

KINDLER, A. "New types of Palestinian city-coins", *ALON* 3 (2), 1968, pp.49-50, pl.2/8 (Hebrew).

KINDLER, A. "Coins of the land of Israel. Bank of Israel collection", Jerusalem 1971, p.133/202 (Hebrew).

KINDLER, A. "The status of cities in the Syro-Palestinian area as reflected by their coins", *INJ* 6-7, 1982/3, pp.80, 81.

KIRKBRIDE, A.S. "Currencies in Transjordan", *PEQ* 1939, p.156.

KLIMOWSKY, E.W. "The monetary function of city coins", International numismatic convention in Jerusalem (1963), proceedings (A. Kindler, ed.), Tel-Aviv 1967, pp.132, 164, 166, 168, 172, 177.

KLIMOWSKY, E.W. "Roman imperial 'Virtutes' on contemporaneous city coins" in "On ancient Palestinian and other coins, their symbolism and metrology", *PINS* 7, Tel-Aviv 1974, p.87. Same in *INJ* 3, 1965/6, p.15.

LAMBERT, C. "Coins in the Palestine Museum, II", *QDAP* 1, 1931/2, p.134, pl.55/19.

LIEBE, C.S. "Gotha numaria sistens Thesauri Fridericiani..", Amsterdam 1730, pp.334-335.

MANNS, F. "Gemmes de l'époque Gréco-Romaine provenant de Palestine", LA 28, 1978, pp.157-158, pl.26/16.

MATSSON, G.O. "The gods, goddesses and heroes on the ancient coins of Bible Lands", Stockholm 1969, pp.144-145, 167-168, 228-229, pl.6/88a, b.

MESHORER, Y. "An anonymous coin of Nysa-Scythopolis", IEJ 25 (2-3), 1975, pp.142-143, pl.14.

MESHORER, Y. "A hoard of coins from Migdal", ATIQOT, Es 11, 1976, pp.55, 56, 65-76, pls.13/107-116; 14/117-120.

MESHORER, Y. "Another coin of Nysa-Scythopolis", IEJ 27 (1), 1977, pp.40-41, pl.4.

MESHORER, Y. "The city coins of Eretz-Israel and the Decapolis in the Roman period", Jerusalem 1984, pp.39-42, 114 (Hebrew).

MESHORER, Y. and SPAER, A. "Some additional apparently unpublished city coins", INJ 3, 1965/6, pp.74-75, pl.14/2-4.

MIONNET, T.E. "Description de médailles antiques, grecques et romaines", Paris 1806-1837, vol. V, pp.511-512, vol. VIII, suppl., pp.355-356.

OVADIA, A. "Greek cults at Beth-Shean/Scythopolis in the Hellenistic and Roman periods", EI 12, 1975, p.121 (Hebrew).

PRICE, M.J. and TRELL, B.L. "Coins and their cities", London 1977, p.283.

NYSA-SCYTHOPOLIS

REICHARDT, H.C. "Unpublished Greek Imperial coins", NC, Ns 2, 1862, p.113.

RESHEF, M. "A coin of Nysa-Scythopolis countermarked with the name of the city", ALON 1 (3), 1967, pp.41-43, pl.2/1-4 (Hebrew).

RESHEF, M. "An unknown coin of Gabinius struck at Nysa-Scythopolis", ALON 5 (1), 1973, pp.7-8, pl.1/3-4 (Hebrew).

RIDER, G. le "Les ateliers monétaires de la côte Syrienne, Phénicienne, Palestinienne, Égyptienne et Cyrénéenne", Congresso Internazionale di numismatica (Roma 1961), vol. I, Relazioni, Roma 1961, p.87.

ROSENBERGER, M. "City-coins of Palestine", vol. III, Jerusalem 1977, pp.27-38.

SAULCY, F. de "Numismatique de la Terre Sainte", Paris 1874, pp.287-290, pl.14/8-13.

SEAR, D.R. "Greek imperial coins and their values", London 1982, nos. 403, 481, 630, 1682, 1802, 2058, 2272, 2461, 2686, 2901, 3123, 3785, 5215.

SESTINI, D. "Classes generales geographiae numismaticae sev monetae urbium, populorum et regum..", Lipsiae 1797, part I, p.71, part II, p.103.

SESTINI, D. "Classes generales sev moneta vetus urbium, populorum et regum..", Florentiae 1821, p.150.

SESTINI, D. "Descrizione delle medaglie antiche greche del Museo Hedervariano", part 3, Firenze 1829, p.110.

SEYRIG, H. "Antiquités Syriennes, 10. Note sure le culte de Déméter en Palestine", SYRIA 13, 1932, pp.357, 360.

SEYRIG, H. "Antiquités Syriennes, 81. Note sur les cultes de Scythopolis à l'époque romaine", SYRIA 39, 1962, pp.210-211.

SEYRIG, H. "Notes on Syrian coins", NNM 119, 1950, p.32.

SEYRIG, H. "Monnaies Hellénistique. XIII Sur quelques ères Syriennes. 3. L'ère de Scythopolis", RN, 6th ser. 6, 1964, pp.65-67.

SNG ANS part 6, 1981, "Palestine - South Arabia", 1981, pl.35/1045-1059.

SNG DNM "Palestine-Characene", 1961, pl.1/22.

SPERBER, D. "Roman Palestine 200-400. Money and prices", Jerusalem 1974, p.143.

SPIJKERMAN, A. "An unknown coin-type of Pella Decapoleos", LA 20, 1970, p.356.

SPIJKERMAN, A. "Cafarnao III. Catalogo delle monete della citta", Jerusalem 1975, pp.29/176; 41/323, pl.1/10.

SPIJKERMAN, A. "The coins of the Decapolis and provincia Arabia", Jerusalem 1978, pp.186-209, 294-295, pls.41-45, suppl. I, 3b, 33b.

STAHL, Z. "The Flavian Emperors and their coins in Eretz-Israel", special brochure of Israel Num. Society, Tel-Aviv branch, 1976, p.7 (Hebrew).

STAHL, Z. "Roman coins of Palestinian cities issued during the Jewish War, 66-70 C.E.", special brochure of Israel

STAHL, Z. (con't) Num. Society, Tel-Aviv branch, 1979, pp.12, 20-21, 25 (Hebrew).

SUTHERLAND, C.H.V. "The pattern of monetary development in Phoenicia and Palestine during the Early Empire", International numismatic convention in Jerusalem (1963), proceedings (A. Kindler, ed.), Tel-Aviv 1967, p.91.

TZORI, N. "On two rare coins from Scythopolis (Beth-Shan)", PEQ 1960, p.70, pl.5.

VLIET, N. van der "Monnaies inédites ou très rares du médaillier de Sainte-Anne de Jérusalem", RB 57, 1950, pp.258-259, pl.5/16.

ZURI, N. "A hoard of bronze and silver coins from Ain Hanaziv", INB 1962 (3-4), p.105. Heb. ed. p.88.

Auction Catalogues and Price Lists

AGORA Tel-Aviv 1974 (1), p.22, no. 132, pl.8.
1975 (2), nos. 181-182, pl.8.

BETTER Haifa 1972 (1), no. 224.
Haifa 1973 (4), no. 184.
Haifa 1974 (8), nos. 153-154.

EIDELSTEIN AND HOLLAND, Haifa, 10 Nov. 1975, no. 172.

HOLZER, H. "The Thomas Ollive Mabbott collection", part I, New York 1969, p.105, no. 2697.

MALTER, J.L. "Journal of Numismatic Fine Arts", Encino, CA, USA 1973 (2/2), p.37/B 79.

MONNAIES ET MÉDAILLES, Basel 1966 (32), p.46, no. 436.

RAUCH, H.D. Wien 1985 (34), nos. 255-257.

SCHLESSINGER, F. (price list), Amsterdam 1938 (9), p.3, no. 666.

STERNBERG, F. Zürich, 25-26 Nov. 1976, p.91, no. 700, pl.30.

SUPERIOR STAMP AND COIN CO., Los-Angeles, June 1976, p.28, nos. 313-314.

TAMAR Ramat-Gan, Israel 1976 (11), p.11, nos. 137-138.
Ramat-Gan, Israel 1976 (12), p.51, nos. 849-851.

PANEAS

BARAG, D. "The 'Iudaea capta' coinage in Eretz-Israel and its implications for the absolute chronology of the reign of Agrippa II", CATHEDRA 8, 1978, p.49 (Hebrew).

BARAG, D. "Tyrian influence in Galilee", INJ 6-7, 1982/3, pp.10, 11.

BARAMKI, D.C. "The coins exhibited in the Archaeological Museum of the American University of Beirut", Beirut 1968, p.74/249-251, pl.7.

BELLINGER, A.R. "The Syrian tetradrachms of Caracalla and Macrinus", ANS NS 3, 1940, p.13.

BERNHART, M. "Dionysos und seine Familie auf griechischen Münzen", JNG 1, 1949, p.170, nos. 1483-1491.

CARSON, R.A.G. "The inflation of the Third Century and its monetary influence in the Near East", International numismatic convention in Jerusalem (1963), proceedings (A. Kindler, ed.), Tel-Aviv 1967, p.242.

ECKHEL, J. "Catalogus Musei Caesarei Vindobonensis numorum veterum..", Vindobonae 1779, part I, p.251.

ECKHEL, J. "Doctrina numorum veterum..", vol. III, Vienna 1794, pp.339-344.

GESSNER, J.J. "Numismata antiqua Imperatorum Romanorum latina et graeca..", Tiguri (Zürich), 18th cent., pl.112/8.

GRANT, M. "The pattern of official coinage in the early principate", in 'Essays in Roman coinage presented to Harold Mattingly, (R.A.G. Carson and C.H.V. Sutherland, eds.), Oxford 1956, pp.98, 103, pl.4/1, 3.

GROSE, S.W. "Catalogue of the McClean collection of Greek coins in the Fitzwilliam Museum", vol. III, Cambridge 1929, p.362/9441, pl.348/14.

HAMBURGER, H. "A hoard of Syrian tetradrachms and Tyrian bronze coins from Gush Halav", IEJ 4 (3-4), 1954, pp.206-207, 222, pl.20. Same in 'Recent studies and discoveries on ancient Jewish and Syrian coins' PINS 1, Jerusalem 1954, pp.70-71, 86, pl.20/128-129.

FROELICH, E. "Quatuor tentamina in re numaria vetere", 2nd ed., Viennae 1737, pp.223-225.

HEAD, B.V. "Historia numorum", Oxford 1911, pp.785-786.

HENDIN, D. "Guide to ancient Jewish coins", New York 1976, pl.95.

JANIS, E. "The other coin cities of Israel", SHEKEL 3 (3), 1970, p.15.

KINDLER, A. "Coins of the land of Israel. Bank of Israel collection", Jerusalem 1971, p.135, no. 204 (Hebrew).

KINDLER, A. "Thesaurus of Judaean coins from the fourth century B.C. to the third century A.D.", Jerusalem 1958, no. 45 (Hebrew).

KINDLER, A. "A new coin-type of Paneas", ALON 1 (3), 1967, pp.58-59, pl.2/7 (Hebrew).

KINDLER, A. "The status of cities in the Syro-Palestinian area as reflected by their coins", INJ 6-7, 1982/3, pp.81, 83.

KLIMOWSKY, E.W. "The monetary function of city coins", International numismatic convention in Jerusalem (1963), proceedings (A. Kindler, ed.), Tel-Aviv 1967, pp.164, 166, 172.

PANEAS

KRAFT, K. "Das System der kaiserzeitlichen Münzprägung in Kleinasien", Berlin 1972, p.101, pl.117/7.

MATSSON, G.O. "The gods, goddesses and heroes on the ancient coins of Bible Lands", Stockholm 1969, pp.149, 152, 231, pl.6/93.

MESHORER, Y. "Coins of the Ancient World", Minneapolis 1975, pp.68, 74. Hebrew version (Jerusalem 1979), p.52. Same in "Münzen, Zeugen der Vergangenheit", Zürich - Köln, 1979, pp.73-74.

MESHORER, Y. "About the problems of the eras of Agrippa II", CATHEDRA 8, 1978, pp.59, 60, 63 (Hebrew).

MESHORER, Y. "The city coins of Eretz-Israel and the Decapolis in the Roman period", Jerusalem 1984, pp.67-69, 118 (Hebrew).

MIONNET, T.E. "Description de médailles antiques, grecques et romaines", Paris 1806-1837, vol. V, p.311-315, vol. VIII, suppl., pp.217-219.

PRICE, M.J. and TRELL, B.L. "Coins and their cities", London 1977, pp.21, 281-282, figs. 10-12, 358.

RAHMANI, L. and SHARABANI, M. "List of coins", in 'Hammath Tiberias' by M. Dothan, Jerusalem 1983, p.72, pl.22/17.

RAYNOR, J. "Numismatic report of Nabratein, 1980", in 'Preliminary report on the 1980 excavations at En-Nabratein, Israel', BASOR 244, 1981, p.20, fig. 11/6.

ROSENBERGER, M. "City-coins of Palestine", vol. III, Jerusalem 1977, pp.38-47.

SAULCY, F. de "Numismatique de la Terre Sainte", Paris 1874, pp.313-324, pl.18.

SCHOLZ, J. "Griechische Münzen aus meiner Sammlung", NZ 33, 1901, p.48.

SEAR, D.R. "Greek imperial coins and their values", London 1982, nos. 1672, 2046, 3019, 3103, 3214, 3253.

SESTINI, D. "Descriptio numorum veterum..", Lipsiae 1796, p.530, pl.12/2-3.

SESTINI, D. "Classes generales geographiae numismaticae sev monetae urbium, populorum et regum..", Lipsiae 1797, part I, p.67, part II, pp.99-100.

SESTINI, D. "Descrizione delle medaglie Greche e Romani del Fu Benkowitz", Berlino 1809, pp.32-33.

SESTINI, D. "Classes generales sev moneta vetus urbium, populorum et regum..", Florentiae 1821, p.143.

SESTINI, D. "Descrizione d'alcune medaglie Greche del museo del Signore Carlo D'Ottavio Fontana", Firenze 1822, p.13.

SESTINI, D. "Descrizione delle medaglie antiche Greche del Museo Hedervariano", part 3, Firenze 1829, p.72.

SEYRIG, H. "Irenopolis-Neronias-Sepphoris", NC, 6th ser. 10, 1950, pp.286, 287.

SEYRIG, H. "Irenopolis-Neronias-Sepphoris, an additional note", NC, 6th ser. 15, 1955, pp.157, 158.

SNG ANS part 6, "Palestine - South Arabia", 1981, pls.27-28, figs. 858-888.

PANEAS

SNG DNM "Syria, Cities", 1959, pl.12/446-447.

SNG FM vol. IV, part 8, "Syria-Nabathaea", 1971, pl.132/5974.

SPERBER, D. "Roman Palestine 200-400. Money and prices", Jerusalem 1974, p.143.

SPIJKERMAN, A. "Cafarnao III. Catalogo delle monete della citta", Jerusalem 1975, p.51/429.

STAHL, Z. "Women in the life of Emperor Nero on coins related to Eretz-Israel", special brochure of Israel Num. Society, Tel-Aviv branch, 1978, pp.8-14 (Hebrew).

STEVENSON, S.W. "A dictionary of Roman coins", London 1964 (rp), pp.161-162.

VAILLANT, J. "Numismata imperatorum, augustarum et caesarum a populis Romanae ditionis Graece loquentibus..", Paris 1698, pp.56, 73, 78, 95, 106, 120, 142, 238, 354-356.

WICZAY, M. "Musei Hedervarii numi antiqui..", Vindobonae 1814, part I, p.278, nos. 6024-6027, pl.26/565.

WROTH, W. BMC, Galatia, Cappadocia and Syria, 1899, pp.lxxx-lxxxii, pp.298-299, pl.37/6-7.

WROTH, W. "Greek coins acquired by British Museum in 1900", <u>NC,</u> 3rd ser. 20, 1900, pp.294-295.

<u>Auction Catalogues and Price Lists</u>

AGORA Tel-Aviv 1974 (1), p.21, nos. 126-127, pl.7.

BETTER Haifa 1972 (1), no. 236.
Haifa 1972 (2), no. 349.

BUTTON, E. (price list), Frankfurt 1938 (37), p.28, no. 5529.

GANS, E. "Numismatic Fine Arts" (Mail bid sale), Berkeley CA, USA 1955 (15), p.27, no. 459.

GANS, E. "Numismatic Fine Arts", Berkeley CA, USA
1956 (18), p.3, no. 4240.
1956 (20), p.15, no. 4970.

GLENDINING London, 19 July 1950, p.45, no. 332.

HESS, A. Frankfurt 1936 (224), p.57, no. 1702.

HOLZER, H. "The Thomas Ollive Mabbott collection", part I, New York 1969, p.102, nos. 2620-2623.

MALTER, J.L. "Journal of Numismatic Fine Arts", Encino CA, USA 1973 (2/2), p.37/B 64.

MONNAIES ET MÉDAILLES, Basel 1966 (32), p.48, no. 459-460, pl.28.

MÜNZEN UND MEDAILLEN, Basel 1958 (176), p.3, no. 40.
1978 (398), p.1, no. 1.

SCHULMAN, H.M.F., New York, 14-15 Dec. 1970, p.18, no. 963.
6-7 Apr. 1971, p.24, no. 441.

SEABY London 1966 (575), p.216, no. A 472.

SPINK AND SON London 1902 (10/116), no. 85063.
1905 (13/149), no. 13825.
1931 (39/8), no. 9255.
1960 (68/1), p.12, no. 11.

STERNBERG, F. Zürich, 25-26 Nov. 1976, p.87, nos. 672-673, pl.28.

SUPERIOR STAMP AND COIN CO., Los-Angeles, June 1976, p.28, no. 315.

PELLA

BELLINGER, A.R. "The Syrian tetradrachms of Caracalla and Macrinus", ANS NS 3, 1940, p.14.

CARRADICE, I. "Coinage in Judaea in the Flavian period, AD 70-96", INJ 6-7, 1982/3, p.17.

DOWLING, T.E. "Interesting coins of Pella and Bittir", PEF 25, 1907, pp.295-296.

ECKHEL, J. "Catalogus Musei Caesarei Vindobonensis numorum veterum..", Vindobonae 1779, part I, p.252.

ECKHEL, J. "Doctrina numorum veterum..", vol. III, Vienna 1794, pp.350-351.

FROELICH, E. "Quatuor tentamina in re numaria vetere", 2nd ed., Viennae 1737, p.225.

HEAD, B.V. "Historia numorum", Oxford 1911, p.787.

HERZFELDER, H. "Contribution à la numismatique de la Décapole", RN, 4th ser. 39, 1936, pp.285-291.

KINDLER, A. "The coinage of Bostra", Warminster, England 1983, pp.58, 144.

KIRKBRIDE, A.S. "Currencies in Transjordan", PEQ 1939, p.156.

KLIMOWSKY, E.W. "The monetary function of city coins", International numismatic convention in Jerusalem (1963), proceedings (A. Kindler, ed.), Tel-Aviv 1967, pp.166, 172.

KUBITSCHEK, W. "Münzen von Pella in Palästina", NZ 42, 1909, pp.25-32.

MESHORER, Y. "The city coins of Eretz-Israel and the Decapolis in the Roman period", Jerusalem 1984, pp.92, 121 (Hebrew).

MIONNET, T.E. "Description de médailles antiques, grecques et romaines", Paris 1806-1837, vol. V, pp.329-330; vol. VIII, suppl., p.232.

PRICE, M.J. and TRELL, B.L. "Coins and their cities", London 1977, pp.39, 44, 282, figs. 56, 72.

REGLING, K. "Nachlese zu den Münzen von Sinope und Pella (Dekapolis)", NZ 42, 1909, pp.17-18.

REICHARDT, H.C. "Unpublished Greek Imperial coins", NC, Ns 2, 1862, p.105.

RIDER, G. le "Les ateliers monétaires de la côte Syrienne, Phénicienne, Palestinienne, Égyptienne et Cyrénéenne", Congresso Internazionale di numismatica (Roma 1961), vol. I, Relazioni, Roma 1961, p.87.

ROSENBERGER, M. "The coinage of Eastern Palestine", Jerusalem 1978, pp.58-60.

SAULCY, F. de "Numismatique de la Terre Sainte", Paris 1874, pp.291-293, pl.16/8.

SEAR, D.R. "Greek imperial coins and their values", London 1982, nos. 878, 1911, 2052, 3109.

SESTINI, D. "Classes generales geographiae numismaticae sev monetae urbium, populorum et regum..", Lipsiae 1797, part I, p.68.

SESTINI, D. "Lettere e dissertazioni numismatiche", t.IX, Firenze 1820, p.90.

PELLA

SESTINI, D. "Classes generales sev moneta vetus urbium, populorum et regum..", Florentiae 1821, p.144.

SEYRIG, H. "Antiquités Syriennes, 73. Temples, cultes et souvenirs historiques de la Décapole", SYRIA 36, 1959, pp.68-70, 78, pl.13/22-26.

SNG ANS part 6, "Palestine - South Arabia", 1981, pl.46/1353-1358.

SPIJKERMAN, A. "An unknown coin-type of Pella Decapoleos", LA 20, 1970, pp.353-358.

SPIJKERMAN, A. "The coins of the Decapolis and provincia Arabia", Jerusalem 1978, pp.210-217, 293, pls.46-47.

VLIET, N. van der "Monnaies inédites ou très rares du médaillier de Sainte-Anne de Jérusalem, RB 57, 1950, pp.252-253, pl.5/11.

WROTH, W. BMC, Galatia, Cappadocia and Syria, 1899, p.lxxxix.

Auction Catalogues and Price Lists

MÜNZEN UND MEDAILLEN, Basel 1978 (398), p.1, no. 5.

SCHLESSINGER, F. (price list), Amsterdam 1938 (9), p.2, no. 626.

PETRA

ARIEL, T.D. "A survey of coin finds in Jerusalem", LA 32, 1982, pp.292, 318.

BABELON, J. "Catalogue de la collection de Luynes", vol. IV, Paris 1936, p.55, no. 3507, pl.130.

BARAG, D. "Tyrian currency in Galilee", INJ 6-7, 1982/3, pp.9, 11.

BARAMKI, D.C. "Note on a cemetery at Karm-ak-Shaikh, Jerusalem. Summary of coins found", QDAP 1, 1931/2, p.7.

BEN-DAVID, A. "'Dinarei Arba' and silver coins called 'Harubim', ALON 5 (2), 1974, p.28 (Hebrew).

BEN-DOR, S. "Petra colonia", BERYTUS 9, 1947/8, pp.41-43, pl.14/1-5.

ECKHEL, J. "Doctrina numorum veterum..", vol. III, Vienna 1794, pp.503-504.

HANSON, R.S. "Meiron coins: 1974-75", AASOR 43, 1976, p.99.

HANSON, R.S. "Tyrian influence in the Upper Galilee", Cambridge 1980, p.52.

HEAD, B.V. "Historia numorum", Oxford 1911, p.812.

HILL, G.F. BMC, Arabia, Mesopotamia and Persia, 1922, pp.xxxvii-xxxix, pp.34-36, pl.5/10-15.

HILL, G.F. "Greek coins acquired by the British Museum in 1923", NC, 5th ser. 4, 1924, pp.16-17.

PETRA

KINDLER, A. "Thesaurus of Judaean coins from the fourth century B.C. to the third century A.D.", Jerusalem 1958, nos. 43, 44 (Hebrew).

KINDLER, A. "The status of cities in Syro-Palestinian area as reflected by their coins", INJ 6-7, 1982/3, pp.82, 84.

KINDLER, A. "The coinage of Bostra", Warminster, England 1983, pp.16, 25, 36, 37, 38, 39, 52, 56, 78, 98, 142, 145.

KIRKBRIDE, A.S. "Currencies in Tansjordan", PEQ 1939, p.155.

KIRKBRIDE, A.S. "Some rare coins from Transjordan", BASOR 106, 1947, p.8, figs. 3-4/4-5.

KLIMOWSKY, E.W. "The monetary function of city coins, International numismatic convention in Jerusalem (1963), proceedings (A. Kindler, ed.), Tel-Aviv 1967, pp.164, 166, 172.

KNOBLOCH, F. "Inedited and rare coins of Petra in Arabia", Numismatic Review 3 (1), 1946, New York, p.13.

MACDONALD, G. "Catalogue of Greek coins in the Hunterian collection", Glasgow 1905, vol. III, p.300.

MESHORER, Y. "The city coins of Eretz-Israel and the Decapolis in the Roman period", Jerusalem 1984, pp.106, 122-123 (Hebrew.

MIONNET, T.E. "Description de médailles antiques, grecques et romaines", Paris 1806-1837, vol. V, pp.587-589, vol. VIII, suppl., pp.387-388.

NEGEV, A. "Kurnub", Bible et Terre Sainte 90, 1967, p.17.

NEGEV, A. "Seal impressions from Tomb 107 at Kurnub (Mampsis)", IEJ 19 (2), 1969, pp.90, 94, 103.

PATIN, C. "Imperatorum Romanorum numismata ex aere mediae et minimae formae descripta et enarrata..", Amsterdam(?), 1671, p.200.

PATRICH, J. "Prohibition of a graven-image among the Nabateans - the testimony of the Massebot-cult", CATHEDRA 26, 1982, p.66 (Hebrew).

PLANT, R. "Greek coin types and their identification", London 1979, no. 609.

PRICE, M.J. and TRELL, B.L. "Coins and their cities", London 1977, pp.156, 285, fig. 274.

REED, W.L. "The excavation at Dibon (Dhibān) in Moab. The second campaign, 1952. The coins", AASOR 36-37, 1964, p.61/3, pl.82/5.

ROBINSON, E.S.G. "Coins from Petra, etc.", NC, 5th ser. 16, 1936, pp.288-291.

ROSENBERGER, M. "The coinage of Eastern Palestine", Jerusalem 1978, pp.61-66.

SAULCY, F. de "Numismatique de la Terre Sainte", Paris 1874, p.351-353, pl.20/1-6.

SEAR, D.R. "Greek imperial coins and their values", London 1982, nos. 1254, 1511, 1714, 2065, 2281, 2698, 2906, 3137.

SESTINI, D. "Classes generales geographiae numismaticae sev monetae urbium, populorum et regum..", Lipsiae 1797, part I, p.73.

SESTINI, D. "Classes generales sev moneta vetus urbium, populorum et regum..", Florentiae 1821, p.156.

PETRA

SESTINI, D. "Descrizione delle medaglie antiche Greche del Museo Hedervariano", part 3, Firenze 1829, p.123.

SNG ANS part 6, "Palestine - South Arabia", 1981, pl.47/1359-1377.

SNG DNM "Palestine-Characene", 1961, pl.5/150.

SPIJKERMAN, A. "The coins of Decapolis and provincia Arabia", Jerusalem 1978, pp.218-241, 276, 296, pls.48-53.

TIEPOLO, L. and F. "Musei Theupoli antiqua numismata..", Venetiis 1736, series 6, pp.879, 999.

VAILLANT, J. "Numismata imperatorum, augustarum et caesarum a populis Romanae ditionis Graece loquentibus..", Paris 1698, pp.36, 61, 100, 246, 254, 478.

VLIET, N. van der "Monnaies inédites ou très rares du médaillier de Sainte-Anne de Jérusalem", RB 57, 1950, pp.127-129, pl.3/28-30.

Auction Catalogues and Price Lists

AGORA Tel-Aviv 1975 (2), nos. 236-237, pl.10.

BETTER Haifa 1972 (1), nos. 276-278.
Haifa 1972 (2), nos. 371-373.
Haifa 1973 (4), nos. 270-273.
Jaffo 1974 (7), nos. 279-282.
Haifa 1974 (8), nos. 184-186.

CAHN, A.E. Frankfurt 1931 (71), p.69, no. 1122, pl.33/1121.

EIDELSTEIN AND HOLLAND Haifa, 10 Nov. 1975, no. 175.

GANS, E. "Numismatic Fine Arts", (Stock cat.), New York 1943 (2), pp.25 (7316), 26 (6322).

GLENDINING London, 10 March 1965, p.23, nos. 181-183, pl.6.

HOLZER, H. "The Thomas Ollive Mabbott collection", part I, New York 1969, p.112, nos. 2878-2881.

MALTER, J.L. "Journal of Numismatic Fine Arts", Encino, CA, USA 1973 (2/2), p.37/B 80, pl.11.

MONNAIES ET MÉDAILLES, Basel 1966 (32), p.51, nos. 512-517, pl.30.

MÜNZZENTRUM KÖLN, 1979 (36), p.28, no. 187.

RAUCH, H.D. Wien 1985 (34), no. 258.

SCHLESSINGER, F. (price list), Amsterdam 1938 (9), p.5, nos. 697-700.

SEABY London 1961 (513), p.73, no. A 167.
1968 (604), p.433, no. A 934,
1969 (616), p.437, no. A 1146.
1972 (647), p.279, no. A 836.

SPINK AND SON London 1932 (40/1), no. 12411.
1970 (78/11), no. 12425.
1974 (82/7-8), no. 6116.

STERNBERG, F. Zürich, 25-26 Nov. 1976, p.87, nos. 674-676, pl.28.

SUPERIOR STAMP AND COIN CO., Los-Angeles, June 1976, p.28, nos. 316-317.

TAMAR Tel-Aviv 1975 (9), p.8, nos. 178-179.
Tel-Aviv 1975 (10), p.10, nos. 164-166.
Ramat-Gan, Israel 1976 (11), p.11, no. 147.
Ramat-Gan, Israel 1976 (12), p.53, no. 890.

PHILADELPHIA

ARIEL, D.T. "A survey of coin finds in Jerusalem", _LA_ 32, 1982, pp.292, 317.

BARAG, D. "Tyrian currency in Galilee", _INJ_ 6-7, 1982/3, p.11.

BARAMKI, D.C. "The coins exhibited in the Archaeological Museum of the American University of Beirut", Beirut 1968, p.76/258, pl.7.

BELLINGER, A. "Coins from Jerash 1928-1934", _NNM_ 81, 1938, pp.9, 31, no. 48.

BREZINA, A. "Darstellung von Meteoriten auf antiken Münzen", _Monatsblatt der numismatischen Gesellschaft in Wien_ 70, 1889, p.314, fig. 8.

CARRADICE, I. "Coinage in Judaea in the Flavian period, AD 70-96", _INJ_ 6-7, 1982/3, p.17.

DECLOEDT, A. "Monnaies de Syrie (Dora, Philadelphie, Nabatéenne, moules araméen et arabe)", _RN_, 4th ser. 15, 1911, p.367.

ECKHEL, J. "Catalogus Musei Caesarei Vondobonensis numorum veterum..", Vindobonae 1779, part I, p.238.

ECKHEL, J. "Doctrina numorum veterum..", vol. III, Vienna 1794, p.351.

FLESCH, M. "Group of city coins", in 'Collector's choice', Bezalel National Museum, Jerusalem 1964, p.15/73.

FRANCESCO DE DOMINICIS "Repertorio numismatico", Napoli 1826, t.I, pp.203, 571.

FROELICH, E. "Quatuor tentamina in re numaria vetere", 2nd ed., Viennae 1737, pp.192, 195.

GESSNER, J.J. "Numismata antiqua Imperatorum Romanorum latina et graeca..", Tiguri (Zürich), 18th cent., pls.70/49; 103/16.

HADIDI, A. "Some bronze coins from Amman", ADAJ 18, 1973, p.52, pl.32/1-2.

HAMBURGER, L. "Die beiden palästinensischen Münzstätten Nikopolis-Emmaus", (Sonder-Abdruck aus den Frankfurter Münzblättern 1, 1899, nos. 8, 9), p.13.

HARDING, G.L. "A roman tomb in Amman", ADAJ 1, 1951, p.33.

HEAD, B.V. "Historia numorum", Oxford 1911, p.787.

HILL, G.F. BMC, Arabia, Mesopotamia and Persia, 1922, pp.xxxix-xli, pp.37-41, pl.6/1-13.

IMHOOF-BLUMER, F. "Zur griechischen und römischen Münzkunde, II", SNR 14, 1908, p.128.

KADMAN, L. and KINDLER, A. "Coins in Palestine throughout the ages", Tel-Aviv 1963, p.40, pl.18/8 (Hebrew).

KINDLER, A. "Thesaurus of Judaean coins from the fourth century B.C. to the third century A.D.", Jerusalem 1958, no. 46 (Hebrew).

KINDLER, A. "New types of Palestinian city-coins" ALON 4 (3), 1970, pp.47-48, pl.4/2 (Hebrew).

KINDLER, A. "The coinage of Bostra", Warminster, England 1983, pp.16, 36, 37, 38, 55, 58, 67.

PHILADELPHIA

KIRKBRIDE, A.S. "Currencies in Transjordan", PEQ 1939, p.155.

KLIMOWSKY, E.W. "The monetary function of city coins", International numismatic convention in Jerusalem (1963), proceedings (A. Kindler, ed.), Tel-Aviv 1967, pp.150, 160, 162, 164, 166, 170, 172.

LAMBERT, C. "Coins in the Palestine Museum, II", QDAP 1, 1931/2, p.138, pl.56/32-33.

MATSSON, G.O. The gods, goddesses and heroes on the ancient coins of Bible Lands", Stockholm 1969, pp.32, 56, 109, 202, 209-210, 218, pls.2/24; 3/42; 4/62b.

MESHORER, Y. "The 'Cista Mystica' and worship of Kore-Persephone at Samaria", EI 15, 1981, p.356, pl.70/4 (Hebrew).

MESHORER, Y. "The city coins of Eretz-Israel and the Decapolis in the Roman period", Jerusalem 1984, pp.96, 121-122 (Hebrew).

MESHORER, Y. and SPAER, A. "Some additional apparently unpublished city coins", INJ 3, 1965/6, p.75.

MIONNET, T.E. "Description de médailles antiques, grecques et romaines", Paris 1806-1837, vol. V, pp.330-333, vol. VII (Notes et observ.), p.110, vol. VIII, suppl., pp.232-236.

NEGEV, A. "Seal impressions from Tomb 107 at Kurnub (Mampsis)", IEJ 19 (2), 1969, p.91.

PATIN, C. "Imperatorum Romanorum numismata ex aere mediae et minimae formae descripta et enarrata..", Amsterdam(?) 1671, p.200.

PRICE, M.J. and TRELL, B.L. "Coins and their cities", London 1977, p.285.

RIDER, G. le "Les ateliers monétaires de la côte Syrienne, Phénicienne, Palestinienne, Égyptienne et Cyrénéenne", Congresso Internazionale di numismatica (Roma 1961), vol. I, Relazioni, Roma 1961, p.87.

ROSENBERGER, M. "The coinage of Eastern Palestine", Jerusalem 1978, pp.66-74.

SAULCY, F. de "Numismatique de la Terre Sainte", Paris 1874, pp.386-392, pl.22/3-9.

SEAR, D.R. "Greek imperial coins and their values", London 1982, nos. 781, 796, 879, 1255, 1525, 1688, 1715, 1880, 2066, 3138, 5220.

SESTINI, D. "Classes generales geographiae numismaticae sev monetae urbium, populorum et regum..", Lipsiae 1797, part I, p.68.

SESTINI, D. "Lettere e dissertazioni numismatiche..", t.IX, Firenze 1820, pp.90-94.

SESTINI, D. "Classes generales sev moneta vetus urbium, populorum et regum..", Florentiae 1821, p.144.

SESTINI, D. "Descrizione delle medaglie antiche Greche del Museo Hedervariano", part 3, Firenze 1829, pp.75-76, pl.31/7.

SEYRIG, H. "Antiquités Syriennes, 10. Note sur le culte de Déméter en Palestine", SYRIA 13, 1932, p.357.

SNG ANS part 6, "Palestine - South Arabia", 1981, pls.47-48, nos. 1378-1401.

PHILADELPHIA

SNG DNM "Syria, Cities", 1959, pl.12/451-454.

SPIJKERMAN, A. "An unknown coin-type of Pella Decapoleos", LA 20, 1970, pp.355-356.

SPIJKERMAN, A. "Cafarnao III. Catalogo delle monete della città", Jerusalem 1975, p.51/436.

SPIJKERMAN, A. "The coins of the Decapolis and provincia Arabia", Jerusalem 1978, pp.242-257, 297, pls.54-57.

TIEPOLO, L. and F. "Musei Theupoli antiqua numismata..", Venetiis 1736, series 6, pp.782, 902.

VAILLANT, J. "Numismata imperatorum, augustarum et caesarum a populis Romanae ditionis Graece loquentibus..", Paris 1698, p.20, 23, 25, 30, 38, 50, 64, 73, 251, 273, 377-378.

VLIET, N. van der "Monnaies inédites ou très rares du médaillier de Sainte-Anne de Jérusalam", RB 57, 1950, pp.253-258, pl.5/12-15.

WIZCAY, C.M. "Musei Hedervarii numi antiqui..", Vindibonae 1814, part I, p.279/6034.

WROTH, M. BMC, Galatia, Cappadocia and Syria, 1899, pp.lxxxix-xci, p.306, pl.38/9-10.

ZAYADINE, F. "A Greek inscription from the forum of Amman-Philadelphia, A.D.189", ADAJ 14, 1969, p.34.

Auction Catalogues and Price Lists

AGORA Tel-Aviv 1974 (1), p.27, nos. 170-171, pl.10.
1975 (2), nos. 231-232, pl.10.

BETTER Haifa 1972 (1), nos. 279-282.
Haifa 1972 (2), no. 374.
Haifa 1973 (4), no. 282.
Jaffo 1974 (7), nos. 283-284, 291.
Haifa 1974 (8), nos. 175, 187.

BUTTON, E. (price list), Frankfurt 1938 (35), p.5, no.3065.

GANS, E. "Numismatic Fine Arts", (Stock cat.), New York 1943 (2), p.21, no. 6321.

GANS, E. "Numismatic Fine Arts", Berkeley CA, USA 1956 (20), p.16, no. 4990.

GLENDINING London, 10 March 1965, pp.22-23, nos. 176-177, pl.6.

HESS-LEU Luzern 1965 (28), p.42, no. 301, pl.13.

HOLZER, H. "The Thomas Ollive Mabbott collection", part I, New York 1969, p.104, nos. 2666-2671.

MALTER, J.L. "Journal of Numismatic Fine Arts", Encino CA, USA 1973 (2/2), p.37/B 81.

MONNAIES ET MÉDAILLES, Basel 1966 (32), p.52, nos. 518-522, pl.30.

MÜNZEN UND MEDAILLEN, Basel 1955 (152), p.12, no. 238.
1969 (305), p.3, no. 49.
1984 (468), p.14, no. 175.

MÜNZZENTRUM KÖLN, 1979 (36), p.29, nos. 190-193.

RAUCH, H.D. Wien 1985 (34), no. 259.

SALTON-SCHLESSINGER, M.M. (price list), New York 1958 (27), p.7, no. 136.

PHILADELPHIA

SCHLESSINGER, F. (price list), Amsterdam 1938 (9), p.2, nos.627-633.

SCHULMAN, H.M.F., New York, 14-15 Dec. 1970, p.18, no. 967.

SEABY London 1960 (510), p.461, no. A 961.
1969 (616), p.438, no. A 1174.

SPINK AND SON London 1902 (10/116), nos. 85073-85075.
1905 (13/149), nos. 13832-13834.
1932 (40/1), nos. 12412-12413.
1934 (42/10), nos. 36198-36200.
1971 (79/6), p.252, no. 6612.
1977 (85/7), p.318, no. 6647.

STERNBERG, F. Zürich, 25-26 Nov. 1976, pp.87-88, nos. 677-681, pls. 28-29.

SUPERIOR STAMP AND COIN CO., Los-Angeles, June 1976, pp.28-29, nos. 318-321.

TAMAR Ramat-Gan, Israel 1976 (11), p.11, nos. 148-149.

PHILIPPOPOLIS

ARRIGONI, O. "Numismata quaedam cujuscunque formae..", Tarvisii, part I, 1741, Numismata in coloniis percussa a J. Vaillant non relata, pl.11/167.

BELLINGER, A.R. "Coins from Jerash 1928-1934", NNM 81, 1938, p.9, 26-27, nos. 29-31.

BEN-DAVID, A. "'Dinarei Arba' and silver coins called 'Harubim'", ALON 5 (2), 1974, p.28 (Hebrew).

BENTINCK, de "Catalogue d'une collection de médailles antiques", Amsterdam 1788, suppl., p.105.

ECKHEL, J. Doctrina numorum veterum..", vol. III, Vienna 1794, p.504.

HEAD, B.V. "Historia numorum", Oxford 1911, p.812.

HILL, G.F. BMC, Arabia, Mesopotamia and Persia, 1922, pp.xli-xlii, pp.42-43, pl.6/14-17.

KINDLER, A. "The status of cities in the Syro-Palestinian area as reflected by their coins", INJ 6-7, 1982/3, p.82.

KINDLER, A. "The coinage of Bostra", Warminster, England 1983, pp.37, 38, 141.

KIRKBRIDE, A.S. "Currencies in Transjordan", PEQ 1939, p.155.

KUBITSCHEK, W. "Zur Geschichte von Städten des römischen Kaiserreiches. Epigraphisch-numismatische Studien", heft 1, Wien 1916, p.41.

MACDONALD, G. "Catalogue of Greek coins in the Hunterian collection", Glasgow 1905, vol. III, p.300, pl.78/23.

PHILIPPOPOLIS

MESHORER, Y. "The city coins of Eretz-Israel and the Decapolis in the Roman period", Jerusalem 1984, pp.70, 118 (Hebrew).

MIONNET, T.E. "Description de médailles antiques, grecques et romaines", Paris 1806-1837, vol. V, p.589; vol. VIII, suppl., p.388.

PLANT, R. "Greek coin types and their identification", London 1979, nos. 137, 597.

ROSENBERGER, M. "The coinage of Eastern Palestine", Jerusalem 1978, p.74.

SAULCY, F. de "Numismatique de la Terre Sainte", Paris 1874, pp.395-398, pl.24/1-4.

SEAR, D.R. "Greek imperial coins and their values", London 1982, nos. 3969, 4064, 4156, 4161.

SEQUIN, P. "Selecta numismata antiqua", Paris 1684, p.182.

SESTINI, D. "Classes generales geographiae numismaticae sev monetae urbium, populorum et regum..", Lipsiae 1797, part II, p.104.

SESTINI, D. "Classes generales sev moneta vetus urbium, populorum et regum..", Florentiae 1821, p.156.

SNG ANS part 6, "Palestine - South Arabia", 1981, pls.48-49, nos. 1402-1412.

SNG DNM "Palestine-Characene", 1961, pl.5/151-152.

SPIJKERMAN, A. "The coins of the Decapolis and provincia Arabia", Jerusalem 1978, pp.258-261, 298, pl.58.

STEVENSON, S.W. "A dictionary of Roman coins", London 1964 (rp), p.624.

TIEPOLO, L. and F. "Musei Theupoli antiqua numismata..", Venetiis 1736, series 4, pp.743, 749.

VAILLANT, J. "Numismata aera imperatorum, augustarum et caesarum in coloniis, municipiis et urbibus..", Paris 1688, part II, pp.249-250, 274.

WADDINGTON, W.-H. "Sur l'emplacement de Philippopolis d'Arabie et sur les médailles de Marin et de Pacatien", _RN,_ Ns 10, 1865, pp.56-66.

WEBSTER, W. "List of unedited Greek coins - copper", _NC,_ Ns 1873, p.40.

Auction Catalogues and Price Lists

AGORA Tel-Aviv 1975 (2), nos. 214-215, pl.9.

HOLZER, H. "The Thomas Ollive Mabbott collection", part I, New York 1969, p.112, nos. 2882-2884.

MONNAIES ET MÉDAILLES, Basel 1966 (32), p.52, no. 523, pl.30.

RIGO Nürnberg 1959 (40), p.16, no. 340.

SEABY London 1969 (616), p.439, no. A 1183.
1977 (702), p.68, no. C 118.

SPINK AND SON London 1932 (40/1), no. 12414.
1973 (81/4), p.156, no. 2953.

STERNBERG, F. Zürich, 25-26 Nov. 1976, p.88, no. 682, pl.29.

RABBAT-MOBA

BELLINGER, A.R. "The excavations at Dura-Europos. Final report VI. The coins", New Haven, USA 1949, p.87/1856.

BEN-DAVID, A. "'Dinarei Arba' and silver coins called 'Harubim'", ALON 5 (2), 1974, p.28 (Hebrew).

ECKHEL, J. "Doctrina numorum veterum..", vol. III, Vienna 1794, pp.504-505.

HEAD, B.V. "Historia numorum", Oxford 1911, p.812.

HILL, G.F. BMC, Arabia, Mesopotamia and Persia, 1922, pp.xlii-xliv, p.44, pl.7/1-2.

KINDLER, A. "The coinage of Bostra", Warminster, England 1983, pp.16, 37, 38, 53, 54, 142, 144.

KIRKBRIDE, A.S. "Currencies in Transjordan", PEQ 1939, p.155.

KLAWANS, Z.H. "An outline of ancient coins", Wisconsin, USA 1959, p.134.

KLIMOWSKY, E.W. "The monetary function of city coins", International numismatic convention in Jerusalem (1963), proceedings (A. Kindler, ed.), Tel-Aviv 1967, pp.166, 172.

MATSSON, G.O. "The gods, goddesses and heroes on the ancient coins of Bible Lands", Stockholm 1969, pp.19, 20, 198, p.1/11.

MESHORER, Y. "The city coins of Eretz-Israel and the Decapolis in the Roman period", Jerusalem 1984, pp.102, 122 (Hebrew).

MIONNET, T.E. "Description de médailles antiques, grecques et romaines", Paris 1806-1837, vol. V, pp.590-591, vol. VIII, suppl., pp.388-389.

NEGEV, A. "Kurnub", Bible et Terre Sainte 90, 1967, p.17.

NEGEV, A. "Seal impressions from Tomb 107 at Kurnub (Mampsis)", IEJ 19 (2), 1969, pp.93, 96-97, 104.

PRICE, M.J. and TRELL, B.L. "Coins and their cities", London 1977, pp.166, 285, fig. 419.

ROSENBERGER, M. "The coinage of Eastern Palestine", Jerusalem 1978, pp.74-78.

SAULCY, F. de "Numismatique de la Terre Sainte", Paris 1874, pp.354-358, pl.20/7-12.

SEAR, D.R. "Greek imperial coins and their values", London 1982, nos. 2282, 2466, 2699, 2907, 3139.

SESTINI, D. "Classes generales geographiae numismaticae sev monetae urbium, populorum et regum..", Lipsiae 1797, part I, p.73, part II, p.104.

SESTINI, D. "Classes generales sev moneta vetus urbium, populorum et regum..", Florentiae 1821, p.156.

SESTINI, D. "Descrizione delle medaglie antiche Greche del Museo Hedervariano", part 3, Firenze 1829, p.123, pl.32/2.

SEYRIG, H. "Antiquités Syriennes, 3. Numismatique supposée de Chalcis au Liban", SYRIA 12, 1931, p.324.

SEYRIG, H. "Antiquités Syriennes, 89. Les dieux armés et les Arabes en Syrie. (4. Les dieux armés hors de Palmyre)", SYRIA 47, 1970, p.96, fig. 17.

RABBAT-MOBA

SNG ANS part 6, "Palestine - South Arabia", 1981, pl.49/1413-1420.

SPIJKERMAN, A. "The coins of the Decapolis and provincia Arabia", Jerusalem 1978, pp.262-277, 299, pls.59-62.

TIEPOLO, L. and F. "Musei Theupoli antiqua numismata..", Venetiis 1736, series 6, p.999.

VAILLANT, J. "Numismata imperatorum, augustarum et caesarum a populis Romanae ditionis Graece loquentibus..", Paris 1698, pp.100, 130, 188, 247, 366-367.

VLIET, N. van der "Monnaies inédites ou très rares du médaillier de Saint-Anne de Jérusalem", _RB_ 57, 1950, p.129, pl.3/31.

Auction Catalogues and Price Lists

AGORA Tel-Aviv 1974 (1), p.27, no. 173, pl.10.
1975 (2), no. 235, pl.10.

BETTER Haifa 1972 (1), nos. 283-284.

CAHN, A.E. Frankfurt 1931 (71), p.69, no. 1123, pl.33.

GLENDINING London, 10 March 1965, pp.23(nos.184-186), 27(no.220), pls.6, 8.

HOLZER, H. "The Thomas Ollive Mabbott collection", part I, New York 1969, p.112, no. 2885.

MALTER, J.L. "Journal of Numismatic Fine Arts", Encino, CA, USA 1973 (2/2), p.37/B 82.

MONNAIES ET MÉDAILLES, Basel 1966 (32), p.52, nos. 524-525, pl.30.

MÜNZEN UND MEDAILLEN, Basel 1980 (424), p.17, no. 208.
1981 (436), p.14, no. 161.

SEABY London 1958 (476), p.20, no. AG 86.

STERNBERG, F. Zürich, 25-26 Nov. 1976, p.90, no. 698, pl.30.

SUPERIOR STAMP AND COIN CO., Los-Angeles, June 1976, p.29, nos. 328-329.

TAMAR Ramat-Gan, Israel 1976 (11), p.11, no. 150.
Ramat-Gan, Israel 1976 (12), p.53, no. 889a.

RAPHIA

ANONYMOUS — CH 1, 1975, p.34/124.

ARIEL, D.T. — "A survey of coin finds in Jerusalem", LA 32, 1982, p.318.

BARAMKI, D.C. — "The coin collection of the American University of Beirut Museum. Palestine and Phoenicia", Beirut 1974, p.68.

BARAMKI, J. — "Coins in the Palestine Archaeological Museum, III", QDAP 8, 1939, p.79, pl.41/12.

BELLINGER, A.R. — "The Syrian tetradrachms of Caracalla and Macrinus", ANS NS 3, 1940, p.13.

BELLINGER, A.R. — "The excavations at Dura-Europos. Final report VI. The coins", New Haven, USA 1949, p.89/1897.

BERNHART, M. — "Dionysos und seine Familie auf griechischen Münzen", JNG 1, 1949, pp.64/211-212; 123/955-956; 135/1079.

CARSON, R.A.G. — "The inflation of the Third Century and its monetary influence in the Near East", International numismatic convention in Jerusalem (1963), proceedings (A. Kindler, ed.), Tel-Aviv 1967, p.242.

ECKHEL, J. — "Doctrina numorum veterum..", vol. III, Vienna 1794, pp.454-455.

FORRER, L. — "The Weber collection, vol. III, part 2: Greek coins", London 1929, p.800/8123, pl.299.

GESSNER, J.J. — "Numismata antiqua Imperatorum Romanorum latina et graeca..", Tiguri (Zürich), 18th cent., pl.127/85.

HAMBURGER, A. "Gems from Caesarea Maritima", ATIQOT, Es 8, 1968, p.9/52-53.

HAMBURGER, L. "Die beiden palästinensischen Münzstätten Nikopolis-Emmaus", (Sonder-Abdruck aus dem Frankfurter Münzblättern 1, 1899, nos. 8, 9), p.10, pl.7/15-16.

HARDUIN, J. "Nummi antiqui populorum et urbium illustrati", Parisiis 1684, pp.417-418.

HEAD, B.V. "Historia numorum", Oxford 1911, p.806.

HENDIN, D. "Guide to ancient Jewish coins", New York 1976, p.116, pl.9/269.

HENDIN, D. "Coins of ancient Israel", SHEKEL 11 (6), 1978, p.28.

HILL, G.F. "Some Palestinian cults in the Graeco-Roman age", Proceedings of the British Academy, vol. V, London 1912, p.415, pl./4.

HILL, G.F. BMC, Palestine, 1914, pp.lxxxi-lxxxiii, pp.171-174, pl.18/1-13.

JANIS, E. "The other coin cities of Israel", SHEKEL 3 (3), 1970, p.15.

JONAS, R. "Mythology on Palestinian coins", internal circular no. 2, Israel Num. Society, Haifa branch, 1959, p.4.

KADMAN, L. and KINDLER, A. "Coins in Palestine throughout the ages", Tel-Aviv 1963, p.35, pl.15/21-22 (Hebrew).

KINDLER, A. "Thesaurus of Judaean coins from the fourth century B.C. to the third century A.D.", Jerusalem 1958, no. 30 (Hebrew).

RAPHIA

KINDLER, A. "A new coin-type of Raphiah", ALON 3 (1), 1968, p.20, pl.1/13 (Hebrew).

KINDLER, A. "Coins of the land of Israel. Bank of Israel collection", Jerusalem 1971, p.139, no. 207 (Hebrew).

KINDLER, A. "The status of cities in the Syro-Palestinian area as reflected by their coins", INJ 6-7, 1982/3, p.81.

KLAWANS, Z.H. "An outline of ancient Greek coins", Wisconsin, USA 1959, p.135.

KLIMOWSKY, E.W. "The monetary function of city coins", International numismatic convention in Jerusalem (1963), proceedings (A. Kindler, ed.), Tel-Aviv 1967, pp.164, 166, 168, 172, 177.

KLIMOWSKY, E.W. "Roman imperial 'Virtutes' on contemporaneous city coins", in "On ancient Palestinian and other coins, their symbolism and metrology", PINS 7, Tel-Aviv 1974, pp.87, 91, 96, 98, pl.7/51. Same in INJ 3, 1965/6, pp.15, 18, 23, 25, pl.6/51.

LAMBERT, C. "Coins in the Palestine Museum, II", QDAP 1, 1931/2, pp.132-133, pl.54/10-12.

MANNS, F. "Gemmes de l'époque Gréco-Romaine provenant de Palestine", LA 28, 1978, pp.155, 164, pls. 25/6; 30/46-47.

MATSSON, G.O. "The gods, goddesses and heroes on the ancient coins of Bible Lands", Stockholm 1969, pp.125, 222, pl.5/73.

MESHORER, Y. "Monnaies de Raphia", RN, 6th ser. 18, 1976, pp.57-68, pls.3-7.

MESHORER, Y. "The city coins of Eretz-Israel and the Decapolis in the Roman period", Jerusalem 1984, pp.32, 113 (Hebrew).

MIONNET, T.E. "Description de médailles antiques, grecques et romaines", Paris 1806-1837, vol. V, pp.551-552, vol. VIII, suppl., pp.376-377.

PLANT, R. "Greek coin types and their identification", London 1979, no. 506.

REICHARDT, H.C. "Unpublished Greek Imperial coins", NC, Ns 2, 1862, p.122.

ROSENBERGER, M. "City-coins of Palestine", vol. III, Jerusalem 1977, pp.48-53, 86.

SAULCY, F. de "Numismatique de la Terre Sainte", Paris 1874, pp.237-240, pl.12/7-9.

SEAR, D.R. "Greek imperial coins and their values", London 1982, nos. 1718, 2061, 2277, 3129, 3379, 3787, 3967, 4154.

SESTINI, D. "Descriptio numorum veterum..", Lipsiae 1796, pp.546-547.

SESTINI, D. "Classes generales geographiae numismaticae sev monetae urbium, populorum et regum..", Lipsiae 1797, part I, p.71.

SESTINI, D. "Classes generales sev moneta vetus urbium, populorum et regum..", Florentiae 1821, p.152.

SESTINI, D. "Descrizione delle medaglie antiche Greche de Museo Hedervariano", part 3, Firenze 1829, p.116, pl.31/19.

RAPHIA

SNG ANS — part 6, "Palestine - South Arabia", 1981, pl.35/1060-1066.

SNG DNM — "Palestine-Characene", 1961, pl.2/55.

SPERBER, D. — "Roman Palestine 200-400. Money and prices", Jerusalem 1974, p.143.

STAHL, Z. — "The Flavian Emperors and their coins in Eretz-Israel", special brochure of Israel Num. Society, Tel-Aviv branch, 1976, p.7 (Hebrew).

VAILLANT, J. — "Numismata imperatorum, augustarum et caesarum a populis Romanae ditionis Graece loquentibus..", Paris 1698, pp.83, 130, 247, 367-368.

WALCHER de MOLTHEIN, L. "Catalogue de la collection des medailles grecques de M. Le Chevalier", Paris-Vienne 1895, p.273, no. 3209, pl.30/3209.

<u>Auction Catalogues and Price Lists</u>

BETTER — Haifa 1972 (1), nos. 225-228.
Haifa 1972 (2), no. 301.
Jaffo 1974 (7), nos. 256-262.

CAHN, A.E. — Frankfurt 1931 (71), p.68, nos. 1117-1119, pl.33.

HOLZER, H. — "The Thomas Ollive Mabbott collection", part I, New York 1969, p.106, 2723.

MALTER, J.L. — "Journal of Numismatic Fine Arts", Encino, CA, USA 1973 (2/2), p.37/B 83.

MONNAIES ET MÉDAILLES, Basel 1954 (13), p.72, no. 938, pl.34.
1966 (32), p.46, no. 437.

MÜNZEN UND MEDAILLEN, Basel 1958 (176), p.4, no. 58.

SCHLESSINGER, F. (price list), Amsterdam 1938 (9), p.4, no. 691.

SUPERIOR STAMP AND COIN CO., Los-Angeles, June 1976, p.29, no. 330.

TAMAR Tel-Aviv 1975 (9), p.7, no. 155.
Tel-Aviv 1975 (10), p.10, nos. 151-153.
Ramat-Gan, Israel 1976 (11), p.11, nos. 139-140.

SEBASTE

ANGLO-JEWISH HISTORICAL EXHIBITION, Catalogue, London 1888, p.161, no. 2353 (3846).

ANONYMOUS "Roman legionary coins", INJ 1963 (4), p.88.

ARIEL, D.T. "A survey of coin finds in Jerusalem", LA 32, 1982, p.318.

BARAG, D. "The countermarks of the Legio Decima Fretensis", International numismatic convention in Jerusalem (1963), proceedings (A. Kindler, ed.), Tel-Aviv 1967, pp.119, 120, 121, 124.

BARAG, D. "Tyrian currency in Galilee", INJ 6-7, 1982/3, p.11.

BARAMKI, D.C. "The coin collection of the American University of Beirut Museum, Palestine and Phoenicia", Beirut 1974, pp.32-33, pls.6/7-10.

BARAMKI, J. "Coins in the Palestine Archaeological Museum, III", QDAP 8, 1939, pp.79-80, pl.41/15-17.

BELLINGER, A.R. "The Syrian tetradrachms of Caracalla and Macrinus", ANS NS 3, 1940, p.13.

BERNHART, M. "Dionysos und seine Familie auf griechischen Münzen", JNG 1, 1949, p.143, no. 1184.

CARRADICE, I. "Coinage in Judaea in the Flavian period, A.D. 70-96", INJ 6-7, 1982/3, p.17, pl.2/11.

CARSON, R.A.G. "The inflation of the Third Century and its monetary influence in the Near East", International numismatic

CARSON, R.A.G. (con't) convention in Jerusalem (1963), proceedings (A. Kindler, ed.), Tel-Aviv 1967, p.242.

CHAIX, E. "Recherche des monnaies coloniales Romaines non décrites dans l'ouvrage de H. Cohen", ASFN 16, 1892, pp.223-224.

COHEN, H. "Médailles Imperiales", Leipzig 1930 (rp), vol. I, pp.532-533/750-755; vol. III, p.375/1188-1191; vol. IV, pp.135/336-338; 237-238/915-918; 286/310; 383/19; 398/70.

ECKHEL, J. "Doctrina numorum veterum..", vol. III, Vienna 1794, pp.440-441.

HARDUIN, J. "Nummi antiqui populorum et urbium illustrati", Parisiis 1684, p.443.

HEAD, B.V. "Historia numorum", Oxford 1911, p.803.

HENDIN, D. "Guide to ancient Jewish coins", New York 1976, p.107.

HENDIN, D. "Coins of ancient Israel", SHEKEL 11 (6), 1978, p.30.

HEYMANN, H. "Roman legionary coins from Phoenicia", INJ 1963 (3), p.49.

HILL, G.F. "Some Palestinian cults in the Graeco-Roman age", Proceedings of the British Academy, vol. V, London 1912, p.413.

HILL, G.F. BMC, Palestine, 1914, pp.xxxvii-xli, pp.78-81, pl.8/8-15.

JANIS, E. "The other coin cities of Israel", SHEKEL 3 (3), 1970, p.14.

SEBASTE

KADMAN, L. "When was Aelia Capitolina named 'Commodiana' and by whom?" IEJ 9 (2), 1959, p.139 (note 18).

KADMAN, L. "Numismatic evidence of the architectonic revolution in the Second Century C.E.", INB 1962 (3-4), p.72. Heb. ed. p.65.

KADMAN, L. and KINDLER, A. "Coins in Palestine throughout the ages", Tel-Aviv 1963, pp.36-37, pl.16/11-15 (Hebrew).

KINDLER, A. "Thesaurus of Judaean coins from the fourth century B.C. to the third century A.D.", Jerusalem 1958, no. 31 (Hebrew).

KINDLER, A. "New types of Palestinian city-coins", ALON 3 (2), 1968, pp.50-51, pl.2/9 (Hebrew).

KINDLER, A. "The coin issues of the Roman administration in the provincia Judaea during the reign of Domitian", ALON 3 (4), 1969, p.92, pl.6/19 (Hebrew).

KINDLER, A. "The 'Damnatio memoriae' of Elagabal on city-coins of the Near East", SM 117, 1980, pp.4, 5, 6, 7, figs. 5-6, 9-10.

KINDLER, A. "The status of cities in the Syro-Palestinian area as reflected by their coins", INJ 6-7, 1982/3, pp.81, 85 (note 44).

KINDLER, A. "The coinage of Bostra", Warminster, England 1983, pp.28, 37, 64.

KLAWANS, Z.H. "An outline of ancient Greek coins", Wisconsin, USA 1959, p.138.

KLIMOWSKY, E.W. "The monetary function of city coins", International numismatic convention in Jerusalem (1963), proceedings

KLIMOWSKY, E.W. (con't) (A. Kindler, ed.), Tel-Aviv 1967, pp.132, 154, 155, 164, 166, 172.

KLIMOWSKY, E.W. "Roman imperial 'Virtutes' on contemporaneous city coins", in "On ancient Palestinian and other coins, their symbolism and metrology", PINS 7, Tel-Aviv 1974, pp.87, 95, pl.5/10-11. Same in INJ 3, 1965/6, pp.15, 22, pl.4/10-11.

KUBITSCHEK, W. "Zur Geschichte von Städten des römischen Kaiserreiches. Epigraphisch-numismatische Studien", heft 1, Wien 1916, pp.6, 14-15.

LAMBERT, C. "Coins in the Palestine Museum, II", QDAP 1, 1931/2, pp.134-135, pl.55/20.

MANNS, F. "Gemmes de l'époque Gréco-Romaine provenant de Palestine", LA 28, 1978, p.161, pl.28/34-35.

MATSSON, G.O. "The gods, goddesses and heroes on the ancient coins of Bible Lands", Stockholm 1969, pp.76, 159, 179, 216, 232, 239, pls.4/57a; 6/97; 7/110a.

MESHORER, Y. "The 'Cista Mystica' and worship of Kore-Persephone at Samaria", EI 15, 1981, pp.356-357, pl.70/2-3 (Hebrew).

MESHORER, Y. "The city coins of Eretz-Israel and the Decapolis in the Roman period", Jerusalem 1984, pp.43-45, 114-115 (Hebrew).

MIONNET, T.E. "Description de médailles antiques, grecques et romaines", Paris 1806-1837, vol. V, pp.513-516, vol. VIII, suppl., pp.356-359.

NEUMANN, F. "Populorum et regum numi veteres inediti..", part II, Vindobonae 1783, pp.82-84, pl.3/5.

SEBASTE

PRICE, M.J. and TRELL, B.L. "Coins and their cities", London 1977, p.283.

REICHARDT, H.C. "Unpublished Greek Imperial coins", NC, Ns 2, 1862, p.113.

RIDER, G. le "Les ateliers monétaires de la côte Syrienne, Phénicienne, Palestinienne, Égyptienne et Cyrénéenne", Congresso Internazionale di numismatica (Roma 1961), vol. I, Relazioni, Roma 1961, p.96.

ROSENBERGER, M. "City-coins of Palestine", vol. III, Jerusalem 1977, pp.54-60.

ROSENBERGER, M. "The coinage of Eastern Palestine", Jerusalem 1978, p.84.

SAULCY, F. de "Numismatique de la Terre Sainte", Paris 1874, pp.275-281, pl.14/4-7.

SEAR, D.R. "Greek imperial coins and their values", London 1982, nos. 883, 2687, 2902, 3218, 3257.

SESTINI, D. "Descriptio numorum veterum..", Lipsiae 1796, p.544.

SESTINI, D. "Classes generales geographiae numismaticae sev monetae urbium, populorum et regum..", Lipsiae 1797, part I, p.71.

SESTINI, D. "Classes generales sev moneta vetus urbium, populorum et regum..", Florentiae 1821, pp.150-151.

SESTINI, D. "Descrizione delle medaglie antiche Greche del Museo Hedervariano", part 3, Firenze 1829, p.110.

SEYRIG, H. "Antiquités Syriennes, 10. Note sur le culte de Deméter en Palestine", SYRIA 13, 1932, P.357.

SEYRIG, H. "Notes on Syrian coins", NNM 119, 1950, p.32.

SNG ANS part 6, "Palestine - South Arabia", 1981, pl.36/1067-1084.

SPERBER, D. "Roman Palestine 200-400. Money and prices", Jerusalem 1974, p.143.

SPIJKERMAN, A. "Herodion III. Catalogo delle monete", Jerusalem 1972, p.98.

SPIJKERMAN, A. and STARCKY, J. "Un nouveau lot de monnaies palestiniennes", RB 65, 1958, pp.569, 581-582, pl.20/81-87.

STAHL, Z. "The Flavian Emperors and their coins in Eretz-Israel", special brochure of Israel Num. Society, Tel-Aviv branch, 1976, p.7 (Hebrew).

STEVENSON, S.W. "A dictionary of Roman coins", London 1964 (rp), p.725.

SUTHERLAND, C.H.V. "The pattern of monetary development in Phoenicia and Palestine during the Early Empire", International numismatic convention in Jerusalem (1963), proceedings (A. Kindler, ed.), Tel-Aviv 1967, pp.94, 95, 98.

TIEPOLO, L. and F. "Musei Theupoli antiqua numismata..", Venetiis 1736, series 6, p.929.

VAILLANT, J. "Numismata aera imperatorum, augustarum et caesarum in coloniis, municipiis et urbibus..", Paris 1688, part II, pp.30-31.

VAILLANT, J. "Numismata imperatorum, augustarum et caesarum a populis Romanae ditionis Graece loquentibus...", Paris 1698, pp.16, 84, 110, 248, 369-371.

SEBASTE

VLIET, N. van der "Monnaies inédites ou très rares du médaillier de Sainte-Anne de Jérusalem", RB 58, 1950, pp.125-126, pl.3/26.

WICZAY, C.M. "Musei Hedervarii numi antiqui..", Vindobonae 1814, part I, p.288, nos. 6210-6211, pl.26/574.

Auction Catalogues and Price Lists

AGORA Tel-Aviv 1974 (1), p.22, no. 133, pl.8.
1975 (2), nos 183-185, pl.8.

BETTER Jaffo 1974 (7), no. 263.
Haifa 1974 (8), no. 155.

CAHN, A.E. Frankfurt 1931 (71), p.66, no. 1092, pl.32.

GANS, E. "Numismatic Fine Arts", (Mail bid sale) Berkeley CA, 1955 (15), p.23, no. 373.

GLENDINING London, 19 July 1950, p.46, no. 334.
10 March 1965, p.21, no. 160.

MALTER, J.L. "Journal of Numismatic Fine Arts", Encino CA, USA
1972 (1/5), p.100, no. A 19.
1973 (2/2), p.37/B 84, pl.11.

SCHLESSINGER, F. (price list), Amsterdam 1938 (9), p.3, no. 667.

SPINK AND SON London 1931 (39/9), nos. 10043/10044.
1936 (44/1), nos. 48037-48039.

STERNBERG, F. Zürich, 25-26 Nov. 1976, p.58, no. 455, pl.18; p.91, nos. 701-704, pl.30.

SUPERIOR STAMP AND COIN CO., Los-Angeles, June 1976, pp.29-30, nos. 331-335.

TAMAR Ramat-Gan, Israel 1976 (12), p.51, no. 852.

SEPPHORIS

ANONYMOUS SHEKEL 7 (3), 1974, p.15.

BARAG, D. "Tyrian currency in Galilee", INJ 6-7, 1982/3, pp.10, 11, 13.

BARAMKI, D.C. "The coins exhibited in the Archaeological Museum of the American University of Beirut", Beirut 1968, p.89/299-301, pl.8.

BARAMKI, D.C. "The coin collection of the American University of Beirut Museum. Palestine and Phoenicia", Beirut 1974, pp.1-2, pl.1/1-4.

BELLINGER, A.R. "Coins from Jerash 1928-1934", NNM 81, 1938, pp.9, 25, no. 24.

BELLINGER, A.R. "The Syrian tetradrachms of Caracalla and Macrinus", ANS NS 3, 1940, p.13.

CARSON, R.A.G. "The inflation of the Third Century and its monetary influence in the Near East", International numismatic convention in Jerusalem (1963), proceedings (A. Kindler, ed.), Tel-Aviv 1967, p.242.

ECKHEL, J. "Catalogus Musei Caesarei Vindobonensis numorum veterum..", Vindobonae 1779, part I, p.246, pl.4/13.

ECKHEL, J. "Doctrina numorum veterum..", vol. III, Vienna 1794, pp.425-426.

FLESCH, M. "Group of city coins", in 'Collector's choice', Bezalel National Museum, Jerusalem 1964, p.16/80.

GEIGER, J. "Sepphoris and the 'War of Qitos'", CATHEDRA 8, 1978, pp.69-70 (Hebrew).

HAMBURGER, H. "The coin issues of the Roman administration from the mint of Caesarea Maritima", <u>IEJ</u> 20 (1-2), 1970, pp.85-86, 89.

HAMBURGER, L. "Die Münzprägungen während des letzten Aufstandes der Israeliten gegen Rom", (Sonder-Abdruck aus der Zeitschrift für Numismatik 18, 1892), p.101.

HARDUIN, J. "Nummi antiqui populorum et urbium illustrati", Parisiis 1684, pp.449-450.

HEAD, B.V. "Historia numorum", Oxford 1911, p.802.

HENDIN, D. "Guide to ancient Jewish coins", New York, 1976, pp.100-101, pl.8/237-238.

HENDIN, D. "Coins of ancient Israel", <u>SHEKEL</u> 10 (6), 1977, p.21.

HILL, G.F. BMC, Palestine, 1914, pp.xi-xii, pp.1-4, pl.1/1-7.

JANIS, E. "The other coin cities of Israel", <u>SHEKEL</u> 3 (3), 1970, p.14.

KADMAN, L. and KINDLER, A. "Coins in Palestine throughout the ages", Tel-Aviv 1963, p.36, pl.16/8-10 (Hebrew).

KADMAN, L. "Numismatic evidence of the architectonic revolution in the Second Century C.E.", <u>INB</u> 1962 (3-4), p.72. Heb. ed. p.65.

KINDLER, A. "Thesaurus of Judaean coins from the fourth century B.C. to the third century A.D.", Jerusalem 1958, nos. 35-36 (Hebrew).

KINDLER, A. "Two remarks", <u>CATHEDRA</u> 8, 1978, pp.66-67 (Hebrew).

SEPPHORIS

KINDLER, A. "Coins of the land of Israel. Bank of Israel collection", Jerusalem 1971, p.136/205 (Hebrew).

KINDLER, A. "The status of cities in the Syro-Palestinian area as reflected by their coins", *INJ* 6-7, 1982/3, pp.80, 81, 82.

KINDLER, A. "The coinage of Bostra", Warminster, England 1983, pp.28, 61.

KIRKBRIDE, A.S. "Currencies in Transjordan", *PEQ* 1939, p.156.

KLIMOWSKY, E.W. "The monetary function of city coins", International numismatic convention in Jerusalem (1963), proceedings (A. Kindler, ed.), Tel-Aviv 1967, pp.144, 153, 154, 160, 162, 164, 166, 170, 172.

KUBITSCHEK, W. "Zur Geschichte von Städten des römischen Kaiserreiches. Epigraphisch-numismatische Studien", heft 1, Wien 1916, pp.73-80.

MACDONALD, G. "Catalogue of Greek coins in the Hunterian collection", Glasgow 1905, vol. III, p.275.

MANNS, F. "Gemmes de l'époque Gréco-Romaine provenant de Palestine", *LA* 28, 1978, p.158, pl.27/18.

MESHORER, Y. "Coins from the excavations at Khorazin", *EI* 11, 1973, p.158, pl.29/2 (Hebrew).

MESHORER, Y. "Coins of the Ancient World", Minneapolis 1975, p.68. Hebrew version (Jerusalem 1979), pp.55-56. Same in "Münzen, Zeugen der Vergangenheit", Zürich - Köln, 1979, pp.68, 73.

MESHORER, Y. "A hoard of coins from Migdal", *ATIQOT,* Es 11, 1976, pp.55, 56, 69-70, pl.15/141-148.

MESHORER, Y. "The coins of Sepphoris as a historical source", ZION 43 (3-4), 1978, Jerusalem, pp.185-200 (Hebrew).

MESHORER, Y. "About the problems of the eras of Agrippa II", CATHEDRA 8, 1978, p.60 (Hebrew).

MESHORER, Y. "Jewish symbols on Roman coins struck in Eretz Israel", IMN 14, 1978, pp.60, 61-63, nos. 4-10.

MESHORER, Y. "Sepphoris and Rome", in 'Greek numismatics and archaeology', Essays in honour of Margaret Thompson (O. Mørkholm and N. Waggoner, eds.), Wetteren 1979, pp.159-171.

MESHORER, Y. "The city coins of Eretz-Israel and the Decapolis in the Roman period", Jerusalem 1984, pp.36-37, 113-114 (Hebrew).

MIONNET, T.E. "Description de médailles antiques, grecques et romaines", Paris 1806-1837, vol. V, pp.482-483, vol. VIII, suppl., pp.331-332.

NARKISS, M. "The Sepphorenes and Vespasian", BIES 17 (3-4), 1953, pp.108-120, pls.1-2 (Hebrew).

PATIN, C. "Imperatorum Romanorum numismata ex aere mediae et minimae formae descripta et enarrata..", Amsterdam(?) 1671, p.183.

PELLERIN, J. "Recueil de médailles de peuples et de villes", part 6, suppl., Paris 1763, p.246, pl.134/2.

PRICE, M.J. and TRELL, B.L. "Coins and their cities", London 1977, p.283.

SEPPHORIS

RIDER, G. le "Les ateliers monétaires de la côte Syrienne, Phénicienne, Palestinienne, Égyptienne et Cyrénéenne", Congresso Internazionale di numismatica (Roma 1961), vol. I, Relazioni, Roma 1961, p.95.

ROSENBERGER, M. "City-coins of Palestine", vol. III, Jerusalem 1977, pp.60-63.

SAULCY, F. de "Numismatique de la Terre Sainte", Paris 1874, pp.325-330, pl.17/1-7.

SEAR, D.R. "Greek imperial coins and their values", London 1982, nos. 1090, 1504, 2681.

SESTINI, D. "Descriptio numorum veterum..", Lipsiae 1796, pp.541-542.

SESTINI, D. "Classes generales geographiae numismaticae sev monetae urbium, populorum et regum..", Lipsiae 1797, part I, p.70, part II, p.102.

SESTINI, D. "Classes generales sev moneta vetus urbium, populorum et regum..", Florentiae 1821, p.149.

SESTINI, D. "Descrizione delle medaglie antiche Greche del Museo Hedervariano", part 3, Firenze 1829, p.103.

SEYRIG, H. "Irenopolis-Neronias-Sepphoris", NC, 6th ser. 10, 1950, pp.284-289.

SEYRIG, H. "Irenopolis-Neronias-Sepphoris. An additional note", NC, 6th ser. 15, 1955, pp.157-159.

SNG ANS part 6, "Palestine - South Arabia", 1981, pls.36-37, nos. 1085-1096.

SNG DNM "Palestine-Characene", 1961, pl.1/1-3.

SNG FM vol. IV, part 8, "Syria-Nabathaea", 1971, pl.136/6101-6102.

SPANHEMIUS, E. "Dissertationes de praestantia et de usu numismatum antiquorum", new ed., t.I, London 1706, p.353.

SPERBER, D. "Roman Palestine 200-400. Money and prices", Jerusalem 1974, p.143.

SPIJKERMAN, A. "Cafarnao III. Catalogo delle monete della citta", Jerusalem 1975, pp.24/121; 25/135; 32/210; 38/282, pl.1/8.

STAHL, Z. "The Flavian Emperors and their coins in Eretz-Israel", special brochure of Israel Num. Society, Tel-Aviv branch, 1976, p.7 (Hebrew).

STAHL, Z. "Roman coins of Palestinian cities issued during the Jewish War, 66-70 C.E.", special brochure of Israel Num. Society, Tel-Aviv branch, 1979, pp.12, 19-20, 25 (Hebrew).

SUTHERLAND, C.H.V. "The pattern of monetary development in Phoenicia and Palestine during the Early Empire", International numismatic convention in Jerusalem (1963), proceedings (A. Kindler, ed.), Tel-Aviv 1967, p.91.

TIEPOLO, L. and F. "Musei Theupoli antiqua numismata..", Venetiis 1736, series 6, p.867.

VAILLANT, J. "Numismata imperatorum, augustarum et caesarum a populis Romanae ditionis Graece loquentibus..", Paris 1698, pp.23, 30, 248.

WALCHER de MOLTHEIN, L. "Catalogue de la collection des médailles grecques de M. Le Chevalier", Paris-Vienne 1895, p.268, nos. 3164-3165, pl.30/3164.

SEPPHORIS

WICZAY, C.M. "Musei Hedervarii numi antiqui..", Vindobonae 1814, part I, p.287/6186.

<u>Auction Catalogues and Price Lists</u>

AGORA Tel-Aviv 1974 (1), p.20, nos. 118-120, pl.7.
1975 (2), nos. 166-169, pl.7.

BETTER Haifa 1972 (1), nos. 229-230.
Haifa 1972 (2), nos. 302-303.
Haifa 1973 (3), nos. 340-347.
Haifa 1973 (4), nos. 215-218.
Jaffo 1974 (5), no. 157.
Jaffo 1974 (7), nos. 264-265.
Haifa 1974 (8), nos. 156-157.

CAHN, A.E. Frankfurt 1930 (68), p.95, no. 1580.
1931 (71), p.66, no. 1083, pl.32.

COIN GALLERIES (price list), New York 1959 (17), p.16, no. A 236.

EIDELSTEIN AND HOLLAND (price list), Haifa, summer 1976, no. 191.

GANS, E. "Numismatic Fine Arts", Berkeley CA, USA
1956 (18), p.1, no. 4201.
1956 (20), p.14, no. 4950.

GLENDINING London, 21-23 Feb. 1961, p.98, no. 3004.
10 March 1965, p.20, no. 152.

HESS, A. Frankfurt 1936 (224), p.58, no. 1733.

HESS-LEU Luzern 1970 (45), p.47, no. 383.

MALTER, J.L. "Journal of Numismatic Fine Arts", Encino CA, USA 1973 (2/2), p.37/B 85, pl.11.

MONNAIES ET MÉDAILLES, Basel 1954 (13), p.71, no. 930, pl.33.
1966 (32), p.46, nos. 438-441, pl.27.

MÜNZEN UND MEDAILLEN, Basel 1952 (112), p.6, no. 128.
1955 (151), p.12, no. 231.
1969 (305), p.3, nos. 50-54.
1980 (424), p.17, no. 218.

MÜNZZENTRUM KÖLN, 1981 (43), p.36, no. 214.

NUMISMATICA WIEN, 1975 (9), p.23, no. 127.

NUMISMATIC FINE ARTS, Beverly Hills CA, USA 1983 (12), no. 103.

RAUCH, H.D. Wien 1985 (34), nos. 261-262.

SCHLESSINGER, F. (price list), Amsterdam 1938 (9), p.3, no. 642.

SPINK AND SON London 1905 (13/153), nos. 18155-18160.
1925 (33/11-12), no. 45404.
1930 (38/10), no. 962.
1931 (39/9), no. 10017.
1934 (42/8-9), no. 35047.
1936 (44/1), nos. 48001-48002.
1939 (47/3), nos. 78584-78586.
1945 (53/6), p.166, nos. 31062-31063.
1977 (85/12), p.553, no. 13057.

STERNBERG, F. Zürich, 25-26 Nov. 1976, p.92, nos. 706-710, pl.30.

SUPERIOR STAMP AND COIN CO., Los-Angeles, June 1976, p.30, nos. 336-341.

TAMAR Tel-Aviv 1975 (9), p.7, nos. 156-157A.
Tel-Aviv 1975 (10), p.10, nos. 154-155.

SEPPHORIS

TAMAR (con't)	Ramat-Gan, Israel 1976 (11), pp.11, 12, nos. 141, 169.
	Ramat-Gan, Israel 1976 (12), pp.50-51, nos. 833-837.
VINCHON, J.	"Monnaies Juives", Paris, 13 Fév. 1970, no. 93.

TIBERIAS

ANONYMOUS — CH 1, 1975, p.34/123.

ANONYMOUS — "City-coins of ancient Israel", JIN 1 (2), 1966, pp.48, 49.

ARIEL, D.T. — "A survey of coin finds in Jerusalem", LA 32, 1982, pp.292, 318.

AVI-YONAH, M. — "The foundation of Tiberias", IEJ 1 (3), 1950/51, p.168.

BARAG, D. — "Tyrian currency in Galilee", INJ 6-7, 1982/3, pp.10, 11, 13.

BARAMKI, D.C. — "The coins exhibited in the Archaeological Museum of the American University of Beirut", Beirut 1968, pp.89-90, nos. 302-304, pl.8.

BARAMKI, D.C. — "The coin collection of the American University of Beirut Museum. Palestine and Phoenicia", Beirut 1974, pp.3-5, pl.1/5-13.

BELLINGER, A.R. — "The Syrian tetradrachms of Caracalla and Macrinus", ANS NS 3, 1940, p.13.

BENTINCK, de — "Catalogue d'une collection de médailles antiques", Amsterdam 1787, part II, p.1072.

ECKHEL, J. — "Catalogus Musei Caesarei Vindobonensis numorum veterum..", Vindobonae 1779, part I, pp.245-246, pl.4/12.

ECKHEL, J. — "Doctrina numorum veterum..", vol. III, Vienna 1794, pp.426-428.

TIBERIAS

FLESCH, M. "Group of city coins", in 'Collector's choice', Bezalel National Museum, Jerusalem 1964, p.16/81.

FORRER, L. "Weber collection, vol. III, part 2: Greek coins", London 1929, p.795/8104, pl.299.

GESSNER, J.J. "Numismata antiqua Imperatorum Romanorum latina et graeca..", Tiguri (Zürich), 18th cent., pls.82/45-47; 92/24-29, 58.

HAMBURGER, A. "Gems from Caesarea Maritima", ATIQOT, Es 8, 1968, p.12/85-88.

HAMBURGER, H. "The coin issues of the Roman administration from the mint of Caesarea Maritima", IEJ 20 (1-2), 1970, pp.82, 85.

HANSON, R.S. and BATES, M.L. "Numismatic report" in 'Ancient synagogue excavations at Khirbet Shema, Upper Galilee, Israel, 1970-1972', AASOR 42, 1976, p.153, pl.6.2/4 (R 1551).

HANSON, R.S. "Tyrian influence in the Upper Galilee", Cambridge 1980, p.53.

HEAD, B.V. "Historia numorum", Oxford 1911, p.802.

HENDIN, D. "Guide to ancient Jewish coins", New York 1976, pp.98-99, pl.8/230-233.

HILL, G.F. "Some Palestinian cults in the Graeco-Roman age", Proceedings of the British Academy, vol. V, London 1912, p.413, pl./9-10.

HILL, G.F. BMC, Palestine, 1914, pp.xiii-xv, pp.5-10, pls.1/8-14; 2/1-6.

HUBER, C.W. Unedirte Bronzemünze in Tiberias Galilaeae unter Commodus geprägt", NZ 1, 1869, pp.401-414.

JONAS, R. "Mythology on Palestinian coins", internal circular no. 2, Israel Num. Society, Haifa branch, 1959, p.5.

KADMAN, L. and KINDLER, A. "Coins in Palestine throughout the ages", Tel-Aviv 1963, pp.35-36, pl.16/1-7 (Hebrew).

KINDLER, A. "Thesaurus of Judaean coins from the fourth century B.C. to the third century A.D.", Jerusalem 1958, no. 34 (Hebrew).

KINDLER, A. "The coins of Tiberias", Tiberias 1961.

KINDLER, A. "New types of Palestinian city-coins", ALON 3 (2), 1968, pp.51-52, pl.2/10-11 (Hebrew).

KINDLER, A. "The coins of Tiberias in the Roman period", in 'The book of Tiberias' (O. Avissar, ed.), Jerusalem 1973, pp.50-59 (Hebrew).

KINDLER, A. "The status of cities in the Syro-Palestinian area as reflected by their coins", INJ 6-7, 1982/3, p.84.

KINDLER, A. "The coinage of Bostra", Warminster, England 1983, pp.28, 61.

KIRKBRIDE, A.S. "Currencies in Transjordan", PEQ 1939, p.156.

KLIMOWSKY, E.W. "The monetary function of city coins", International numismatic convention in Jerusalem (1963), proceedings (A. Kindler, ed.), Tel-Aviv 1967, pp.131, 144, 160, 162, 164, 166, 170, 172.

KLIMOWSKY, E.W. "Roman imperial 'Virtutes' on contemporaneous city coins" in "On ancient Palestinian and other coins, their symbolism and metrology", PINS 7, Tel-Aviv 1974, p.97, pl.7/41, 56. Same in INJ 3, 1965/6, p.24, pl.6/41.

TIBERIAS

MACDONALD, G. "Catalogue of Greek coins in the Hunterian collection", Glasgow 1905, vol. III, p.275.

MATSSON, G.O. "Two unpublished Roman city coins of Palestine", NCirc 64 (1), 1956, pp.9-10, fig. 2.

MATSSON, G.O. "The gods, goddesses and heroes on the ancient coins of Bible Lands", Stockholm 1969, pp.156, 244, pl.8/118b.

MESHORER, Y. "Coins of Tiberias", in "All the land of Naftali..", 24th Archaeological convention in Jerusalem (1966), Jerusalem 1967, pp.192-194 (Hebrew).

MESHORER, Y. "Coins of the Ancient World", Minneapolis 1975, p.68. Hebrew version (Jerusalem 1979), pp.50-51. Same in "Münzen, Zeugen der Vergangenheit", Zürich - Köln, 1979, p.8.

MESHORER, Y. "Catalogue of coins" in 'Ships and parts of ships on ancient coins' (Ben-Eli, A.L., ed.), part I, National Maritime Museum of Haifa, 1975, p.56/45-46.

MESHORER, Y. "A hoard of coins from Migdal", ATIQOT, Es 11, 1976, pp.55, 56, 67-68, pl.14/121-130.

MESHORER, Y. "Jewish symbols on Roman coins struck in Eretz Israel", IMN 14, 1978, pp.61-62, nos. 1-3.

MESHORER, Y. "The city coins of Eretz-Israel and the Decapolis in the Roman period", Jerusalem 1984, pp.33-35, 113 (Hebrew).

MEYSHAN, J. "Chronology of the coins of the Herodian dynasty", EI 6, 1960, pp.109. Same in 'Essays in Jewish numismatics', PINS 6, Jerusalem 1968, pp.71-72.

MIONNET, T.E. "Description de médailles antiques, grecques et romaines", Paris 1806-1837, vol. V, pp.483-486; vol. VIII, suppl., pp.332-333.

PATIN, C. "Imperatorum Romanorum numismata ex aere mediae et minimae formae descripta et enarrata..", Amsterdam(?) 1671, pp.185, 205.

PRICE, M.J. and TRELL, B.L. "Coins and their cities", London 1977, p.283.

RAHMANI, L. and SHARABANI, M. "List of coins" in 'Hammath Tiberias' by M. Dothan, Jerusalem 1983, p.72, pl.22/13.

RAYNOR, J. "Numismatic report of Nabratein, 1980", in 'Preliminary report on the 1980 excavations at En-Nabratein, Israel' BASOR 244, 1981, p.20, fig.11/4.

RIDER, G. le "Les ateliers monétaires de la côte Syrienne, Phénicienne, Palestinienne, Égyptienne et Cyrénéenne", Congresso Internazionale di numismatica (Roma 1961), vol. I, Relazioni, Roma 1961, p.96.

ROSENBERGER, M. "City-coins of Palestine", vol. III, Jerusalem 1977, pp.63-67.

SAULCY, F. de "Numismatique de la Terre Sainte", Paris 1874, pp.333-338, pl.17/9-14.

SCHONWALTER, R. "Numismatic evidence from the Dead Sea", NUMISMATIST 71 (7), 1958, p.796.

SEAR, D.R. "Greek imperial coins and their values", London 1982, nos. 480, 1091, 1247, 2055.

SESTINI, D. "Descriptio numorum veterum..", Lipsiae 1796, pp.542-543.

TIBERIAS

SESTINI, D. "Classes generales geographiae numismaticae sev monetae urbium, populorum et regum..", Lipsiae 1797, part I, p.70, part II, p.102.

SESTINI, D. "Descrizione delle medaglie Greche e Romane del Fu Benkowitz", Berlino 1809, p.35.

SESTINI, D. "Classes generales sev moneta vetus urbium, populorum et regum..", Florentiae 1821, p.149.

SESTINI, D. "Descrizione d'alcune medaglie Greche del museo del Signore Carlo D'Ottavio Fontana", Firenze 1822, p.13.

SESTINI, D. "Descrizione delle medaglie antiche Greche del Museo Hedervariano", part 3, Firenze 1829, pp.104-105, pl.31/15.

SEYRIG, H. "Antiquités Syriennes, 73. Temples, cultes et souvenirs historiques de la Decapole", SYRIA 36, 1959, p.74.

SNG ANS part 6, "Palestine - South Arabia", 1981, pl.37/1097-1118.

SNG DNM "Palestine-Characene", 1961, pl.1/4.

SNG FM vol. IV, part 8, "Syria-Nabathaea", 1971, pl.136/6103.

SOFER-OVADIA, R. "A bronze figurine of Tyche", SEFUNIM 1, 1966, p.24, pl.6/2. Heb. ed. p.22

SPANHEMIUS, E. "Dissertationes de praestantia et usu numismatum antiquorum", new ed., t.I, London 1706, p.526.

SPERBER, D. "Roman Palestine 200-400. Money and prices", Jerusalem 1974, pp.142, 143.

SPIJKERMAN, A. "Monete della sinagoga di Cafarnao", LA 20, 1970, pp.107/8; 113/96.

SPIJKERMAN, A. "Cafarnao III. Catalogo delle monete della citta", Jerusalem 1975, pp.23/116; 41/319; 50/422; 51/432, pl.1/12.

STAHL, Z. "The Flavian Emperors and their coins in Eretz-Israel", special brochure of Israel Num. Society, Tel-Aviv branch, 1976, p.7 (Hebrew).

TIEPOLO, L. and F. "Musei Theupoli antiqua numismata..", Venetiis 1736, series 4, pp.868, 880.

VAILLANT, J. "Numismata imperatorum, augustarum et caesarum a populis Romanae ditionis Graece loquentibus..", Paris 1698, pp.30, 37, 49, 250, 374, 478.

WICZAY, C.M. "Musei Hedervarii numi antiqui..", Vindobonae 1814, part I, p.287, nos. 6187-6188.

Auction Catalogues and Price Lists

AGORA Tel-Aviv 1974 (1), p.21, nos. 121-125, pl.7.
1975 (2), nos. 163-165, pl.7.

BETTER Haifa 1972 (2), nos. 304-306.
Haifa 1973 (3), nos. 332-339.
Haifa 1973 (4), nos. 219-223.
Jaffo 1974 (5), nos. 158-160.
Jaffo 1974 (7), nos. 266-267.
Haifa 1974 (8), nos. 158-159.

CAHN, A.E. Frankfurt 1930 (68), p.95, nos. 1581-1582.
1931 (71), p.66, nos. 1084-1086, pl.32.

TIBERIAS

COIN GALLERIES (mail bid sale), New York, 13 July 1954, nos. 1190-1191.

EIDELSTEIN AND HOLLAND, Haifa, 10 Nov. 1975, nos. 173-174.

GANS, E. "Numismatic Fine Arts", (Stock cat.), New York
1943 (2), pp.14 (no.7313), 15 (no.7323), 16 (no.6111).
1943 (3), p.9, nos. 6111, 7313, 7323.

GANS, E. "Numismatic Fine Arts" (Mail bid sale), Berkeley CA, USA 1955 (15), p.23, no. 369.

GANS, E. "Numismatic Fine Arts", Berkeley CA, USA 1956 (20), no. 4951.

GIBBONS, S. London, 9-10 Oct. 1972, p.2, no. 14.

HOLZER, H. "The Thomas Ollive Mabbott collection", part I, New York 1969, p.104, no. 2673.

MALTER, J.L. "Journal of Numismatic Fine Arts", Encino CA, USA 1973 (2/2), p.37/B 86, pl.11.

MONNAIES ET MÉDAILLES, Basel 1951 (10), p.13, no. 147.
1954 (13), p.72, no. 931.
1962 (25), p.22, no. 543, pl.9.
1966 (32), pp.46-47, nos. 442-449, pl.27.

MÜNZEN UND MEDAILLEN, Basel 1950 (96), p.2, no. 21.
1952 (112), p.6, no. 129.
1968 (293), p.4, nos. 51-55.
1978 (398), p.1, no. 6.
1980 (424), p.17, no. 219.
1981 (430), p.2, no. 16.
1981 (436), p.14, no. 152.
1982 (448), p.1, no. 13.

MÜNZEN UND MEDAILLEN (con't) 1984 (464), p.15, no. 192.
1985 (475), p.2, no. 30.

MÜNZZENTRUM KÖLN, 1979 (36), p.29, nos. 194-195.
1983 (48), p.32, no. 209.

NUMISMATIC FINE ARTS (Winter mail bid sale), Beverly Hills, CA, USA, Jan. 1982, no. 264.

RAUCH, H.D. Wien 1985 (34), no. 263.

SCHLESSINGER, F. (price list), Amsterdam 1938 (9), p.3, nos. 643-644.

SCHULMAN, H.M.F. New York, 18-19 Nov. 1955, p.71, nos. 1938-1939.

SCHULMAN, J. Amsterdam 1966 (243), p.37, no. 1317.

SEABY, London 1949 (373), p.288, no. A. 1655.
1949 (378), p.536, nos. AM 331-334.
1967 (584), p.159, no. A 380.
1970 (624), p.287, no. A 744.
1971 (637), p.336, no. A 850.
1979 (733), p.301, no. C 977.

SPINK AND SON London 1905 (13/153), no. 18161.
1925 (33/11-12), nos. 45407-45408.
1931 (39/9), nos. 10018-10023.
1934 (42/8-9), nos. 35052-35053.
1934 (42/10), no. 36207.
1936 (44/1), nos. 48003-48004.
1939 (47/3), nos. 78587-78589.
1945 (53/6), p.166, nos. 31064-31071.
1952 (60/4), p.214, nos. 3387-3388.
1977 (85/7-8), p.318, no. 6645.

STERNBERG, F. Zürich, 25-26 Nov. 1976, p.93, nos. 713-717, pl.30.

TIBERIAS

SUPERIOR STAMP AND COIN CO., Los-Angeles, June 1976, pp.30-31, nos. 344-346.

TAMAR Tel-Aviv 1975 (9), p.8, no. 158.
Tel-Aviv 1975 (10), p.10, nos. 156-157.
Ramat-Gan, Israel 1976 (11), p.11, nos. 142-144.
Ramat-Gan, Israel 1976 (12), p.50, no. 832.

VECCHI, V.C. "Bonhams", London 1982 (8), p.30, no. 403, pl.19.

APPENDIX I

ABBREVIATIONS

Archaeology

AASOR	Annual of the American Schools of Oriental Research. Jerusalem and Baghdad, Cambridge (Mass.) USA.
ADAJ	Annual of the Department of Antiquities. Amman, Jordan.
AJA	American Journal of Archaeology. Archaeological Institute of America, New York.
ATIQOT	Atiqot. Department of Antiquities, Jerusalem.
BA	Biblical Archaeologist. American Schools of Oriental Research, Jerusalem and Baghdad, Cambridge (Mass.) USA.
BASOR	Bulletin of the American Schools of Oriental Research. Jerusalem and Baghdad, Cambridge (Mass.) USA.
BERYTUS	Berytus. American University of Beirut, Museum of Archaeology, Beirut.
BIES	Bulletin of the Israel Exploration Society (Hebrew). Jerusalem. Continuing BJPES.
BJPES	Bulletin of the Jewish Palestine Exploration Society (Hebrew). Jerusalem.
CATHEDRA	Cathedra for the History of Eretz-Israel and its Yishuv (Hebrew). Jerusalem.
IEJ	Israel Exploration Journal. Israel Exploration Society, Department of Archaeology, Hebrew University, Department of Antiquities, Ministry of Education and Culture, Jerusalem.

APPENDIX I

IMN	The Israel Museum News. The Israel Museum, Jerusalem.
JPOS	Journal of the Palestine Oriental Society. Jerusalem.
LA	Liber Annuus. Studium Biblicum Franciscanum, Jerusalem.
MHB (MHY)	Museum Ha'aretz Bulletin (Museum Ha'aretz Yearbook). Museum Ha'aretz, Ramat-Aviv, Israel.
PEFA	Palestine Exploration Fund Annual. London.
PEFQSt	Quarterly Statement of the Palestine Exploration Fund. London.
PEQ	Palestine Exploration Quarterly. Palestine Exploration Fund, London. Continuing PEFQSt.
QDAP	Quarterly of the Department of Antiquities in Palestine. Jerusalem.
RB	Revue Biblique. Paris.
SEFUNIM	Sefunim. Bulletin of the Maritime Museum (Hebrew), Haifa, Israel.
SYRIA	Syria. Revue d'Art Oriental et d'Archéologie. Institut Francais d'Archéologie de Beyrouth, Paris.
TEL-AVIV	Tel-Aviv. Department of Archaeology, University of Tel-Aviv.
YEDIOT	Yediot Behaqirat Eretz-Israel Weatiqoteha (Hebrew). Jerusalem. Continuing BIES.
ZDPV	Zeitschrift des Deutschen Palästina-Vereins. Wiesbaden, Germany.

APPENDIX I

Numismatics

ALON	Alon Hahevra Hanumismatit Le'Israel. Newssheet of the Israel Numismatic Society (Hebrew), Tel-Aviv.
ANS MN	American Numismatic Society, Museum Notes. New York.
ANS NS	American Numismatic Society, Numismatic Studies. New York.
ASFN	Annuaire de la Société Française de Numismatique. Paris.
BMC	A catalogue of the Greek coins in the British Museum. London.
CN	Cahiers Numismatiques. Bulletin de la Société d'Etudes Numismatique et Archéologique, Paris.
CH	Coin Hoards. Royal Numismatic Society, London.
INB	Israel Numismatic Bulletin (Hebrew-English). Israel Coins and Medals Company, Jerusalem.
INJ	Israel Numismatic Journal. Israel Numismatic Society, Tel-Aviv.
JIAN	Journal International d'Archéologie Numismatique. Athens.
JIN	Journal of Israel Numismatics. The independent publication for the collector. International Israel Numismatic Society, New York.
JNFA	Journal of Numismatic Fine Arts. Encino CA, USA.

APPENDIX I

JNG	Jahrbuch für Numismatik und Geldgeschichte. Bayerische Numismatische Gesellschaft, Kallmünz über Regensburg, W. Germany.
NC	Numismatic Chronicle. Royal Numismatic Society, London.
NCirc	Numismatic Circular (Spink Numismatic Circular). Spink and Son Ltd., London.
NNM	Numismatic Notes and Monographs. American Numismatic Society, New York.
NUMISMATIST	Numismatist. Official Publication of the American Numismatic Association, Colorado Springs, Colorado, USA.
NZ	Numismatische Zeitschrift. Numismatische Gesellschaft, Vienna.
PINS	Publications of the Israel Numismatic Society. Tel-Aviv - Jerusalem.
RN	Revue Numismatique. Société Française de Numismatique, Centre National de la Recherche Scientifique, Paris.
SAN	Journal of the Society for Ancient Numismatics. Santa Monica, CA, USA.
SHEKEL	Shekel. American Israel Numismatic Association, New York.
SM	Schweizer Münzblätter (Gazette Numismatique Suisse). Schweizerische Numismatische Gesellschaft (Société Suisse de Numismatique), Basel.

SNG ANS	Sylloge Nummorum Graecorum, American Numismatic Society, New York.
SNG DNM	Sylloge Nummorum Graecorum, Danish National Museum, Copenhagen.
SNG FM	Sylloge Nummorum Graecorum, published for the British Academy by the Oxford University Press and Spink and Son, London. (vol. IV: Fitzwilliam Museum).
SNR	Schweizerische Numismatische Rundschau (Revue Suisse de Numismatique). Schweizerische Numismatische Gesellschaft (Société Suisse de Numismatique), Bern.
ZN	Zeitschrift für Numismatik. Berlin.

APPENDIX II

LIST OF AUTHORS

Akerman, John Jonge
Ariel, Donald T.
Arrigoni, Onorio (Honorius)
Avigad, Nahman
Avi-Yonah, Michael
Babelon, M. Ernest
Babelon, Jean
Baldus, Hans Roland
Banks, Florence Aiken
Barag, Dan
Baramki, Dimitri C.
Baramki, Jalil
Barkay, Gabriel
Bates, Michael L. (& Hanson, R.S.)
Beit Arieh, Itzhaq (& Stern, E.)
Bellinger, Alfred R.
Ben-David, Arye
Ben-Dor, Stella
Bentinck, la Csse Douair, de
Berman, Ariel
Bernhardt, Max
Brett, Agnes Baldwin
Brezina, Aristides
Bull, Robert J.
Campbell, Edward F. jr. (& Bull, R.J.)
Carnig, Paul
Carradice, Ian
Carson, Robert Andrew Glindinning
Cavedoni, Calestino
Chabachoff, B.
Chaix, E.
Chéhab, Maurice
Cohen, Henry
Decloedt, Achille
Donaldson, T.L.
Dowling, Theodore E.
Drexler, W.
Durand, Germer
Dussaud, René
Eckhel, Joseph
Elgavish, Joseph
Flesch, Max
Flusser, David
Forrer, Leonard Steyning
Francesco de Dominicis
Friedländer, Julius
Froelich, Erasmus
Frova, Antonio
Fuks, Gideon
Fulco, William J.
Geiger, Joseph
Gersht, Rivka
Gessner, Johannes Jacob
Gilmore, Peter M.
Goldmann, Zeev
Grant, Michael
Grose, Sidney William
Hadidi, Adnan
Harl, Kenneth W.
Hamburger, Anit
Hamburger, Herbert
Hamburger, Leopold
Hanson, Richard Simon
Harding, G. Lankester
Harduin, Jean (Harduinus, Joannes)
Head, Barclay Vincent
Hendin, David
Herzfelder, Hubert
Heymann, H.

Hill, George Francis
Horn, Siegfried H.
Howgego, Christopher
Huber, C.W.
Imhoof-Blumer, Friedrich
Janis, Edward
Jesselsohn, David
Johnson, Sherman E.
Jonas, Rudolf
Kadman, Leo
Kanael, Baruch
Kanitz, L. Eliezer
Kasher, Arie
Kellner, Wendelin
Kenneth, A. Jacob
Kindler, Arie
Kirkbride, Alec Seath
Kirschner, Bruno Israel
Klimowsky, Ernst Werner
Knobloch, Frederick S.
Kontorini, Vassa
Kraay, Colin W.
Kraft, Konrad
Kubitschek, Wilhelm
Lambert, Charles
Lapp, Nancy L.
Lederer, Philipp
Levine, Lee L.
Levy, Moritz Abraham
Liebe, Christian Sigismund
Macdonald, George
Madden, Fréderic W.
Maltiel-Gerstenfeld, Jacob
Manns, Frederic
Matsson, G.O.
McCown, Chester Charleston
Mendelsson, Edwin
Meshorer, Ya'akov
Meyshan, Josef
Mildenberg, Leo
Mionnet, Théodore Edme
Morey, C.R.
Münsterberg, Rudolf
Narkiss, Mordechai
Negev, Avraham
Neumann, Francisco
Newell, Edward Theodore
Östreicher, Bruno
Ovadia, Asher
Patin, Charles
Patrich, Joseph
Pellerin, J.
Piccirillo, Michele
Plant, Richard
Price, Martin Jessop
Qedar, Shraga
Raffaeli, Samuel
Rahmani, Levi Yizhaq
Rappaport, Uriel
Raynor, Joyce
Reed, William L.
Redling, Kurt
Reichardt, Henry C.
Reifenberg, Adolf
Reinach, Théodore
Reshef, Moshe
Rider, Georges le
Ringel, Josef
Robinson, E.S.G.
Rogers, Edgar
Rosenberger, Mayer
Rosenthal-Heginbottom, Renate
Rouvier, Jules
Sarfatti, Gad B.

APPENDIX II

Saulcy, Félicien de

Schnitzler, Otto

Scholz, J.

Schonwalter, Robert

Schuman, Edward

Scott, W.H.

Sear, David R.

Seguin, P. (Seguinus, Petrus)

Sellers, Ovid Rogers

Sestini, Domenico

Seyrig, Henri

Shahaf, Nahum

Sharabani, Marcia

Sofer-Ovadia, Ruth

Soloveichik, Max

Spaer, Arnold

Spanhemius, Ezechiel

Sperber, Daniel

Spijkerman, Augustus

Stahl, Zvi

Stern, Ephraim

Starcky, Jean (& Spijkerman, A.)

Stevenson, Seth William

Stieglitz, Robert R.

Svoronos, John N. (& Head, B.V.)

Sukenik, Eliezer Lipa

Sutherland, Carol Humphrey Vivian

Tierch, H.

Tiepolo, Federico (& Tiepolo, L.)

Tiepolo, Lorenzo (Theupolus, L.)

Tolkowsky, Samuel

Trell, Bluma L.

Vaillant, Joannes

Vaux, Roland de

Vliet, N. van der

Waage, Dorothy B.

Wacks, Mel

Waddington, W.H.

Walcher de Molthein, L.

Webster, W.

Weder, Marcus

Wiczay, Michael C.

Wroth, Warwick

Yadin, Yigael

Zayadine, Fawzi

Zuri, Nehemia

APPENDIX III

LIST OF AUCTION CATALOGUES AND PRICE LISTS

AGORA Ltd, Tel-Aviv, auctions
no. 1, 14 May 1974
no. 2, 21 May 1985

ANTIQUITY IMPORTS, Fixed price catalog no.1, spring 1976, Minneapolis, Minnesota, USA.

BETTER (Auction Company Ltd.), auctions
no. 1, Haifa, 4-6 July 1972
no. 2, Haifa, 27-28 Dec. 1972
no. 3, Haifa, 4 March 1973
no. 4, Haifa, 30 Aug. 1973
no. 5, Jaffo, 12 March 1974
no. 7, Jaffo, September 1974
no. 8, Haifa, 5 Dec. 1974

BUTTON, Elizabeth "Frankfurter Münzhandlung", Frankfurt am Main
Verzeichnis nr. 35, März 1938
nr. 37, Sept. 1938

CAHN, Adolf E., Frankfurt am Main, Auktionen
Auktionskatalog 68, 26 Nov. 1930
71, 14 Oct. 1931
80, 27 Feb. 1933

COIN GALLERIES New York
Mail bid sale, 13 July 1954
Fixed price list no. 17, Feb.-March 1959
Auction, 24-25 May 1963

EGGER BRÜDER "Verzeichnis verkäuflicher Münzen und Medaillen", nr. 56, Apr. 1930, Wien.

APPENDIX III

EIDELSTEIN AND HOLLAND, Haifa
Mail auction sale, 10 Nov. 1975
Summer price list, 1976

GANS, Edward "Numismatic Fine Arts", Stock catalogue with fixed prices, New York
no. 1, April 1942
no. 2, Jan. 1943
no. 3, Oct. 1943

GANS, Edward "Numismatic Fine Arts", Mail bid sale no. 15, Berkeley CA, USA, 4 May 1955.

GANS, Edward "Numismatic Fine Arts", price list, Berkeley CA, USA
list no. 18, pre-spring 1956
no. 20, fall 1956
no. 24, fall 1958
no. 26, fall 1960
no. 28, spring 1962

GIBBONS, Stanley (Auction Ltd.), auction 9-10 Oct. 1972, London.
GLENDINING AND CO., Ltd., London, auctions.

HAMBURGER, Leo, Auktions-katalog 96, 25-26 Oct. 1932, Frankfurt am Main.

HESS, Adolf, Nachfolger, Katalog 224, 18-19 Feb. 1936, Frankfurt am Main.

HESS-LEU auction 28, 5-6 Mai in Luzern.

HIRSCH, Gerhard "Münzen und Medaillen", München, Auktionen
nr. 37, 10-11 Dez. 1963
nr. 45, 9-10 Dez. 1965
nr. 75, 22-24 Nov. 1971
nr. 84, 27-20 Juni 1973

HOLZER, Hans (catalogue by) "The Thomas Ollive Mabbott collection", part I: Coins of the Greek World, auction, 6-11 June 1969, the Hans Schulman gallery, New York.

KRAUS, Franz Ferdinand "Braunschweiger Münzverkehr", Braunschweig, Germany April/Juni 1928, no. 2
Jan./Juni 1929, no. 1/2

KRESS, Karl "Münchner Münzhandlung", München, Auktionen
nr. 98, 20 April 1955
nr. 108, 10 Juni 1958
nr. 119, 6 Sept. 1961
nr. 124, 29 Nov. 1962
nr. 139, 19 Juni 1967
nr. 167, 21-22 Oct. 1976
nr. 172, 29-30 Juni 1978
nr. 185, 15-16 März 1983

MALLOY, Alex G., price list no. 20, Dec. 1970/Jan. 1971, New York.

MALTER, Joel L. "Journal of Numismatic Fine Arts", Encino CA, USA
vol. I, no. 5, July-Sept. 1972
vol. II, no. 2, summer 1973
vol. IV, no. 1, Aug. 1975
vol. VI, no. 1, spring 1977

MALTER, Joel L. and McNall, Bruce P. (consultants), "Constantinopole Fine Arts", Encino CA, USA, fixed price list no. 1, 1970(?).

MONNAIES ET MÉDAILLES S.A. (Münzen und Medaillen A.G.), Basel, Ventes publiques
no. 10, 22-23 Juin 1951
no. 13, 17-19 Juin 1954
no. 25, 17 Nov. 1962
no. 32, 20 Oct. 1966
no. 41, 18-19 Juin 1970

APPENDIX III

MÜNZEN UND MEDAILLEN, A.G. (Monnaies et Medáilles S.A.), Basel, price list.

MÜNZZENTRUM KÖLN (Albrecht-Hoffmann GmbH), Lagerliste 2, Feb./März 1970.

MÜNZZENTRUM KÖLN (Albrecht-Hoffmann), Auktionen
nr. 36, 7-9 Nov. 1979
nr. 42, 10-13 Nov. 1980
nr. 43, 27-30 Apr. 1981
nr. 47, 10-12 Nov. 1982
nr. 48, 27-29 Apr. 1983
nr. 53, 13-15 Nov. 1984

MYERS, Robert J. (Myers/Adams), New York, auctions
no. 1, 18-19 Nov. 1971
no. 2, 11-12 May 1972
no. 5, 15-16 March 1973

NUMISMATICA WIEN, Münzaktion 9, 20-21 Nov. 1975.

NUMISMATIC FINE ARTS, Inc., Beverly Hills, CA, USA, auctions
no. 1, 9-11 Nov. 1973
no. 3, 27 March 1976
no. 5, 23-24 Feb. 1978
no. 6, 27-28 Feb. 1979
no. 12, 23-24 March 1983
Winter mail bid sale, January 1982

PEUS, Busso, Nachfolger, Lagerliste 14, März 1970, Frankfurt am Mein

RAUCH, Hans Dieter (Auktionshaus), Wien, Auktionen
nr. 7, 4-5 Juni 1971
nr. 34, 14-17 Jan. 1985

RIGO (Richard Götze), Lagerliste 40, Nürnberg 1959(?).

SALTON-SCHLESSINGER, Mark M., fixed price list no. 27, fall 1958, New York.

SCHLESSINGER, Felix, Münz-Auktion, 26 Feb. 1934, Berlin- Charlottenburg.

SCHLESSINGER, Felix, liste 9, 1938, Amsterdam.

SCHULMAN, Hans M.F., New York, auctions

SCHULMAN, Jacques, N.V., cat. 243, 8-10 June 1966, Amsterdam.

SEABY, Coin and Medal bulletin, London.

SIMONETTI, Luigi "Bollettino Numismatico", Firenze

SPINK AND SON Ltd., "Numismatic Circular", London

STACK'S (Stack, Benjamin and Harvey), New York, auctions

STERNBERG, Frank, Zürich, Auktionen nr. 7, 24-25 Nov. 1977
nr. 12, 18-19 Nov. 1982
"Antike Münzen", 25-26 Nov. 1976

SUPERIOR STAMP AND CO., Inc., auction, 15-19 June 1976, Los-Angeles (Beverly Hills, CA, USA).

TAMAR (Auction Company Ltd.), auctions
no. 9, 23 March 1975, Tel-Aviv
no. 10, 16 July 1975, Tel-Aviv
no. 11, 27 Jan. 1976, Ramat-Gan, Israel
no. 12, 22 March 1976, Ramat-Gan, Israel

VECCHI, V.C. AND SONS (Vecchi/Bonhams), Sale no. 8, 11-12 Oct. 1982, London.

VINCHON, Jean "Monnaies Juives", vente publique, 13 Fév. 1970, Paris.

www.ingramcontent.com/pod-product-compliance
Lightning Source LLC
Chambersburg PA
CBHW041158150926
51501CB00052B/1672